"Ellie is bright, funny, and interesting. She captures her audience and holds it close by combining a great message with an entertaining delivery. She helped inspire our group and she has my top endorsement."

—Major General Steve Goldfein,
Former USAF Vice-Director, The Joint Chiefs of Staff

"Commanders at all levels know that readiness never takes a day off. This is certainly true for our nation's military personnel at home and abroad, and it is equally true for those heroes who remain on the home front. These home-front spouses and families need help and hope for their critical role in maintaining strong families and securing our nation's future. Ellie Kay has captured this essential need in *Heroes at Home,* an important tool for spouses, troops, and commanders."

—Major General Bob Dees,
USA (Retired)
Associate Vice President for Military Outreach at Liberty University
Military Director for American Association
of Christian Counselors (AACC)
Senior Military Advisor for DNA Military

"*Heroes at Home* is uplifting and encouraging. These are more than just words on a page and good tips; there is obviously a love for what our military families and the members serving in uniform do. I, personally, am pleased to have been thanked by America for my service from the hand and heart of Ellie Kay. She is truly an American spokesperson bent on ensuring our military members and families are loved and thanked, and that they know they are serving with support."

—Command Chief Master Sergeant
Vance M. Clarke, USAF (Retired)
52nd Fighter Wing, Spangdahlem, Germany

"Ellie is amazing! I don't think she ever sleeps! Ellie provides great information and is always a fun guest on the show."

—Bill Griffith, Former host, CNBC's *Power Lunch*
Current host, CNBC's *Closing Bell*

HEROES *at* HOME

HEROES *at* HOME

★ ★ ★ ★ ★ ★ ★

HELP AND HOPE FOR AMERICA'S MILITARY FAMILIES

ELLIE KAY

BETHANY HOUSE PUBLISHERS

a division of Baker Publishing Group
Minneapolis, Minnesota

Third edition, 2012

Published by Bethany House Publishers
11400 Hampshire Avenue South
Bloomington, Minnesota 55438

Bethany House Publishers is a division of
Baker Publishing Group, Grand Rapids, Michigan.

Printed in the United States of America

Library of Congress Cataloging-in-Publication Data
Kay, Ellie.
    Heroes at home: help and hope for America's military families / Ellie Kay.—3rd ed.
      p. cm.
    Includes bibliographical references.
    Summary: "From the wife of an Air Force pilot, this is a compilation of unique insights and practical tips on how to physically and mentally survive being the spouse of an active military member"—Provided by publisher.
    ISBN 978-0-7642-0981-9 (pbk. : alk. paper)
    1. Families of military personnel—United States. I. Title.
UB403 .K38 2012
355.1'20973—dc23
                                                2011044059

Cover design by Dan Pitts

12   13   14   15   16   17   18   7   6   5   4   3   2   1

green
press
INITIATIVE

CONTENTS

ACKNOWLEDGMENTS

When people ask me what I do, I tell them that being America's Family Financial Expert® is my *profession,* but bringing *Heroes at Home* to military troops and their families is my *passion.* This book started with an idea to fill the gap in the marketplace for a resource that would help meet a military family's unique needs. Bethany House Publishers had the vision to bring help and hope through this book, which has now become a vital resource for more than one hundred thousand military families around the world.

I want to thank the professional partners who have helped to provide copies of this book for these amazing families, and they include USAA, James Robison of the *Life Today* television show, my friends at Military Ministry, as well as Andy and Joan Horner of Premier Designs. These partners have purchased and distributed thousands of copies of *Heroes at Home* with one thought in mind: to help military families with a free gift and a timely resource.

My original editor at Bethany House was Steve Laube, who contracted the first edition of this book. Then he became a literary agent and is now an advocate for the book as well as my literary representative. I want to thank Steve for believing in my work for almost a decade and partnering with me to bring entertainment, encouragement, and education to people around the world. I also want to thank Julie Smith, at Bethany House, whom I've known for a decade and partnered with in many projects. I appreciate your professionalism, kindness, and the fact that you don't require that I do formatting work (since I don't understand all those styles and forms).

This book was made all the more authentic from the profiles and work submitted by various heroes at home. I want to thank Keri Powers Pye, Bobbie Kennedy, Jessica Culley, Kara Siert, Stephanie Theis, Michelle Cuthrell, Joann Patrick, Myra Hinote, Brenda Taylor, and Paquita Rawleigh for their writing and their profiles. The diversity among this group is remarkable and represents all military ranks, demographics, and branches of the service. I say, "Semper Fi, Hoo-ah, and Aim High" to all of you!

When I gave my very first *Heroes at Home* presentation to a handful of military families, I had a professional partner with me: Wendy Wendler. She was a friend as well as my personal assistant. We had no idea that this message would someday go on tour and eventually speak to eight thousand people in an auditorium, where they stood on their feet and cheered for our heroes. Wendy was my right hand and I thank her for nine years of service.

I want to thank my precious family for being such good sports with my crazy life as an author and speaker. They've given me permission to tell their stories and show their pictures. They've stepped up to the plate in taking over responsibilities at home while I travel, and they've prayed for our military members and their families. I am so proud of each one of you and wouldn't trade you for anything. I am a wealthy woman because of the riches I have in my husband and children.

INTRODUCTION TO THE THIRD EDITION

When I wrote the first edition of this book, ten years ago, my husband was an active duty Stealth F-117 fighter pilot, on call to make the first run into downtown Baghdad. Times were uncertain in our household, to say the least. Our seven kids ranged in age from six to twenty, and five were living at home, filling our home to overflowing. I had five of these by birth, two by marriage, and all by love. Fast-forward to this third edition, a decade later, and there's only one Kay kid left at home. All the other children are either college graduates or on their way to their degree. Two of those are currently serving in our nation's military with the last one on his way.

The first edition of *Heroes at Home* was met with great enthusiasm by the military community as well as those who love the military. Almost a quarter million people have read this book (the average copy of a book is read 2.2 times), and we've been able to reach some 9 million with the *Heroes at Home* message via live events, television, and radio. It just goes to show that America loves you: the military member and the military family.

I love you too.

I've been so honored to meet many of you face-to-face. I've been at some events where you bring me copies of my book that look like they've been through the washer—their coffee-stained pages a testament to the devotion of the owner. I love signing those kinds of copies of *Heroes at Home* because they remind me of the Velveteen

Rabbit—loved and worn. The book comes to life when it is read over and over and helps the owner weather the storms of military life. It's like we've been having coffee together for years, and that's something that's highly valuable to me. Next time, you bring the chocolate.

Whether I'm coming to your base in order to help the community with an ops tempo issue, or I'm just a keynote speaker for spouse appreciation day, I get to see you. Meeting you is a special treat for me. When we hug as strangers-who-are-close-friends, we share in the military community and legacy that has made our military strong and our nation great. I'll take the face of a young wife in my hands, tears in our eyes, and communicate the truth that what she does has value, worth, and great reward—no matter what it may feel like in the heat of battle. It truly is worth it.

When I get to speak directly to the troops before they go downrange, or immediately after a deployment, it's such a privilege to remind them that they are heroes when they put integrity first, service before self, and excellence in all they do. Sometimes it just takes a mama of seven to speak a good word in due season and remind all of us that it really is worth it. When I travel to your posts and bases, your commanders usually roll out the red carpet, even though that's not what I ask for. They give me coveted unit coins, plaques, and even an occasional adventure—like a ride in an F-15E Strike Eagle. While these acts of kindness and gratitude are very much appreciated, I think that YOU are the ones who deserve these honors, not me. YOU are the ones who put up with the separations, the fear, the life-and-death situations, the short notice moves, and the chaotic schedules because YOU are a patriot of epic proportions.

The generations of Americans who have committed to serve for the last decade have been a volunteer force signing up during a time of war. That makes you and your family very special from day one. Only 1 percent of the American population has the honor and responsibility of protecting the rights and freedoms of the other 99 percent of us.

And we thank you.

We also thank your families.

This book was originally written for all American patriots—military or civilian. The military family has read this and learned how to do things a little better or smarter, while civilians have learned what it's like to live the unique and often challenging lifestyle of an American military family. My hope is that it has helped *all* of us learn how to be better patriots by not only supporting those who serve our country but also by learning how to better understand and support their families.

Over 2.3 million Americans are serving in our nation's active and reserve components—the Air Force, Army, Navy, Marine Corps, and Coast Guard. There are a number of heroes among them, and the most highly decorated individuals will invariably attribute their heroics to a team effort: the humble assertion that there are other people who stand behind the strength, courage, and daring of these individuals. These military men and women deserve their medals, but behind every hero is a unit, a team, or a family—their support consists of people both on and off the battlefield. Without this support, they couldn't be as focused and on top of their game as they need to be. When they can concentrate on their mission, there are fewer accidents. With fewer accidents, there is less loss of life.

Of all the million military members, nearly 60 percent are married with families, and it was to that select group of Americans that this book was originally dedicated. But in the last decade, another critical group has emerged—the parents who send their "babies" into the military. Of which I am now a member. So I dedicate this updated edition to all military families. Their collective stories are hidden, oftentimes unknown to anyone outside their four walls. Some of these spouses have married into the military not fully knowing what they were getting into. I have found that military family members tend to quickly develop four characteristics in order to survive above and beyond the call of duty: (1) a keen sense of humor, (2) a sense of adventure, (3) the ability to develop courage in a variety of challenges, and (4) a strong sense of family.

Humor is at the top of the list: A graduating senior tipped his cap to reveal a taped-on message: *Semper Fi* (the Marine motto meaning "Always Faithful"). They have to look at life in a lighthearted way in order to cope with the heavy stress that accompanies this incredible lifestyle. Many learn to laugh *at* themselves and *with* others, and in the process they find a way to rise above the circumstances that surround them.

Military families are also *adventurous*. They may have to pack up their entire foldaway home into eight huge crates and move it to another country, where they don't know the language or the culture—and then do it again in six months.

Courage also describes the military family. The new bride of three months, who sends her twenty-year-old husband into an unknown venture, while she lives out the separation far from family, learns to be pretty gutsy by the time she celebrates her first anniversary. Faith often undergirds the courage needed to tenderly kiss your spouse good-bye, not knowing when you will see him again or *if* you will see him again.

Because they are likely far from extended family, the military family's appreciation for their *immediate* family is naturally heightened. Often siblings are the built-in playmates that provide continuity amid numerous moves. Absence from the military member also tends to make the heart grow fonder (not to mention the cool gifts Mom or Dad bring back from other countries). The real challenge is to learn to say, "Hi, Mom (or Dad)! I'm glad you're back home!" before yelling, "What did you bring me?"

Humor, adventure, courage, and family—these could very well describe the hero in a blockbuster summer action film! In many ways these families are heroes. They don't get the Navy Cross or the Bronze Star, but they deserve a medal—it could be called the Hidden Heroes award: They're heroes at home.

When military members know that their spouse can hold things together at home, and when they have confidence that their spouse believes in what they do for a living, they are better able to concentrate on their duties. Sometimes that concentration is the difference between life and death.

When Americans support those who support our troops, they play a key role in our nation's defense. This book was designed to educate Americans about military families, because while these families are unique, they are common in their need for affirmation, encouragement, and helping hands. This has also been a guidebook for ways military families can do things more efficiently and effectively.

Every family member is impacted when Mom or Dad, son or daughter, takes the pledge to defend our country and risk his or her life to do so. A three-month-old baby sacrifices when that parent is called away, elementary-aged children pay a price for freedom as they adjust to talking to Mommy or Daddy online or through an AVC hookup. Teenagers, at a time when they need their parents most, also miss a deployed parent (although many would rather eat strained spinach than admit it). The spouse left at home sacrifices by putting on the single-parent hat along with the many other hats he or she already wears. The parent of a military member also has to say good-bye to the one they would die for if given the chance—but instead, their child is willing to pay the ultimate sacrifice for their parents' freedom. This book is a tribute to everyone who has loved someone in the service and supported that one in whatever way they could. *You* are the hero. You may be hidden, but it doesn't diminish the effect of your contribution. When I meet you one day, as I hope I will, I look forward to giving you a hug and telling you: America loves you; we are so proud of you; and together, we will be all right.

CELEBRATING
HIDDEN HEROES

☆ 1 ☆

HIDDEN HEROES

The Top Ten Qualities of a Hidden Hero

During the final days of the Gulf War, I took our three-year-old son, Daniel; his two-year-old brother, Philip; and our infant daughter, Bethany, to watch their father launch his F-4 Phantom II. He was going to the Middle East. His mission: to fight for our nation's freedom.

"When will de Papa be back home, Mama?" asked Daniel as he waved his chubby hand at the roaring jet.

"Soon," I said, as I fought back tears and kissed my baby daughter on her fuzzy blond head. "We are praying he will come home soon."

Philip was excited; he loved watching airplanes: "I wuv you, Papa!" he shouted as he jumped up and down. Then all of a sudden he turned to me, furrowed his brow, and said very seriously, "You know, I weally wuv de Papa." Then he turned to wave at the small speck in the sky as his dad flew off to his mission.

Later that week, Mrs. Phillips, Daniel's Sunday school teacher, told me that Daniel had a special prayer request. She said he asked, "Please pway for all de air farce guys dat fly to betect our fweedoms." Then he paused and added, "And please pway for dem Army guys dat do de same thing—but dey fly and fwight on dem helicopters. Oh, and pray for de Army gulls, too!"

☆ ☆ ☆ ☆ ☆ ☆ ☆

Daniel didn't quite understand what his father did for a living when he was that young child, but he understood a decade later, after 9/11 and the situation in the Middle East. As a military family with seven children, we have long held a keen appreciation for what it takes to keep this nation free. We lived through three wars and knew that my husband would be called upon repeatedly to fly and fight in order to protect our nation's freedoms. The kids and I were the veterans on the home front.

Some have called military families the "hidden heroes at home," but most would not accept such a distinction. After all, we don't wear the uniform, we haven't sworn to offer our life's blood to defend our nation, and we don't eat MRE rations in some faraway place. We merely support those who do.

Since Bob knew that when he returned from his mission he would have a loving family waiting for him, he was better equipped to perform at the height of his capabilities. When he believed that his family would have people in the community who would assist us through the uncertain weeks and months ahead, he rested a little better when he contemplated the stars in a darkened sky half a world away. And in many ways, these families, as well as their communities, have contributed to our national defense, as have all the supportive families of other airmen, sailors, and soldiers.

★ ★ ★ ★ ★ ★ ★

I have always disliked the distinction of "the little woman," who stays at home, wringing her hands, waiting for her husband to come back. Military spouses (men and women) tend to be proactive, courageous, and every now and then a little goofy (in a patriotic kind of way). There are plenty of things we can do ahead of time to prepare effectively for those long and short separations. While we can't be sure the kids won't get sick or the washer won't break down, we can do some preventative maintenance in order to help things run smoothly while our heart anxiously awaits the return of our loved one.

There are some basic things military families can do to be more prepared for the various aspects this lifestyle presents. While some of the things listed here seem pretty basic, others, such as relationship issues, are not as evident. And yet these other aspects of our lives have a great impact on how we are able to cope with the moves, the separations, and the financial constraints. Later in the book there will be dozens of specific helps for the areas we're discussing in this chapter. But for now, here's a general overview of your adventure as a military family.

Network of Military Support

Plug in to your unit's individual family readiness or support group, if not actively, then at least in a casual way. You don't have to head a fund-raiser committee or be the driving force in this group, but it's critically important that you plug in and maybe attend a few coffees or activities. You will need this group when your spouse deploys—for information disbursement as well as support. The time to plug in is *before* you need it.

Network of Non-Military Support

When families live on base/post, their children might attend the base school and participate in youth sports on base, and they might go to the base chapel. They can easily become "base cadets." We need to broaden our scope of influence and our children's through developing relationships with non-military friends. We need a break from military-speak, and these friends can provide that bit of touch with reality. Consider joining groups off base/post or go to a civilian church or synagogue to make sure you have friends who will keep you balanced.

Legal Limitations

If your spouse is going to deploy (it could be for a month that turns into a year), you will need to check with your installation's legal department and get your wills in order and a power of attorney. Make sure that your name is on your checking and savings accounts and that your name is also on the title to your vehicles and your home. Be sure you have all the log-in information and passwords to your mutual accounts. These simple precautions can save you major financial and legal problems.

Budget Binges

If you don't have a budget, look at one of the chapters under the Celebrating a Balanced Budget section of this book to see how you can get one set up for your family, and then get on a budget right away! For an online budget tool, go to www.elliekay.com. Be sure you know about the finances in your home and that you have the power of attorney to handle all the financial decisions that could arise when your spouse is deployed. You might also want to budget for "Fun Funds" to be used when your spouse deploys. This would cover those binges such as extra eating out, going to the movies or a theme park, or even buying a new outfit. If these are funded, they won't be a liability to your budget. Later in the book, I'll give loads of fun, easy ways to stretch these funds—for even more fun!

Learn It, Don't Burn It!

I've heard of more than one person who burned up a car engine because they didn't change the oil! During sustained deployments, your local Family Support Center equivalent (i.e., Army Community Services, Military Fleet and Family Support Center, Marine Corps Community Services Center, Airman and Family Readiness Center) often has programs to help you maintain your vehicle. In the meantime, learn the basics of car maintenance (or where and when to take it to have this service done) and home maintenance. You are quite capable of simple home repairs if you decide you're going to learn how to do it. The key is to learn to be flexible.

For example, when we were stationed in northern New York, I took a snowblower class in early September. Later in the month Bob went TDY to Florida, and we had our first snowstorm—but I was prepared. I simply took our handy-dandy John Deere snowblower and cleared our driveway. Then my neighbor Joy (from Korea) asked me to clear hers—so I did. By the time I was finished with her driveway, Elke (from Germany), my neighbor across the street, was yelling over the wind, asking me to do her driveway. I was not only helping my neighbors but improving international relations as well! By the time I finally shook the snow off my boots and went inside in time to get the kids ready for school, my husband's operations officer called and asked in an "I'll help the little woman out" way: "Would you like me to come over and snowblow your driveway?"

I squared my shoulders, smiled, and held the phone firmly in my hand as I replied, "No, thanks, I've already cleared our driveway—and two more!" LOL!

It's pretty cool to be equipped to blow your own snow (or do other routine maintenance chores). But you have to prepare *before* the storms come.

Scheduled Play

Have a plan for some rest and relaxation before your spouse deploys. Interview baby-sitters, find a reliable friend you can swap kids with, look over the course schedules offered by the local community college or civic center, join a choir or even a yoga class. Check with your military installation for free child-care events. But it's critically important to have scheduled play times for YOU while your spouse is away. If it's not immoral or illegal, build it into your schedule. This will keep you from frantically scrambling at the last minute when you're at your wit's end, looking for someone to watch the kids or trying to find a break that is yours alone to enjoy.

Mend Fences

If you or your spouse has "unfinished business" with each other or with extended family members, home time is THE time to get these issues worked out. It may be hard and may even require the assistance of a counselor or base/post chaplain, but it is vitally important that you make every effort to mend these fences. Many military installations now have a Military Family Life Consultant program (MFLC), or an equivalent, in your branch of service. This is a counseling program that supports military members and their families in overcoming post-deployment, family separation, stress management, grief and loss, parenting, and work/life issues. The pre-deployment as well as the reunion and reintegration period after an extended deployment are critical times for military members and their families. These counselors are experienced in family matters, relationships, raising children, substance abuse, good-byes, and homecomings. Services offered include workshops, group discussions, personal consultations, activities, and organization tips.

If you've at least tried, you can have a clear conscience that you have done your part. I had one of these counselors tell me, "You are 100 percent responsible for your 50 percent" of the marital relationship. I put that into practice in my marriage and found that it really helped. Encourage your spouse to also mend fences with his/her extended family members, such as parents and siblings.

Don't Burn Your Bridges

Remember the classic saying "What goes around comes around"? Well, it's true! Bob found himself to be outranked by guys that he once "trained" (i.e., harassed) as a sophomore at the Air Force Academy. Boy, did HE ever regret acting like a jerk back then! I am happy to say he outgrew that immaturity a very long time ago. Conversely, one of the cadets that used to work for Bob, and who had a few run-ins with him over parking tickets, found himself face-to-face with his old AOC (Air Officer Commanding) when the young pilot graduated from pilot training and went to fighter lead-in school. As a matter of fact, this pilot was in centrifuge training, out of state, when his young wife went into labor three weeks early! They had no one else to call to coach her in childbirth, so they asked me to go to the hospital. The pilot made it back just after his son's birth, and was he surprised to see who helped deliver the baby!

The truth is no matter what walk of life you're in, you never know when the tables might be turned; a past acquaintance may be in a position to either help you or hurt you. So it's a good idea when you run into "sandpaper" people (who rub you the wrong way) to just walk away—don't get even. You might end up living near them at some point, or worse, your son might marry their daughter!

The Top Ten Qualities of a Hidden Hero

1. **Sense of Humor.** The ability to laugh at oneself and with each other

2. **Flexibility.** What it's called when you create an elaborate candlelight dinner, farm out the kids for the night, and your husband calls to say he's not coming home because they have an inspection coming up

3. **Courageous.** The ability to wave good-bye for the 200th time, fight back the tears, smile, and say, "I love you, I'm proud of you, and I'll be all right."

4. **Extraordinary.** The ability to move 15,000 pounds of household goods in twenty-four hours

5. **Strong.** Nerves of steel (for all those close calls and near misses)

6. **Patriotic.** Unashamed to shed a tear during the presentation of the colors or the singing of the national anthem

7. **Faith-Full.** Brimming over with faith in God and true to your country

8. **Independent.** Confident during solo parenting gigs, but ready to move to interdependence when the spouse comes back home

9. **Acronym Reader.** The ability to decode three-letter acronyms (TDY, PCS, UOD, MRE, OIC, SOF, BDU, SOL)

10. **Superhero.** The capability to conquer new lands, stay in touch with old friends, keep the home fires burning, jump buildings in a single bound, and stay out of the funny farm

2

ANGELS AMONG US

Practical Ways to Help Military Families

G ot your backpacks?" I shouted above the clamor of five children in the car as they prepared to go to school.

Yes!

"*Lunches?*"

Yes!

"*Homework?*"

Yes! and Um . . .

"*Um? Did I hear an 'um'?*" As "Drill Sergeant Mom," I glared at my seventh-grade boy and said calmly, "Go get it!"

He scrambled out of the car while the others fought over who got to talk to Dad first when he called later that night from his deployment to Red Flag. And I quietly wondered how "roughing it in Las Vegas" constituted serving your country. But as my homework cadet reported in from parole, it was time to continue the roll call.

"*Permission slips?*"

Yes!

"*Water bottles?*"

Yes!

"*Shoes?*"

Yes! and Um . . .

"*Um? Did I hear an 'um'?*" Once again the drill sergeant cast her steely eyes on the guilty party. This time I zeroed in on my youngest, our first-grade son (aka "Turbo Dude" for his ability to hustle, which of course comes in handy when he's so forgetful!).

"You forgot your shoes again?!" I exclaimed as he squirmed under my laser-beam stare. "And if I hadn't asked you about it, you'd end up at the drop-off zone at school like you did last week—Shoeless Joe Jackson! Now go get them, quickly!"

The little guy scrambled out of the car, grabbed his shoes off the shoe rack in the garage, and "turboed" back into the vehicle at record speed. I fondly observed my "baby" and mentally counted the days until his dad would return home to play checkers with the chubby-cheeked cherub. This was day one, and there would be twenty-nine more days of this particular absence.

With the roll call complete, this temporarily single mom began to back the huge white Suburban out of the garage, when suddenly she heard a sickening scrape of metal on metal, followed by her children's screams:

Mom, STOP!

"Oh, no! No!"

You hit the garage door! It fell off the tracks and landed on the back of the car!

"Oh, no! No!"

I lost it, along with the kids. "Who left the garage door partially open?" I asked incredulously. The automatic door lifts it all the way up, and someone had to have purposefully stopped it before it was raised!

Suddenly the whole car became oddly quiet, and then one little voice broke the silence. It was the voice of Sweet Pea, our eight-year-old nearly perfect child.

"Um . . . Mama? Papa said that when the weather is hot like this, we need to leave the garage door partly open. Since Papa is gone, I'm doing his job, and I left it partly open." A wave of tears filled his huge hazel eyes and spilled down his cheeks. "Did I do something wrong?"

Letting out a huge sigh and mustering a semblance of control and the kindest reply I could manage, I answered, "Well, Sweet Pea, I know you're being a big helper. But your dad meant the garage should be partially opened from the bottom when we're at home, not partially opened from the top when we're leaving."

Only twenty-nine days to go!

* * * * * * *

I well remember those days of multiple deployments throughout the years. As a veteran wife and mom, I saw my share of "accidents" at home while Dad was away. Any military spouse will tell you that it seems as soon as the troops deploy, the children get sick, the computer crashes, the washer breaks down, or a distracted mom absentmindedly plows through a partially opened garage door. We purchased *two* garage doors during that year. In fact, Overhead Custom Doors carried our door in stock, ready for the next deployment!

But how do you describe what a deployment is to those who don't know? MCpl Ed Thompson is a husband, father of three, and a serving member of the Canadian forces. Here's his definition:

Most often we think of deployments as a time when a member departs for an extended period to some far-off exotic land. In fact, a deployment includes any time a member is separated from their family, such as a two-week assignment in sunny Wainwright or a yearlong assignment to the Middle East. So when you think of deployment, don't think only of our men and women serving overseas, but also think of those who are away from their families on course, training exercise, and assignments.

I had confidence that the Kay family would survive those continued separations, and we did, even though it didn't feel like it at times. One of the ways we managed was through the help of "angels with skin on." These people put their faith into action and came to the rescue when daily routines became unbearable and the mundane issues of life—like mowing lawns and cooking dinner—threatened to be my downfall. They are the angels that walk among us, and their help is simply heavenly.

We all have our limits. Doing the single-mom thing while worrying about my spouse's safety created so much tension that the thought of plowing through the week without help was almost too much to bear. It was precisely at these moments that God provided a strong back to take care of a few of Dad's chores or we received a hot meal when I was too exhausted to cook.

In times of national concern, people ask themselves (or the military family) how they can reach out in practical ways to help the heroes at home. Americans really do care about each other, as is most evidenced during times of national tragedy. Often people—even extended family members—don't know how to help; that's what this section is for. It will help you help others to help you.

The other problem military families have is that sometimes well-meaning people think what they're doing is helping when it really isn't. For example, the in-laws that want to come and welcome the ship back into port. That seems like a very natural thing to do, and to suggest otherwise could be deemed ungrateful. However, a closer look at the nature of military separations and reentry issues indicates that it would probably be better if the in-laws gave the sailor a couple of weeks to readjust to his nuclear family before they come to visit. That's why putting a copy of this book in the hands of your family and friends will help you and a lot of other military members.

Here are some suggestions that you may want to pass along to those who want to be angels with skin on, from those who think the *right kind* of help is simply divine!

Phone Calls and Text Messages

Initially after a deployment, there are usually quite a few phone calls, cards, and letters of support received when military members leave or when the TDY begins. This can be a great source of encouragement, but here are a few tips to make the most of your support:

Brevity. Keep the initial phone calls, texts, or emails brief and to the point, such as: "I just wanted to let you know that we're here for you and want to support you in any way we can."

Sensitivity. Be mindful that sometimes people will want to talk and other times they won't, because they can feel bombarded by phone calls and emails as well as the enormity of their circumstances.

Leave a Message. Due to the number of phone calls, some families may just let their calls go into voicemail. If you get the recording, don't hang up; just leave a short message expressing your care and concern.

Visits

If you are related to a military family (as a parent, in-law, or sibling), your initial reaction might be to go and help them, which may be exactly what they need. Here are some items to keep in mind if you are considering a visit. These guidelines can also be copied and sent to your extended family members so they will know how to best help you.

Ask First. Don't call your daughter or son-in-law and simply announce your intentions to come to their rescue. Ask permission to come, and be prepared for a "no" or a "please, not right now" answer.

It's Not About You. If you get one of the two negative responses about a visit, remember that this is not about you. Don't make life harder for these family members by insisting on your so-called "family rights" or "responsibility" to help.

Asset, Not Liability. If the military family feels that your visit would be a real asset during this time, carefully consider the living arrangements. If your family lives in military housing, it is more than likely very small. Consider staying at an inexpensive hotel, at billeting on base/post, or even renting an RV to stay in during your visit. Close quarters can make for added stress.

Permissive Help. If it is determined that you will go to visit your family, decide ahead of time to help without taking over. I've had many friends whose families show up and then let the military spouse do all the cooking for the additional family members, thereby adding to their burden! Ask permission to help; then once you get a green light, by all means clean, cook, do laundry, take the children to the zoo, mow the lawn, change the oil in the car, fix the broken door handles, run errands, buy chocolate . . . well, you get the idea.

Keep Those Cards and Notes Coming

During the initial war in Iraq, no one had any idea how long it would last—but few thought it would continue for many years. Once the media frenzy of the initial deployment wears off, people get on with their lives and tend to forget the families that remain alone for many weeks, months, and even years in some cases. Here are ways not to forget:

Mark Your Calendars. Make a weekly reminder note in your phone or calendar to send a card, text, tweet, email, or make a call. A small note makes a *big* difference. I use an online card service such as Hallmark.com and set the days for weeks in the future. It takes ten minutes to keep ten e-cards coming for ten weeks.

Humor Helps. Humor can be an incredibly healing balm and provide a much-needed release so you might want to send a funny card, a poem, cartoon, book, photo, or family-oriented DVD.

Unconditional Love. Do not require a response from your friend or family member. Your card may have meant a lot, but your friend may be so distracted by the stress of the deployment that he or she may forget to thank you (at least right away). The usual protocols do not always apply during sustained separations from family members.

When in Doubt, Send Chocolate (or Other Tokens of Support)

Okay, this piece of advice comes from a chocoholic, but the logic is sound: Give the heroes at home small gifts from time to time.

These special treats can make all the difference during a difficult stretch. Small acts of kindness reap big rewards to those holding down the fort at home.

Money Is No Object. Thoughtful reminders that someone is thinking of you don't have to be expensive. Drop off a gift basket filled with your friend's favorite foods (did I mention chocolate?) or a DVD rental of a movie they've been wanting to see (be sure to let them know when it's due back).

Gifts of Time. I've been called the "Coupon Queen" many times, but why not make a coupon booklet as a gift? Include coupons for free baby-sitting, a meal, a favorite batch of cookies, a coffee date, running errands—the possibilities are only limited by your imagination!

Group Gifts. Groups of friends (such as a Sunday school class, civic organization, or work group) could join together and buy a gift certificate for a favorite restaurant or movie passes for a fun night out.

Saving Private Ryan

It can mean a lot to the family at home to know that others are keeping in touch with the military member. Here are some practical ways to reach out:

Prayer. There's an old saying: "There are no atheists in foxholes." Ninety percent of Americans have a spiritual interlude with God every day, according to a study released recently by Brandeis University. In fact, half pray several times a day. No matter what the military member's religious affiliation is, the overwhelming majority of people won't turn down prayer. Let them know you're praying for them regularly.

Prayer/Letter Chains. If you want to take the above tip a step further, organize a group of friends to pray each week. Have the weekly prayer partners write a note to the military member to let him/her know they're praying. But be sure it's all right with the service person before you organize this chain.

Letters. Your family can adopt a single service member. Send photos of your family, drawings from your kids, and letters of appreciation for the service they are rendering our nation.

Gifts. Check with the military member and see what restrictions there are on small gifts. Send them their own copy of this book so they can feel valued in their role as the hero on the field.

Angels With Skin On Go Beyond "If I Can Do Anything"

It's one thing to give a family an open-ended statement: "If there's anything we can do to help, please let us know." Chances are they will never call for your help. Here are some ways to be proactive in your offer for help:

Refusals Permitted. While you offer to help, be sensitive to the fact that they may refuse it. Don't take it personally; just make another offer to help at a later time.

Be Specific. Instead of a blanket proposal for help, offer a tangible form of assistance, such as, "May my son and I come and mow your lawn on Friday or Saturday?" Or "I'd like to bring you a meal one day next week. What day would be good for you to take a break from cooking?"

Group Projects. If your group wants to help, have specific projects in mind. For example, a youth group could clear away all the leaves in the yard. Remember, always have adult supervision and be responsible for those in your group. These projects can be a tremendous blessing to the families involved.

☆ *Hidden Hero Profile* ☆

Name: Jessica Culley

Spouse's Name: John Culley (E-6)

Branch of Service: United States Coast Guard

Kids: Dominic and Marissa

Number of Moves: six total; as a military spouse, four

Years in Service: I served in active duty with the Coast Guard for five years before marrying my husband. I've been married for nearly twelve of his fifteen years of active duty service.

Hobbies: horseback riding, hiking, scrapbooking, surfing, diving, fishing, writing, hula, backpacking

How many times have you deployed in the last six years and where?
The CG doesn't deploy like the other services. My husband deployed on cutters while we were stationed in Florida. He left for three months at a time and did five deployments in a three-year period (that was six to nine years ago). Two years ago, he did a six-month, extended TDY for training. With his current job, he is in and out constantly. He leaves

for several days to several weeks at a time throughout the year. We never know when he is coming or going.

How does living on one income impact your life?

Choosing to live on one income does not allow us to participate in some of the activities we would like. The kids are limited in the number of sports and activities they participate in. Traveling to the other islands and many area attractions are not an option for us. We gladly take advantage of low- and no-cost activities. The most important thing for us is spending time as a family.

My husband especially looks forward to the day I return to work and help ease some of the financial burden. He seems to feel the social pressure more than I do. When everyone else in his office is an officer, civilian, or dual income, it can be challenging. He can't afford to eat out every day and frequently declines social engagements due to a lack of finances. He doesn't complain, but I know there are many things he would like to do but can't due to our financial limitations.

A single income also makes it difficult to see family and travel (especially now that we live in Hawaii). Plane tickets are expensive so traveling as a family is very limited.

Least Favorite Aspect of Military Life:

Moving. Transitions are hard for me and it takes me a while to feel like I "fit in" somewhere after a move. We moved to Hawaii unaccompanied, which was very interesting! New challenges are also arising as the kids get older. Not only do I have to navigate my own issues now, but I also have to help the kids face their individual challenges.

Favorite Aspect of Military Life:

Moving. I think I love moving as much as I dislike it. I love seeing new places and meeting new people. I enjoy living in different areas with different cultures and experiences. While I may not enjoy the challenges of moving at the time, I love how they make our family stronger and closer in the end.

Favorite Quotes:

"Begin to be now what you will be hereafter."—Saint Jerome
"We walk by faith, not by sight."—2 Corinthians 5:7
"In everything give thanks."—1 Thessalonians 5:18

Other Comments You Would Like to Make:

Our family is far from achieving the financial (or any) ideal. We have, however, learned to manage on one income and make the most of what we have. Money is not the source of our family's happiness or security. I believe money has the potential to create as many problems as it solves.

☆ 3 ☆

HIDDEN HERO PORTRAIT— MYRA HINOTE

She's Cool, She's Clever—And She's Got a **Really** *Clean Car*

The base was conducting an exercise, alternating the security requirements between FPCON (Force Protection Condition) Bravo and the more serious FPCON Charlie. Just as any able-minded person wouldn't dare make jokes about guns and bombs while walking through metal detectors at an airport, you wouldn't make jokes when going through the base security check at the main gate. But Myra wasn't really able-minded: Her husband had deployed for the eighth time in six months, and she was fending off three very cute (but very active) preschoolers. In a court of law, I'm sure any jury would declare her temporarily insane after seven straight nights of nursing sick kids with colds and ear infections.

Myra drove up to the security gate in a squeaky-clean van—she'd just been through the car wash for the third time in three days. It seems that Hunter, her three-year-old son, found life's fulfillment by going through the small town's brand-new, automatic, triple deluxe wash system—with colored bubbles! (Who says those marketing researchers didn't know how many minivans they could clean with that sly tactic?) Every time they'd drive by the facility (which happened to be several times a day because it was on the main drag in town), he'd announce from his car seat:

☆ *Profile* ☆

Name: Myra Hinote

Spouse's Name: Clint (COL)

Branch of Service: USAF

Kids: Meg, Hunter, Holly

Number of Moves: Only ten (four in our first six years of marriage)!

Years in Service: eighteen

Work/Employer: Graduate student in Political Science. Professional volunteer at kids' school. Some Web design work. Have had multiple home businesses.

Hobbies: Reading, hiking, biking, scrapbooking, cooking, truffling

Describe your military service before 9/11 and after:

While Clint deployed quite frequently before 9/11 in support of the no-fly zones over Iraq, the nature of the deployments certainly changed after the second war in Iraq. Most Americans aren't aware that we are still sending our military personnel to Korea, "unaccompanied," for a year or more, fifty-five-plus years after the Korean War ended. Unfortunately, we appear to have added a new Korea to our repertoire in Iraq, with thousands of airmen, soldiers, sailors, and Marines rotating in and out of Iraq (and Afghanistan), many for a year or more. This doesn't look likely to end any time soon, especially for our airmen, who will probably be in the theatre for many years after the other services withdraw.

Clint's remote was a direct result of this, and we understand that it is not likely to be the last one he does in the Middle East. On another note, I think 9/11 gave our country a greater awareness of and appreciation for our military. I certainly feel that people go out of their way to express their appreciation for our service to the country.

Least Favorite Aspect of Military Life:

Lack of control over our future, next move, etc.

Favorite Aspect of Military Life:

The community and camaraderie with our squadrons and other military families. Also, feeling as though what we are doing is giving back to society, contributing in some small way. It is much easier for me to support my husband in a demanding military job than I think it would be in a demanding corporate job.

Favorite Quote:

"Joy is the infallible sign of the presence of God."—Madeleine L'Engle

Any other comments you would like to make:

Thank you for continuing to support our military families!

"Car deedy, Mama!"

Just in case Mama hadn't heard how dirty he thought the car was, he'd shout it again.

"Car deedy, Mama!"

Myra ignored him and drove her daughter to school.

"Car deedy, Mama!"

She went by the drive-in cleaners and pulled out her credit card.

"Car deedy, Mama!"

She pulled into the drive-thru bank. He yelled into the teller's microphone, "Car deedy, Mama!"

Moms are good at ignoring kids—for a remarkably long time. But any mom who is honest will tell you that it begins to wear on you about the thirty-second time.

"Car deedy, Mama!" Hunter was no quitter. But Myra was—especially when she was doing the single-mom thang.

Much to Hunter's delight, his life was once again fulfilled for the day as he giggled and shouted over the colorful bubbles. Their van was squeaky clean as Myra drove by the security forces guard at the gate during Threatcon Charlie.

The young airman sported an M-16 on his back as he approached Myra's open window. He wore his Battle Dress Uniform (BDU), which was especially hot on this sweltering day in the New Mexico desert.

He was in no joking mood.

Myra was so relieved that she had a temporary respite from Hunter's endless chattering. She absentmindedly pulled her identification out of her wallet for the guard, who now stood in front of her window.

"Ma'am, we are in Threatcon Charlie; may I see your military identification?"

Myra smiled smugly at her efficiency (who says mothers of young children don't have it together?). She had the card ready; the guard wouldn't have to tap his foot impatiently while she searched for it in her purse.

She thrust it through the window so the policeman could see it clearly.

He looked shocked at first, eyeing Myra suspiciously. Then he took one look at sleeping baby Holly and glanced over at Hunter in his car seat (who was, once again, shouting you-know-what).

For the first time that day, the guard smiled.

"Well, ma'am, that's a really nice credit card, but I'll still need to see your military ID."

* * * * * * *

Myra is *not* your typical security-gate criminal offender. She was offered a scholarship to Berkeley, was accepted to MIT, and graduated from Wellesley with a double major in astrophysics and religion. This background came in really handy when she married her husband, Clint, the number-one graduate in his class at the U.S. Air Force Academy. They ended up living in the middle of a sandy desert in New Mexico with three babies under five. While her classmates were getting partnerships and advanced degrees, she was establishing support groups and chairing fund-raisers for nonprofit organizations.

Does this sound like the life she always envisioned?

No.

Are her days full of joyful (and not so joyful) surprises?

Definitely.

Is she happy?

Are we grading on a curve? Okay, well, most of the time.

Myra is cool, courageous, and clever—she's even got a clean car. She's a hidden hero.

"If I felt that life stopped when the guys deployed, I'd have no life!" That's her basic philosophy regarding TDYs, school, and deployments.

When they were first married, Clint was assigned to Columbus, Mississippi, a small town of around thirty thousand people. For some strange reason there weren't a lot of job openings for astrophysicists who could give running commentary on the world's major religions. So she did what tons of military spouses did: She adapted. When life gave her lemons, she made lemonade—out of chocolate, no less! She turned her hobby of "truffling" into a full-fledged business and became a successful chocolatier, marketing her "to die for" truffles in dark chocolate, raspberry, kahlua, and orange flavors.

In order to verify the truthfulness of this, I asked Myra (okay, so I demanded, begged, and groveled) to:

"Just hand over the chocolate, and no one gets hurt."

So she did.

Now, I have to tell you that I am a chocolate connoisseur; I've tasted so many "Death by Chocolate" creations that I should have passed on long ago (but what a way to go!). I've sampled Godiva, savored Parisian chocolates, and drooled over the best chocos the Belgian Alps had to offer. But NOTHING is as good as Myra's! (I might have to sample a few more just to make sure.)

The week she "charged" through the base gate, she also spearheaded a fund-raiser for a support group called *MOPS* (Mothers of Preschoolers), a group she took to the next level in their second year. As the coordinator and head of the steering committee (or "the leader of all leaders," as one five-year-old put it) of this nonprofit organization, she doubled the membership, thus meeting the needs of dozens of moms with young children throughout the community. Her background as a gourmet chocolatier came in handy, as well. She even organized the creation of two thousand truffles for the fund-raiser!

Fiercely independent, Myra put her computer skills to work by freelancing for an entrepreneurial website designer, who handled some of the best association and industrial sites on the Internet. It's one way she maintains her personal identity despite being a traveling mom who has moved a lot.

Myra was facing every hidden hero's fear: sending her husband to fly F-16s in Korea for a year by himself. She went through the roller coaster emotions that are intensified by the fact that the Air Force may not send him after all. There usually seems to be a Plan B, C, and D. But it's Plan E—the one that no one ever thought of—that comes through most often.

Myra had to decide whether she would leave the network of friends she'd established at her present base and move for that year to be near family. She would be leaving the kids' preschool, her home, friends, church, network of activities, and volunteer work in order to be near family. She would have to establish a new home, find a new school, make new friends, and search for a new church. It's hard for civilians to understand this aspect of military life and the incredible challenge that accompanies it.

One Family Services director employs an excellent exercise to help civilian educators understand what their military students experience on a regular basis. You might try this exercise to help family members, co-workers, or other civilians gain an understanding of the lifestyle. If you're reading this and you are non-military, just follow the directions.

> **Step One** Think about all the things you enjoy most in life right now. These must be things that are on the outside of your home, and they cannot be your own family. For example, you may enjoy the way your neighbor laughs over coffee, the southwest sunset you see from your balcony, or the great gym that you work out in.
>
> **Step Two** Narrow your list to the top three.

Step Three If you are in a group setting, ask the exercise leader to collect all the slips of paper from the participants.

Step Four The leader tells the audience, in a soft, soothing voice, "Thank you for listing these and for passing them forward." Most of the audience expects her to read them aloud, thinking they might guess who wrote them. But instead the leader does something very unexpected with the slips of paper.

Step Five The leader takes all the responses, walks over to the side of the room, and throws them in the trash can as she announces: "You've just moved to a new place and *no one cares.*"

* * * * * * *

Sure, Myra's family cared, but the strangers she met in the new neighborhood, school, grocery store, church, and gym didn't know her. They didn't care. They didn't understand why she was married but didn't have a husband within six thousand miles. She's started all over *again.* What magnifies the difficulty of all the military spouses in Myra's situation is one major factor: *She must do all of this alone.*

There will be

- no one to take turns getting up with the baby (and that baby may not recognize Dad when he comes home next)
- no one to fix the garbage disposal when it jams again
- no one to go out with on a romantic date (romantic dates? I settle for just going out!)
- no one to accompany her to the principal's office
- no one who can meet her at the doctor's clinic
- no one to share the funny little thing that Holly did or Hunter said (only the other parent can find some of these things to be indescribably endearing)
- no male figure for Hunter to play catch with
- no one sitting at the other end of the dining room table
- no one to take Meg to the father/daughter banquet
- no one to share her laughter
- no one to kiss her tenderly
- no one to wipe her tears
- no one who even *knows* she cried herself to sleep
- no one to snuggle with at night.

For an entire year, or more, she is alone.

* * * * * * *

Myra came to terms with this monumental event that was in her future and is now in her past. And just about the time she compartmentalized, internalized, and strategized a way to deal with it, good old Uncle Sam changed the game plan. That's why flexibility is a necessary characteristic of life as a hidden hero.

* * * * * * *

"At the end of your life you'll never regret not having passed one more test or not closing one more deal. You will regret times not spent with a child, a husband, a friend, or a parent."

—First Lady Barbara Bush
in an address to the 1990 graduating class
of Myra's school, Wellesley College

CELEBRATING
FAMILY

☆ 4 ☆

BUNNY TALES

Creating Memories and Managing Holidays

Ever since she was old enough to hold a crayon and find an empty wall, our daughter Bethany has been in the creative business of writing and drawing. She earned the nickname Bunny *because when she was two years old, she made us read* ABC Bunny *and* No, No, Bunny *from the Cottontail series about a gazillion times.*

She not only enjoyed reading, she adored creating, too. By the time she was five years old, she had comprised some 5,247 works of art. We posted them on our refrigerator, my desk, Bob's work computer, and even the toilet seat cover. I couldn't bear to throw them away, so I shipped them by the boxful to grandparents and aunts and uncles as our way of keeping in touch with family. But just like another bunny we know, she kept going, and going, and going. . . . Bethany's creations multiplied as quickly as bunnies do, and I knew if she ever found any of her treasures in the trash it would traumatize her.

What's a mother to do? Well, I started including them in the payment envelope when we mailed the bills—the gas, electric, and phone company all received brightly colored pages from her "Peter Cottontail" coloring book, carefully signed, "Love, Bunny."

I was committed to valuing her self-esteem, so I brought along a few with me in the van when I ran errands. The teller at the bank got a picture of a bunny hopping through the tulips. The dry cleaners proudly displayed "Flowers and Puppies" on their window. Even the auto mechanic took down his Sports Illustrated *cover to put up her "Mama Kitty" drawing and didn't even charge me for repairing our flat tire!*

When I got pulled over for speeding one time, I encouraged her to hand one over to the police officer. She was only three at the time and sat proudly in her car seat, her blond hair gathered on top of her head like Pebbles from The Flintstones. *She flashed her bright blue eyes and happy teeth as she thrust a coloring of a pink blob through the window.*

"What do you think that is?" she asked, convinced that the policeman had stopped us in order to get one of these treasures.

"Uh . . ." He was completely taken off guard as he looked into her bright, eager eyes.

"Uh," he repeated. "It looks like a pink . . . uh, thing?"

"That's right!" she squealed, "It's my pink shoe. I ride it. Like my brudders ride der bike! We can go now, Mama. The policey-man got his picture!"

I glanced over Bunny's head to the previously stern officer. My eyes saw a reflection of what he found in my daughter's—eager and bright.

He caved. Big time. The pressure of a Mama Rabbit and her Bunny was just too much. So instead of a much-deserved ticket, he gave me a warning.

"Ma'am. You were going 45 in a 30. You will need to slow down in the future. And, uh," he turned toward Bethany, "thanks for letting me catch up with you so I could get my picture!"

Unfortunately, that brush with the law only encouraged me. I began to stick her "cottage industry products" on the rearview mirror in the car, the bathroom mirror, and my compact powder mirror. So whenever I looked into a mirror, I saw a reflection of my little Bunny.

* * * * * * *

Bethany's outgoing personality suited our military lifestyle. Bob and I were geographically separated from family the second year of our marriage, and we've never lived within a thousand miles of our extended family since. So the new "friends" Bethany picked up along the way were there to encourage her (okay, they fawned over her) the way her grandparents would if they lived nearby.

Staying in touch with extended family members is just as important to the military family as it is to any American family, but it's often a challenge because of the distance. Sometimes military families just give in, charge three thousand dollars on the credit card, and run home to Mama. Others try to convince themselves that they "don't really miss having grandparents" and try to pretend they're all right, when they're really feeling lonely and disconnected from those they love. Still others give up trying to keep a relationship going with extended family and miss the joy of connection.

But it's not a hopeless cause. On one hand, it takes an extra measure of work to keep that relationship with friends and family going when you live far apart. But on the other hand, it's much easier to keep in touch with Skype, Facebook, Twitter, and smartphones than it was ten years ago!

These relationships are important for us, for our kids, and for our future grandkids. Our children will see the way we've treated our parents, and they may one day treat us the same way. So investing in the lives of your extended family is investing in your future life with your children and grandchildren.

Here are some ways to strengthen the roles of extended family members in your lives, stay connected between visits, and tips on handling the holidays.

Building Memories. Take some of those works of art that your children have created and build a Creative Memories type portfolio for your extended family. Attach photos to the artwork. If your children are old enough, have them write the captions, a short story explaining what they're doing in the picture, or even a poem that expresses their feelings about their family. You can send these to relatives monthly or hold the keepsakes until the end of the year and present them at Christmas as a special memory book. Don't forget school papers, certificates, or special awards that you can photocopy and include. Or you can put together these scanned and JPEG items in a special hardback book through places like shutterfly.com or snapfish.com.

Family Calendars. Your local discount department store's photo department is a great resource for making this a truly personal gift. Take photos year-round and order a gallery calendar for your extended family. Or upload your favorites from Facebook—if the quality isn't good enough, then request the JPEG from the person who took the picture and ask them to email it to you.

Write as many special days as you can on their calendar, including birthdays, first and last days of school, moving day, promotions, beginning of the various sports seasons, or even anniversaries. This reminds extended family that their military family is thinking of them, and it might even encourage them to make phone calls, send notes, and be more involved in the lives of those they love from afar.

Kids' Mugs. If you're related to a military family, consider having your photo printed on a mug. Kids love to have their own special cup, and each time they drink from it, they are reminded that they have family who thinks they are special. This even helps very young children recognize and stay connected to Grandma and Grandpa.

Holidays

Where to spend the holidays can be a great challenge for hidden heroes. It can be costly to travel to see family, and yet there's always the possibility that instead of living one thousand miles away, you'll be ten thousand miles away next Christmas. Consequently, a sense of "now or never" can impact these decisions and can also be a cause for dissension among the ranks.

Let's take a look at the case study of a sailor we'll call Ryan and his wife, Jennifer. The "holiday decision" was one of the most volatile topics in Ryan and Jennifer's first year in the military. But a lot of the tension could have been eliminated if this couple had taken the time to sit down and discuss the holidays long before the season arrived.

Let's face it, the old saying "You can please some of the people some of the time, but you can't please all of the people all of the time" is never more true than when it comes to where you are going to spend the holidays. When you add stepparents, siblings, and grandparents, you can become torn in so many directions that the joy of the holiday can be drained away. The goal is to come up with a plan that is acceptable to both spouses so that everyone comes out a winner.

An exercise that will help get the conversation started toward a win/win result is to take out a sheet of paper and write down each holiday that could possibly be spent outside your family nest.

Next, list the way you would like to spend each holiday individually. This column will likely be largely based on what your family traditions were like while you were growing up. Also list the feelings you have associated with the holiday. Finally, you will have to compromise with lots of understanding and be willing to use positive communication techniques to decide what you will do for each holiday as a couple.

Some of the questions Ryan and Jennifer had to consider were: (1) Do you want to simplify the season? (2) go to parties and be with people? (3) stay within a limited travel budget? (4) spend the day in the comfort of your own home?

Take a look at the following sample of Ryan and Jennifer's list. It is easy to see why it led to a doozy of an argument.

This couple is an extreme case because their expectations for the holidays and diverse backgrounds were on opposite ends of the spectrum. But if they reached resolution, so can you. By sitting down together and discussing the holiday topic, you can avoid future arguments on the same topic and put to rest any smoldering ashes left over from the last disagreement. As you can see from the final column in our chart, each side had to give and take in order to reach a consensus.

In their discussion, they took into account that the decisions they made in the "here and now" would affect their future children and the rest of their family. So they made their decisions based on what would maintain peace, create lasting and loving memories for their own family, and be an asset to their relationship. They also kept in mind the fact that any decision would not be set in stone but could be modified to meet their future real and felt needs, geographical location, and family situation.

Maybe the plan will get you started on how to celebrate your holidays this coming year and for many happy years to come.

Holiday Celebrations Work Sheet/Year of _____

Thanksgiving Day

Jennifer	Ryan	Compromise
1. Watch Macy's parade	1. Sleep in late	1. Ryan sleeps; Jennifer gets her cocoa and watches the parade
2. Lots of food, fine china, and dressy attire	2. Camp out at home in grubbies	2. Every other year they will have a traditional dinner at the relatives' house. The alternate year is spent at home with a menu of Ryan's choice
3. Traditional menu	3. Pizza or whatever	3. They share what they are thankful for
4. Spend entire day with extended family	4. Watch football games all afternoon	4. Alternate Christmas/ Thanksgiving with relatives (when within traveling distance)
5. Each family member shares two things they are thankful for	5. Get to bed early after eating the leftover pizza	

| | Christmas | |
Jennifer	Ryan	Compromise
1. Christmas Eve church services	1. Open presents on Christmas Eve	1. Go to services, when available, and open one gift on Christmas Eve
2. Up at 6:00 A.M. to read Christmas story from the Bible	2. Sleep in late and wear pajamas most of the day	2. Ryan sleeps in, and they read the Bible story when he wakes up (by 10:00 A.M.)
3. Open presents one at a time, thanking between each one	3. Few presents (the holidays were downplayed)	3. Three gifts, opened one at a time
4. Formal dinner at Grandma's house	4. Pizza or whatever (maybe tacos)	4. They realize the holiday can have the significance you give it
5. Ice-skating in the afternoon	5. Watch football games and then take a nap	5. Football in the afternoon and caroling at night (when possible)
6. Christmas-caroling at night	6. No particular traditions (Christmas is just commercialism)	

Thanksgiving

Thankful Tree

Our "Thankful Tree" was featured in a *Woman's Day* magazine one year. It took two photographers *eight* rolls of film and *four* hours to get *one* three-by-five photo in the magazine. Our youngest son, Joshua, who was then three years old, was missing for one roll of film, and we didn't notice until we saw him making faces from *behind* the photographers.

The tip we shared in the magazine is how we stay in touch with family and friends during this holiday. On November 1, we make a Thankful Tree on poster board and put it on our wall or front door. The tree is bare, because the leaves that we make out of construction paper have not yet been gathered. The leaves have the names of friends or individual family members on them and a place for the person to write what they are thankful for. For example, "Grandma Rawleigh is thankful for _____ ." But we leave the tree up bare at the beginning of the season to teach the children how barren our lives are without the giving of thanks.

We make and send the leaves to friends and family around the world along with a self-addressed envelope or we email a leaf for them to fill in and email back. When these leaves begin to come back, the children get excited as they take turns opening them. At dinner that night, we read the leaf and give thanks along with those who are thankful and put the leaf on our tree. By Thanksgiving Day, we have a tree full of thanks. We carefully save the leaves in an envelope marked by the year and keep all of them in our Thanksgiving decoration box. Each year we read the leaves from past years.

We never know when this year's leaf might be someone's last or which family might have a new leaf on next year's tree. So we give thanks.

Five Kernels of Corn

In the first year after our pilgrim forefathers came to America, there were periods of time when food was so scarce that the daily ration consisted of only five kernels of corn. In remembrance of these difficult circumstances upon which our nation was founded, each of our family members receives five pieces of unpopped popcorn and takes turns passing around a basket. As we drop each kernel into the basket, we name five things that we are thankful for this year. One friend who follows this tradition says that at the end of their thanks, "We pop the popcorn and rejoice in how God has 'multiplied' our blessings!"

Christmas

Photo Greeting Cards

We have photos made in October and get the savings of an early-bird discount on photo greeting cards. If you try this beginning in your first year of marriage, it will be fun to see how your family changes as the years go by. We even put together a special Christmas photo album, and it's a wonderful place to display our annual photo greeting cards and an effective way to preserve memories.

Simplify

The reason we keep our gift-giving simple is *not* because we're cheap. It's because we want to keep the focus on the Reason for the Season. Holiday mania detracts from the coming of the Christ Child as God's greatest gift to us.

Three Gifts

Part of the Kay Family Simplification Plan involves the number of gifts each of our children receives. This could also apply to each spouse, before the kids start coming along. I'll never forget one Christmas before we had children. Bob and I watched a little boy get so many gifts for Christmas that he got tired of opening them and quit. Sadly, he was so spoiled by his parents and grandparents that he had the mistaken notion that Christmas was all about him.

Sharing Christmas

Sometimes the gift of time is the greatest gift of all during the holidays. There are a number of ways you and your spouse can brighten the holidays of those around you and share the season. We like to visit nursing homes and spend time with the residents, talking and sharing. If you know of an elderly relative, neighbor, or friend who rarely gets to decorate for the holidays, why not help that person put up a tree and holiday lights? Then after the season is over, help them put the decorations away.

One of the traditions on military bases is a holiday cookie drive. One year we collected ten thousand dozen cookies and distributed them to the police department, the fire department, and others who worked the holiday shift. You could take a basket of goodies to your local fire fighters or police officers on duty. I know they would enjoy these treats on Christmas Eve! We even bake cookies for the mail carriers and sanitation workers. We place these in easy-to-carry plastic bags and include a can of soda pop.

★ ★ ★ ★ ★ ★ ★

"A gift is a demonstration of love from one heart to another. Calvin Miller once sent me an acrostic poem that spelled out my name. You cherish those special, personal gifts."

—Chuck Swindoll
Tale of the Tardy Oxcart

☆ 5 ☆

PILOTS NEVER PANIC

Tips to Surviving Military Moves

7:00   On the morning of September 7, I woke up to get the children ready to take to the sitter because I had an appointment. I was having a few Braxton-Hicks pains.

7:30   My friend Pauline called from Colorado, and I asked her to pray that these contractions would get stronger and turn into the real thing on their own.

7:33   I hung up the phone, and the first hard contraction hit, followed by another strong one *three* minutes later. I remember thinking, *Wow! When Pauline prays, things happen!*

7:36   Daniel helped his younger siblings get into the van, and I drove them to the sitter's house and then headed a few blocks farther to the squadron.

7:40   At the squadron, Bob was about to fly, and he happened to be looking out the window when I drove into the parking lot.

He met my van outside. "Hi, Beloved (his term of endearment for me). Are you dropping off some bread for the guys?"

I put the van in park. "Yeah, honey, I'm dropping something—but it ain't bread!"

I was in between contractions. "This is it; I'm in labor!" I announced.

Even though he's had many children, Bob still panics every time I have a baby.

He stood there in his flight suit just staring at me.

I repeated, "Come on, let's go NOW!"

7:45 Bob ran back into the squadron, dropped his parachute, and shouted to the operations officer, "I'm having a baby!" Then he ran out.

7:59 Our van screamed into the hospital parking lot as Bob pulled into a No Parking slot in front of the ER doors. With the engine running, he dashed into the emergency room, grabbed a wheelchair, and threw me into it.

8:01 Once inside, he ran the halls, ramming me into an occasional wall while turning a corner. I couldn't talk because there were only a few seconds between contractions.

Just then, to my relief, I saw the double doors at the end of the hall to Labor and Delivery. Rapidly my relief turned to concern, because the wheelchair wasn't losing speed, it was gaining momentum as Bob accomplished his mission.

My mind shouted, The door! *It's an automatic door with a button on the side of the wall! It's not designed to be opened by the feet of women in wheelchairs!*

Bob slammed the chair through the double doors, where we faced some shocked nurses. I heard him mumble, "Some automatic doors!"

"Wait a minute! Who are you?" they asked the zealous pilot and his human battering ram.

"I'm Bob, and she"—he pointed to me—"is going to have that baby right now!"

Then, like a drowning man coming up one more time for air, he bellowed, "Oh, my goodness! The van is still running and it's parked in the ER zone!"

In a flash . . . he was gone.

With the Red Baron out of the way, the nurses helped me to the bathroom to change. No sooner had I gotten the robe on than the baby slammed down the birth canal and the nurses helped me to a bed.

8:02 One of the nurses shouted, "She's complete! Emergency delivery! Labor room two! Get Dr. Holzhauer—STAT!"

The other nurse asked, "Where's her husband?"

I answered in my mind, He's parking the car!

Thankfully, the doctor was in the hospital and arrived in seconds, out of breath from running. He knelt by my side and whispered, "All right, Ellie, I'm here."

8:05 With one intense effort, Joshua Steven was born.

8:10 Bob raced back into the room, shouting, "How is she?"

"Mister," said the nurse with her Southern drawl, "you done had yourself a fine baby boy!"

He looked at his 10-pound 8-ounce "Baby Huey." Joshua eventually earned the nickname "Conan the Baby Barbarian" because he always does things in a big way.

* * * * * * *

I wasn't the first military wife to give birth to a baby alone, and I won't be the last. Our situation was better than some, because at least Bob got there right after the birth. On Our *Heroes at Home* World Tour, I've met hundreds of women who have birthed their babies while their husbands were in the Middle East, and their military friends became their "husband." They coached, comforted, and celebrated the births of those babies.

I wasn't fortunate enough to have my mom geographically nearby for any of our children's births. Just like my friends, I had substitute family in my military family, and for their support, they meant the world to Bob, our children, and me. They celebrated the births of our babies and provided meals and child care for the other children, and I even found a couple of labor coaches among the crowd.

But this kind of "family" is never more important than when you're moving—especially if you're moving with a new baby. I remember when Bob worked at the Air Force Academy and we'd just had our fourth child, Jonathan, who was two weeks old. Bob came home *very* excited one day.

"Guess what, Beloved?" He didn't wait for my reply. "I get to stop flying a desk and go back to flying real fighters again! I've been asked to help stand up the AT-38 Squadron in Columbus, Mississippi." He paused only slightly for a quick breath and then delivered the punch line: "Can you move in two weeks?"

* * * * * * *

When you leave one military family, you're sure to find another in your new assignment. You know there will be others there who have pulled up roots more times than they can count. No sooner will you receive your farewell gift from where you are than you'll be sure to find someone on the other end waiting with a welcome gift. That's the beauty of the military family and their network of thousands of others around the world.

In fact, one of the greatest bonds military families have among themselves is the idea that we are from "everywhere and nowhere." While a precious few military families "homestead" or stay put in one area for anywhere from five to ten years, the overwhelming majority of us moves as much as a traveling circus.

In order to gather a variety of perspectives as well as practical advice on the topic of staying connected while moving, I've compiled tips from all the branches of the service. There's so much good advice in this chapter that I'm actually looking forward to our next move! (Did I just *say* that?)

Here is a list of helpful ideas to consider for your next move, contributed by other heroes at [mobile] home:

Family Means "Home"

Home is where the herd is—the Kay herd, that is! Whether you're in a place three months or three years, it's important to make your apartment, set of quarters, or civilian house look and feel like home. Don't ever get into the misconception that you can live somewhere for a short amount of time without the touches of home. If you know you'll only be in an apartment for three months, make a point of keeping out at least a couple of boxes of your favorite photos, art, or other household goods to make it feel like home to you and your children. Yes, you'll have to repack them in just a few weeks, but during those weeks you will be surrounded by a few of your favorite things—and it will feel like home.

Family Means "Friends"

On our world tour we saw that many military members have friends who literally become family when they are so far from home. This is the way we cope with moves and separations, as well. Sometimes these new friends become our family in just a few hours. When we took our *Heroes at Home* Tour to Aviano, Italy, we got the following note from an active duty military member that illustrates this point perfectly:

> Dear Ellie,
> I met you last night at the Aviano theater. My name is Carissa. I wanted to write and thank you for taking time away from your family to come and speak to your other family. Being overseas we have the advantage of getting a fresh view on military

life, its values, honors, and why we do what we
do. For that reason I am so thankful to have the
opportunity to live here.

On the other side, we also have a deeper understanding of sacrifice, separation, hardships, and
what the effects are of what we do. Living outside
of the U.S. has allowed me to look inside from a
different view. I have felt a little more alone in
our fight for freedom, life, and humanity. This is
why I wanted to say thank you for coming and sharing the stories and words from those who appreciate
those who serve. It meant so much and gives us a
reminder that will allow us to charge on.

Thank YOU for serving our country and those who
serve.

> Carissa
> Active Duty Air Force

Remember that "family" comes in all shapes, sizes, ranks, branches,
demographics, and characters. When you open yourself up to this
concept, you'll find that you are never far from home.

Moving Timeline

We ended up moving seventeen times in twenty years by the time my
husband retired from the Air Force. Moving is a natural part of a
military lifestyle for many military families. Reservists and Guardsmen may not move as much, but some will go to a new base that
requires a move as well. Here is a moving timeline that will help you
get organized. Be sure that you bookmark MilitaryOneSource.com
because a lot of points on this timeline can be researched at this site
for your geographical area.

Step 1—As Soon as the Move Is Announced

- *Arrange for child care.* Now would be the time to call in your
  marker from a friend or family member. Arrange for them to
  take care of the little "sweet peas" and "senior mischiefs" in your
  house during packing and moving day. If you have these and also
  a "Conan," then you may have to call in more than one marker!
  (Have a younger child.) You can begin to look for child care at
  your new location as well if you will be working full time. Go
  to MilitaryOneSource.com for referrals.

- *If the military is moving you.* Talk to the relocation office on your base to find out what help you will be receiving. Keep in close touch with this office throughout the move to be sure you know what preparations are needed before moving day.
- *Research schools.* Go to the Community Services Center equivalent for your branch and ask for a relocation packet that will include this information.

Step 2—Two Months Before the Move

- *Get estimates from several moving companies.* With a military move, this is handled as part of your relocation service. Ask for a breakdown of costs and be sure that you know the specifics so that you can compare prices. Be sure to see what it costs for the truck and how many crew members will be working. Also make sure that your insurance (such as USAA) covers this as a part of your policy. But also ask what the moving company's policy is on damage, breakage, and theft. Be sure you find out what they will and will not move.
- *Organize a moving file.* Get a large jacketed folder that is expandable and offers several different sections in order to collect estimates, CDs with photos of your higher valued items, moving expense receipts, and anything you might need in order to file a claim or to claim some of these expenses on your taxes. For more information on what might be tax-deductible, go to TaxAct.com.
- *Shipping paraphernalia.* Do you prefer hang-up wardrobe boxes or the flat, lie-down boxes? Do you want your Lladro collection bubble-wrapped individually? Now is the time to order those special packing boxes and request extra care with your moving company for collectibles and antiques.
- *Throw away, give away, put away.* My good friend Marcia Ramsland wrote a number of organization books including the bestselling *Organize Your Life* (Thomas Nelson, 2004). She recommends you spend fifteen to twenty minutes of hard work time in a room, a closet, garage, or attic and set a timer. You will put things into each of these three piles (throw away, give away, put away), and you'll get organized. If you spend twenty minutes a day in a room doing this, you'll be ready for your move.
- *Donate it.* Be sure to get a tax-deductible receipt for any goods that you donate to an IRS approved nonprofit.
- *Sell it.* When you are cleaning things out, you may want to also put aside some items that you will want to sell. You can have a garage sale, or put things up on eBay or craigslist.

- *Swap it.* Swap.com is leading the swap movement both online and in communities across the globe, and brings families together to swap books, video games, CDs, and DVDs they already have—for things they actually need. The site is extremely easy to use, and families can register for free to set up a "have" list and a "want" list, then the site's two- and three-way swapping algorithms instantly identify trade opportunities with the site's 1.2 million members. There is no currency exchanged—the only cost is shipping, and Swap.com allows for cross-media trades so you can swap out a video game your son no longer plays for a copy of *The Giver,* for example. There's even a mobile app for swapping your stuff (http://iphone.swap.com).

- *Document items.* Pull out your flip video camera or digital still camera and photograph your prized items for documentation for insurance purposes. Have a hard copy master list and indicate on the list which items are photographed, then mail a copy of the photos to a friend or relative for safekeeping. You will bring the CD or digital tape with you on your move (you won't pack it). Add these to your jacketed folder.

- *Forwarding info.* Go to the post office and get a moving packet that will help you notify all the businesses, friends, medical professionals, and others who will need a change of address card.

- *Sponsor families.* If you are in a military move, chances are good you will be given a sponsor family on the other end of the move who will help you adjust to the relocation. Ask them for referrals for medical professions, and try to research this before you move so that you'll have a doctor or dentist in the event you need them right away.

- *Schools.* After you have researched schools, find out what you will need to do to register your child. If you homeschool, check with the HSLDA to see what state requirements might be in place for your new home.

Step 3—Six Weeks Before the Move

- *Finalize the mover.* By now, you should have a mover chosen, but it still wouldn't hurt to go to BBB.org (Better Business Bureau) to find any history of complaints.

- *Acquaint your children with your new location.* The relocation package that you got last month from your Community Services equivalent will have information on your new home. Show your kids photos or go online and look at the points of interest that will involve and engage them in the move.

- *Insurance coverage.* In addition to checking on contents insurance from your homeowners or tenant policy, now is the time to check with your automobile provider to let them know you are moving, as well. Your insurance should transfer if you are with a mainstream company such as USAA, but you'll still need to make the call.
- *Mail change of address cards.* Last month, you researched and wrote the cards with your new address; now is the time to send them.
- *Floor plans.* If you are buying a home, get the floor plan and pictures of your new home so that you can begin to have a sense of where you will put your furniture. The more planning you do ahead of time, the better it is for the movers (and yourself) on the other end. Organization is the key!

Step 4—One Month Before the Move

- *Plan your space.* If you already have housing (or are on a waiting list for a specific floor plan), measure your furniture and decide on an arrangement. This will help as you send the movers into the right room with the boxes or furniture that will go in that room.
- *Kids count too.* Assign bedrooms to your children and let them create a design. Help them to cut out pieces of furniture to fit the allotted space in the room and let them arrange it as they like.
- *Begin packing.* If you are doing a self move or if you are taking some items in the car with you, then now is the time to start packing and organizing the items to be moved. If you are having a moving service pack you up and move you, then realize their liability policies and that they may not insure or be responsible for items you pack and they move. Most of the time, they have to pack the items they put on their truck.
- *Confirm arrival date.* If movers are coming, then now is the time to confirm when packers will arrive and how many will be coming.
- *Transfer records.* If you have not already transferred all records for your children's school, medical, and dental, arrange to transfer those records or get a copy of records that will be transferred.
- *Pull out important documents.* If you keep critical documents (Social Security cards, birth certificates, marriage certificates, passports, or wills) in a desk or file cabinet, pull them out and put them in a special envelope to be taken in your car. You do not want to ship these documents; hand-carry them.
- *File new address notice with DMV.* Be sure your Department of Motor Vehicles has a record of your new address for your car registration and/or driver's licenses. You can usually do this online, or even at an AAA office.

- *Plan the road trip.* If you are flying, you'll need to make plane reservations now. Be sure you know the weight limits and reimbursement policies for extra bags on air trips. If you are traveling by car, map out the trip and make hotel reservations along the way.
- *Plan for pets.* If you are going overseas, know the policies regarding pets. If the quarantine time is too long for the period of time you will be stationed overseas, consider asking a close friend or relative to pet-sit for the next couple of years.

Step 5—Fourteen Days Before the Move

- *Confirm child care.* Several weeks ago, you made arrangements for younger children on moving day. Call and confirm these plans. You do not want to be caught unawares by someone who agreed to help and then forgot to mark it on their calendar.
- *Disconnect services.* Secure a stop date for all services you pay for, including electricity, gas, phone, newspaper, cable TV, Internet, lawn care, pool care, or housekeeping.
- *Dispose of combustibles.* Several weeks ago, you got a list from your mover of items that cannot be moved. Give away those products to your neighbors or friends.
- *Subscribe.* If possible, go online and subscribe to the community paper in your new town with a start date to coincide with your move-in date.
- *Service vehicles.* If a vehicle is going to be towed, make sure there is a minimal amount of gas in the tank. If the vehicle will be driven, then have a safety inspection for that car including a check on oil, tire pressure, brakes, and all fluids.

Step 6—Seven Days Before the Move

- *Moving help.* If you are moving yourself, be sure to call and remind those who promised to show up and help load items or pack.
- *Get any prescriptions refilled.* Have prescriptions transferred to a pharmacy near your new home and/or refill any you will need on the trip.
- *Complete last-minute errands.* This would include trips to the post office, dry-cleaning pickup, return DVDs and library books or other borrowed items.
- *Write thank-you notes.* Before the busy days of packing up and moving, take the time to write notes to your kids' teachers, friends from the community and church, neighbors, and others who have meant a lot to you at this assignment.

Step 7—Forty-eight Hours Before the Move

- *Set aside valuables.* Pack jewelry and collectibles that you will take with you. Put all the items you are moving yourself (kids' luggage, items for the car, etc.) into a special place in your house or garage and mark it "DO NOT MOVE" so that the packers do not pack those items. See the paragraphs after this list for suggested personal items you may want to move yourself.

- *Prepare mover goodies.* Purchase cookies, sodas, and other treats for your movers to consume during moving day.

- *Collect the contents of your safe-deposit box.*

- *First aid.* Make sure you know where the first-aid kit is to take in your car.

- *Clean*—Begin to clean areas of your home that allow for cleaning, such as windows, refrigerators, freezers, stove, etc.

Step 8—Moving Day

- *Kids first.* Make sure you have your children's favorite things, such as a blanket, stuffed animal, toys, pacifiers, games, activities, or snacks you will need for the trip. It's important they have something that can help them feel secure if they are not with you when your home is being packed or even if they are there watching the movers take all of their stuff.

- *Drop off kids.* If your children are going to stay with a friend, arrange to drop them off or have the friend come and get them a little while after the movers arrive. That way, young children can see that the movers are coming with boxes or a truck to move their things so they won't be shocked when they are dropped off at the house later and find everything is gone.

- *Pets are people, too.* We have a large billboard by the highway that has this saying. And while pets may not be people, they are certainly freaked out by people if they are not settled somewhere safe. You might want to kennel them or let them go to a friend's house.

- *Mover walk-through*—It is critical that you or your spouse be there when movers arrive so that you can walk them through the house, giving instructions for collectibles and other items that need extra care or bubble wrap. If possible, have someone in every room where packers are working in order to supervise the packing.

- *Take care of the movers.* Order pizza or sub sandwiches for the movers during lunchtime. Make sure you have plenty of sodas and snacks.

- *Bill of lading.* This is the official document that lists all the boxes individually and the contents of the containers. They also mark damaged items on this list; you need to make sure the items they mark really are damaged in the way that they indicate in order to avoid disputes on possible damages made during the move. Make sure that the moving company has your and your spouse's cell phone numbers in the event they need to get ahold of you during the move.

- *Final house check.* Before the truck pulls out of the driveway, do a walk-through and make sure that everything is packed, especially from cabinets, behind doors, and in out-of-the-way places. Check the attic, sheds, and basement, as well. Part of this final check will be to make sure you have copies of the bill of lading.

New Steps—Upon Arrival at Your New Home

- *Door to door.* If you have been fortunate to be able to meet your movers at the door of your new home, plan on supervising the unloading. If you do not have child-care arrangements at your new place, then one of the spouses may need to stay at the hotel or temporary billeting with the children in order to keep them calm and out of the way of the movers.

- *Critical check for damage.* It's imperative that you check the bill of lading for any missing items and have the movers unload furniture and remove bubble wrap to check for damages. Note all discrepancies on the bill of lading, as well as any damages.

- *Pizza party.* Be sure to order food for your movers at this end of the move. Oftentimes there will be different employees on the receiving end of your household goods. It's important to take care of them, as well.

- *Drive by.* When the movers leave, pack the kids in the car and get to know the basic layout of the base or neighborhood. Drive to the commissary, schools, and playgrounds so your kids can see there are a lot of new and fun things to do at their new home.

- *Unpack kids first.* It's important for your child to find their bed, their toys, and familiar room decorations that will bring a sense of normalcy to their rocking world. If possible, try to unpack their rooms first.

- *Fun time.* It may take many days or even a few weeks to get completely unpacked and settled. It's important that you take care of the kids and yourself by taking breaks from the hard work. Take a break to get ice cream, visit the new school (if it's not in session), or go bowling, miniature golfing, or to the park. Take a healthy, brisk walk with your kids and meet the neighbors, where you might be able to arrange play dates.

- *Sponsor family.* Most military families are assigned a sponsor family who lives in their new community. Take advantage of this connection and ask them about kid activities, places of worship, adult exercise groups or classes, and base support groups.

- *Safety first.* If you have small children, be sure to insert plastic covers on outlets, doorknob covers, and cabinet safety locks. Unpack your fire extinguisher and get it recharged. Check the batteries in the smoke alarms or purchase more smoke alarms if you don't have enough (there should be one in each bedroom, the kitchen, and the hallways). Be sure you know where the first aid kit is and how to get to the hospital. Post emergency numbers by the phone.

- *Write home.* Let your child take pictures of their new home and send an email or regular letter to the friends they left in their old neighborhood.

Self-Moves

Before you decide to move yourself, known as a DITY (do-it-yourself move), and gain a little extra cash—count the cost! We made one move when we were first married, hauling about five thousand pounds of household goods about one hundred miles to our new location, and we made over one thousand dollars (that was many years ago). That was certainly worth it for us! However, the next move was eight thousand pounds and one thousand miles, and after all the expenses of a moving truck, gas, and insurance, we would have only gained about three hundred dollars. The additional stress on our family and the sheer physical energy it would have taken for that move would *not* have been worth it!

DITY Tips

If you are going to move yourself in the DITY program, here are some tips from Military.com that will make it a bit easier for you.

1. **Figure out your move requirements before you begin.** The monetary rewards for a DITY move are real, but only if you're prepared to keep track of all the details. Is the size of your move manageable enough? How much of the move do you want to

handle yourself? Do you have friends or family who can help out? Can you make arrangements for your family and pets when you move?

2. **Above all, remember two things:** The government will pay you an allowance that equals 95 percent of what it would cost them to move you. If your total moving expenses are above that figure, you have to pay the difference yourself. In addition, any extra money you keep from the allowance will be taxable income, so you will need to fill out a W-2 form when you do your tax returns.

3. **Make sure you know all the rules.** When you first apply for a move, make certain all your questions are answered by your Public Transportation Office counselor. Learn what qualifies as an authorized or unauthorized shipment. Find out exactly what you are responsible for. Likewise, get the lowdown on what the government will pay for and any extra benefits and travel allowances you can receive. You may find that you qualify for more than you expected.

4. **You don't have to do it all at once.** One major advantage of a DITY move is that you're not dependent on a moving company coming in at one specified time and taking away all your belongings in one fell swoop. If you can, rent a truck for a few days, and space out the moving process. You can move all the furniture and other heavy items on one day, and then move out smaller items on another day. If you have to make a long-distance move, check out the possibility of renting two or more trucks and getting friends and family to help you.

5. **Always look for a military discount.** Many moving companies and services don't advertise military discounts, but be sure to ask when you contact them. Don't be afraid to place companies in competition with each other by comparing prices and bargaining—you'll end up winning by receiving a lower price.

Agencies

It is an absolute travesty to have the wonderful (not to mention free) resources we have in our military agencies and not use them! Work closely with your military point of contact for the move. If you are going overseas, you need to be sure to read all the information and checklists regarding visas, passports, and allowable household goods. It will vary from country to country. If you are moving CONUS (Continental United States), or even if you're moving overseas, go to your local Airmen and Family Readiness Center/Army Community Services equivalent and request a SITES brochure, which will give you all the information you need to know about your new assignment.

Financial Compensation

Be sure the military member gets all the information straight regarding en route compensation available for family members. Because we're such a large family, and because we can be economical on the road, there was one move where we would actually make three hundred dollars more if we took ten days to reach our destination rather than trying to make it in seven. Compensation varies greatly according to a variety of factors, so be sure you understand these matters before you hit the road.

Use It or Lose It

There are certain items that movers are not allowed to transport. The reason is obvious for flammables, aerosol cans, and opened products. So use all these items up as well as you can (i.e., don't buy extra gas for the lawn mower if you're just going to have to drain the tank before you move it; the same would apply to propane for your barbecue grill).

Also plan a strategy for using up food in the freezer and refrigerator. The month before your move, take inventory of perishable items that you cannot move and make out menus accordingly. Usually glass jars do not transport well, so keep pantry items in mind as you plan menus.

You might even want to have a party if you just bought a side of beef and your assignment orders came two weeks later!

Stuff and Cram

Even if you don't do a complete DITY, what you take with you as "essentials" qualifies for compensation if you are not over your weight allowance. For example, Bob was allowed twenty thousand pounds (give or take a thousand), and the last trip we hauled four thousand pounds (including a full travel trailer) of essentials for our family. The movers hauled seventeen thousand pounds, so we were compensated for three thousand pounds of the weight we hauled with us. But remember not to take more than you can carry! We've learned that the hard way: As I kept bringing stuff out to Bob to "pack" for our last move, he got to the point where we didn't have room for one of the kids because he'd accidentally packed his seat full of stuff!

Prepacking Tips From the Experts

Record Your Contents

Karen Evenson, a former USAF wife, says, "Use your digital camera to record the contents of your house before you pack your belongings. This is not only good for insurance purposes but also for redecorating—so you can remember what kind of arrangement you had in the rooms of your previous home. If there is ever any question as to the quantity, condition, or value of an item, you have the proof. It is also helpful if you don't have time to do a detailed inventory of books and small items. Just make sure to move your camera slowly and close up. And speaking of small items, you can put the TV remotes in plastic bags and tape them directly to the TV."

Utensils and Small Items

"Put all your silverware and other utensils in gallon-size plastic bags. That way they stay clean, and you don't have to wash them when you get to your destination. They go right into the drawer," says Jill Mingear, wife of an Army helicopter pilot. She adds, "Use two-gallon-size bags for toys with many parts or for games. Use one of these bags for screws, bolts, and nuts for the larger pieces of furniture, such as beds. Tape these bags to a drawer or the back of the furniture."

Sheets

Air Force wife Bonnie Weida says, "Put clean sheets in a plastic bag and zip them into the mattress before a move. This makes them easy to find without going through boxes."

Trash and Treasure

"Empty all your trash cans and wash them out before they are moved. Movers will even box up the garbage!" says Jody Dale, USA wife and mother of three. She adds, "Keep the kids' CDs, DVDs, and books out for traveling and put them in a neighbor's home for the day. The movers can pack so quickly that these 'travel necessities' could find themselves inside the moving van rather than your minivan!"

Pets

Karen Evenson also says, "If you have a cat, get the disposable-type kitty litter box for while you're moving and setting up your new household. They also fit on the floor of the car or under the seat in a van and can be covered up when not in use. They usually don't smell, and when you are done with your move, the entire box goes into the trash."

Many pets can get in the packers' way and even harm themselves. Consider putting them in a neighbor's yard or kennel for the big day. Ask your veterinarian for sleeping or travel sickness pills to help your pet sleep during travel days. Think about your pet's safety and comfort as you travel and plan accordingly. For example, be sure an animal is never left in the car on hot days. Be sure that your pet's tags have current and accurate information printed on them. For example, if you move from New Mexico to Germany and your pet gets lost in Illinois, the "finder" needs the phone number of a relative or veterinarian who knows where you are!

Survival Box

Karen also recommends making a "survival box." She makes sure it is the last item ON the truck and the first one OFF. It should contain toilet paper, Kleenex, an iron, towels, bedding, and a shower curtain.

Children

Young children should be in the care of a family member or neighbor on moving day to ensure their safety. However, it's important that they see part of moving day so they know their stuff didn't just disappear—it went into a box and is on the way to the new home!

More Tips for Packing Day

On the day the packers arrive, be prepared. Know how many packers will come and how much they plan to accomplish that day. If they do not show up on time, have too few workers, or stop working excessively early, call the representative from the relocation office. If you have a friend or two who have offered to help you on that day, ask them to stay in rooms where packers are working while you are with other packers.

Ask for *stand-up wardrobe boxes,* where you can hang your clothing on hangers. Not only do the lay-down boxes wrinkle clothing more easily, you have to re-hang perhaps hundreds of items. If you have a special collectible, such as an antique clock or fragile figurine, ask the packers to create a *custom packing box* for that item with extra packing inside.

Mark It! and Bless 'Em!

Army spouse Cindy Musselwhite says, "Make sure the boxes are marked appropriately. I was once six months pregnant when we moved and thought we had all the boxes marked 'clothes' sent to our temporary quarters. My maternity clothes never arrived, and I finally had to break down and buy more. When we got on post, I was eight months pregnant, and we finally found the clothes in a box marked 'garden hoses.' "

Jody Dale, an Army chaplain's wife, offers this perspective: Take good care of your packers. She says, "Carry a magic marker and put specific labels on the boxes. It will make for a less hectic unpacking day. Put all the clothes and personal items that you're taking with you in your car or put them in a neighbor's house." Jody adds, "We bless the movers/packers with food, kindness, and laughter. We believe many people pick on them and abuse them, giving them a hard time due to past experiences. But we have had some great guys and gals respond to our kindness by being extra careful with our stuff."

The morning they arrive, let the crew know you're buying pizza for lunch and ask them what kind of soda they like. These are small offers of thoughtfulness, but they mean a lot. It can also mean the difference between the packers *throwing* your stuff in a box versus carefully *packing* your prized possessions!

En Route

It's very common for families who are relocating to want to visit extended family members and friends as they travel from point A to point B. It's important, however, to remember that this is a stressful time, when you may not be at your personal best! Moving is one of the top ten stress factors families face, and the added stress of a military move can make it even harder. Carefully consider who you are going to visit and how much time you will be adding to an already challenging road trip. Have your extended family and friends read this section of the book so they will know that you are under considerable stress and your entire nuclear family may not be operating at their peak in terms of propriety and thoughtfulness. An extra special amount of grace is required when hosting a family en route.

Another good rule of thumb is that you travel no more than the daily allowed miles for *per diem* compensation. These mileage numbers are usually lower than what "conquer the road at any cost" types will like. However, it's critical that you think of your kids and spouse in this big adventure. Map out your hotel route and search the Internet for ones with pools and free breakfast buffets. Plan to leave after a good breakfast and arrive at the next destination early enough to enjoy the swimming pool and then rest up for the next day.

Once You Arrive

Jody Dale says, "Label each room in the house with a number so you can simply tell the movers to put it in rooms. Know exactly where you want large pieces of furniture placed and assembled—especially the beds. I've even marked off these areas in a room with masking tape."

Personally, I believe that moving is a surefire way of determining whether you own your things—or they own you! I was so upset when the movers broke the delicate leg of my grandma's antique cherrywood side table—it made my stomach hurt! It's best to expect some things to be broken and realize that we can either get it fixed or we can't. Being upset for months or years is only going to give us an ulcer!

Be Patient

It's important to realize that Rome wasn't built in a day, and your new home won't be put together in one day, either! Pick one room at a time and concentrate on getting it squared away. Play some upbeat, energizing music. Grab a mop, sing along, and keep in step. Your kids will think you've lost your mind, but they will also get a much-deserved laugh after a big transition.

Get Help

Have the movers put together the beds the first night, and then have them come back again to unpack boxes—if you want their help. We usually dismiss them that first day, but I've had friends who schedule them back in three days just to unpack the knickknacks that go into curio cases: it takes her many hours to do what two packers and she can do in one hour.

If you have kids, put them in charge of unpacking their own rooms, giving them only as much responsibility as their ages dictate—anything else will only lead to frustration on your part and theirs.

If your sponsor or new neighbor offers to make you dinner—accept! You can return the favor when they make a future move and need a meal while staying in temporary housing.

Even if your children will not be enrolled in base day care on a regular basis, consider letting them go for the first few days when your house is a complete wreck. They will see more of the home they remember each night when they come home from child care, and they'll get to play with new friends while you work at home.

If your new lawn needs immediate attention and your equipment is in the bottom of a box—who knows where—ask your neighbors if they know of a teen that does yard work. Even if you don't employ yard care regularly, this one-time job will be worth the expense, as it relieves the pressure of getting the job done right away.

If you're living on base and notice things in your new home that are in need of repair, report them immediately. The same would apply if you're renting a civilian dwelling or apartment; get the landlord to make things right as soon as possible. It will cut down on additional nitpicky stressors!

Unpack It!

Cindy Musselwhite says, "Unpack alongside your packers. We didn't have the packers stay in the same room, and we had a brand-new electric train stolen because of this. We didn't unpack all our boxes at the next assignment, and therefore we didn't discover the theft in time to get reimbursement for the loss."

Treat Yourself!

Major Edith Eckerle, USAF, says, "I find the transit part of moving more tolerable by packing comfy slippers for the trip and a fluffy neck pillow (sprayed with a lilac scent). I bring along a candle for the hotel room, a fave comfy blankie (lightweight wool, fleece, or cotton throw), and bubble bath or salts for bath time. I also do AM/PM overall stretches and drink LOTS of water."

When it comes to the other end of moving—unpacking—try playing positive mind games. Set goals, and once you achieve them, treat yourself to something special. For example, if you want to get the dishes and cookware unpacked and put away in your kitchen, once you've done this, treat yourself to a cup of coffee at the neighborhood Starbucks and go by the garden store to pick up a flowering plant for the kitchen. Once you've organized the pantry, buy a new color of nail polish or a magazine that looks interesting and relaxing. After you've got one of the bathrooms completely finished (walls and everything), buy a new scented candle and a bottle of bubble bath and take a long, hot bath!

Join the base's yoga class or take a walk once a day. It will relieve stress and give you a chance to meet your new neighbors. At the half-way point of your unpacking, go out and get a pedicure, and once the house is completely done, get a manicure at the base beauty salon. If you had one *before* your work was done, you'd only ruin it.

Consider getting a totally new hairstyle when you arrive someplace new. If it turns out really "different," your new friends won't know how good you used to look, and you'll only look better as it grows out!

Treat yourself by treating your house. While it's important to stick to a budget, now is the time to add new color to your living room with a throw and pillows or a new wallpaper border. These modest, low-cost changes are also the splurge you need as you transition to your new home. You could also arrange the furniture differently than it was in your last home.

One a Day

Once you've gotten your home somewhat settled, do only one errand a day. If you're going to wait a couple of hours to get a new driver's license, don't wait two more hours to get your car plates on the same day! Do your grocery shopping on one day and enroll the kids in school on another.

Family Fun

Make a ceremony with your kids of putting out the welcome mat. Tell them that it is the first thing you put out and the last thing you pack up when you move, because a home should always welcome new and old friends no matter how many times you move.

Make time for scheduled breaks with your kids. Get a good book and take them to the park. Take them to the base pool and let them wear themselves out while you sun yourself by the baby pool. After they've finished arranging their shelves of toys or books in their rooms, take them out for a hot-fudge sundae!

Take Notes

Buy a fresh spiral notebook that will fit into your purse or pocket or take notes on your smartphone. When someone recommends a baby-sitter, barber, hairstylist, cleaners, or restaurant, take notes with addresses and phone numbers. Write down the names of your neighbors and their house numbers so you know who lives where. Jot down your unit's welcome representative and his or her phone number. Have your kids add the names of their new friends to your notebook and where they live, then make a note to introduce yourself to their parents if they don't come over to see you first.

As you walk from room to room, write down a list of things you'll need for each room; since you're keeping this with you, you'll have it when you need it in the store later. Tape fabric swatches, paint chips, or wallpaper samples to a page in your notebook so you have them when you see a good sale on accessories, curtains, valances, or bedding.

Make a list of things you need to do in your new place: Call the Welcome Wagon (for discounts, freebies, and leads); call the Chamber of Commerce to send you a packet of information; check your insurance policies; get a driver's license and plates; get a new library card; subscribe to the local newspaper (ask for new-customer discounts); find a church; introduce yourself to your mail carrier; make out a list of emergency numbers.

Ways to Make New Friends and Get Used to Your New Home

Get the Thursday paper and a good map and hit the garage sales on Friday and Saturday. You'll familiarize yourself with the neighborhood and make new friends at the same time (unless you ask them if they'll take less for that toaster).

If you have a home business, host a party or host one for someone else who has a home business. Check out www.mops.org to find the local MOPS (Mothers of Preschoolers) group in your area. Have your own "Open House" and invite all your neighbors. One friend with a great sense of humor taped a new sign over the *For Sale/ Sold* sign in her front yard. It read: "Wanted: New friend with a short memory and a long sense of humor." She found her new best friend that way!

* * * * * * *

"For many couples, their major goal in moving is to stay married. . . . I know that moving can rank right up there on the 'fun things to experience' list along with wallpapering, root canals, pet-sitting a pit bull, and having your twelve-month-old triplets all start to teethe at the same time."

—John Trent
from the Foreword of *After the Boxes Are Unpacked*
by Susan Miller

A Special Moment in the Line of Duty

My hubby may have panicked when our babies were born, but he never panicked in the line of duty. He faithfully fulfilled his oath of commissioning for twenty-five years. One of the greatest privileges an officer can have is to administer the oaths of enlistment or commissioning. I've watched my husband administer these oaths as the families looked proudly on. But the greatest joy we had was when Bob administered the oath of enlistment to our son Philip at the United States Naval Academy on induction day. Then again, when Philip graduated with honors, Bob administered the oath at his son's Marine Corps commissioning.

Here are the current oaths of enlistment and commissioning:

I, _____, do solemnly swear (or affirm) that I will support and defend the Constitution of the United States against all enemies, foreign and domestic; that I will bear true faith and allegiance to the same; and that I will obey the orders of the President of the United States and the orders of the officers appointed over me, according to regulations and the Uniform Code of Military Justice, so help me God. (Title 10, U.S. Code; Act of 5 May 1960, replacing the wording first adopted in 1789, with amendment effective 5 October 1962.)

I, _____, [Social Security Account Number (SSAN)] having been appointed an officer in the _____ [branch of service] of the United States, as indicated above in the grade of _____, do solemnly swear (or affirm) that I will support and defend the Constitution of the United States against all enemies, foreign or domestic, that I will bear true faith and allegiance to the same; that I take this obligation freely, without any mental reservations or purpose of evasion; and that I will well and faithfully discharge the duties of the office upon which I am about to enter, so help me God. (DA Form 71, 1 August 1959, for officers.)

HIDDEN HERO PORTRAIT— BRENDA TAYLOR

Gorgeous in Guam and Happy in Hawaii

Military life has a way of drawing courage out of the timid and an adventurous spirit out of those with deep roots, and that is what happened in Brenda's case. "I was not yet twenty when I married my Air Force husband," says soft-spoken Brenda in a slight Southern drawl as she puts strands of her long brown hair behind her ear and smiles shyly. "My family wondered if it would work out, especially since we were moving to Guam immediately after the wedding."

The couple honeymooned in Hawaii en route to the island of Guam, their sunny paradise for the next two years. Brenda noticed that her husband, Drew, seemed to have so much fun flying the B-52 that she decided she'd get in on the action, too, and applied for a job as a flight attendant with Continental Air Micronesia.

Tall and slender, Brenda donned the uniform of her new job: a pink and white floral muumuu that was fitted with a long straight skirt with slits on both sides. She looked gorgeous and was an immediate favorite among the passengers who flew her routes. She went from sunny Florida to the skyways of Bali, Indonesia; Sydney, Australia; Manila, Philippines; Tokyo, Japan; Honolulu, Hawaii; and even one memorable trip to Papua New Guinea.

☆ Profile ☆

Name: Brenda Taylor

Spouse's Name: Lt. Col. Andrew "Drew" Taylor

Branch of Service: USAF

Kids: Lauren and Jonathan

Number of Moves: eight

Years in Service: twenty-four

Work/Employer: Premier Designs Jewelry

Hobbies: Reading, jazzercising, shopping, singing in choir, teaching Bible studies

Describe your military experience before 9/11 and after:
We now have longer work hours and greater commitments because of the smaller force left in the States to support those overseas.

Least Favorite Aspect of Military Life:
Leaving behind friends when you move and the uncertainty of "what's next."

Favorite Aspect of Military Life:
Making all of those friends! Seeing the country/world. Wonderful benefits; job security

Favorite Quote:
"I'd like to be the sort of friend that you have been to me; I'd like to be the help that you've been always glad to be; I'd like to mean as much to you each minute of the day as you have meant, old friend of mine, to me along the way."—Edgar A. Guest

Brenda's Quote:
God has been faithful to us every time we've moved. We've always been able to find a church family, friends, and a safe place to live and raise our family.

Brenda looked at her work as mainly a day job: "I flew out in the morning and was home in time for dinner. I traded off overnight trips with other flight attendants so I could be home with my husband in the evenings. But sometimes I wasn't able to trade off a trip." That's how she was in a position to have her one and only trip to the outer regions of civilization in New Guinea.

Even though Brenda was making great strides in her independence, she still preferred to spend her nights at home as a newlywed with her husband. For a full year she managed to strategically trade off her trips and avoid as many layovers as possible, but every now and then she would be required to have a layover. In fact, she managed to have a layover in Hawaii about once every two months in order to shop! As she served refreshments to the passengers, she thought of their destination and what lay ahead. She tried not to think about the strange hotel, the unusual culture of the people there, and the fact that she would be alone in a place she'd never been before. Instead, she looked over the passengers in the seating area. They were flying a 727 designed to carry one-half cargo and one-half passengers. The crew fondly called these specially configured jets "NuJu" and "JuJu."

As the airline made its final approach to the narrow airstrip in Papua New Guinea, Brenda buckled into her flight attendant's seat and looked out the window. She described it as "always amazing to me how we'd approach the island from the ocean and then the runway would appear, looking like a postage stamp from the air." She saw what looked like a fenced field on either side of the primitive runway, but the most amazing thing was that it looked like there were crowds of people pressing against the fences, their tiny figures distinguishable even from the airplane's landing altitude. But she had no idea what these people looked like until the plane landed.

Brenda was surprised at what she saw when the jet turned and headed toward the "terminal" buildings in this exotic land. The people she viewed from inside the 727 were clearly visible from the window. They were half-naked with tattooed, exotic faces, their bare bodies an expression of their culture.

As Brenda disembarked after the passengers, the wind took her (and her muumuu) by surprise. The people crowded the fences to get a closer look at the Western world. Brenda said, "We felt like animals in a zoo exhibit as they crowded to see what Westerners looked like." At the time, all Brenda could think of was a National Geographic documentary about the cannibalistic customs of primitive tribal villages in the region.

She looked at the faces and thought, Cannibals? No, I won't even THINK about that!

She began to hear a chant going up among one of the groups of people huddled together by the fence, and she stole another side-glance at them.

They were smiling at her and nodding their heads enthusiastically.

And they looked hungry.
Very hungry.

* * * * * * *

The dilapidated hotel bus drove her to a typical hotel on the island. As the vehicle bumped down the dirt road, she tried to talk herself out of the apprehension she felt for the unknown. She reasoned: *I have no other choice; I'm not a child. I've had layovers before. I'm a professional, and this is part of my new job. Other flight attendants make this stopover all the time. I know I've never been here before, but I've survived a lot of new experiences in the past year, and I know I can do this.*

The ancient clerk at the desk, dressed in a brightly colored Hawaiian-print shirt with khaki pants, appeared to be somewhat preoccupied with the organization of a ring of room keys he was sorting. He smiled a wary grin at Brenda but managed to understand her well enough to assign her a room.

Brenda tried the lock on her door, and it seemed to be stable enough. The room was much larger than she'd ever had before and was neat and clean. She closed the door behind her and locked it. There was a rickety chain on the door that looked as if it would give out at the slightest pressure, but she hooked it to the doorframe for added security. She noticed a phone on the nightstand and thought, *At least I can call Drew if I get scared—it would only take him ten hours to get here.*

She pulled out her Bible and read her favorite psalm that always seemed to calm her when she faced something new and different—in fact, she'd read it often since marrying her Air Force husband. All the tension finally caught up with her as she fell asleep, completely spent emotionally and physically from the long flight.

Suddenly she was wide awake.

There was a noise at the door!

Jolted from her deep sleep, she sat straight up in bed and struggled to remember where she was and why she had such a fearful feeling inside. She swiftly glanced around the room, her eyes focusing on the digital clock: 2:30 A.M.

The door rattled a second time.

Then someone fit a key into the lock and began to open the door.

From somewhere deep within, she discovered a newfound courage and shouted, "What are you doing here? This room is occupied!"

Her demand was answered by a voice that replied in broken English, "Dey give key to dis room at desk. So sorry."

It turned out the distracted clerk had booked the room twice!

She never returned to Papua New Guinea. (But she *did* go back to Hawaii!)

That was years and assignments ago. Today Brenda is a veteran hero on the home front, having completed her college degree as a military spouse. She taught first grade, started a home business as an independent jeweler for Premier Designs, and has two children. She's lived in Minot, North Dakota, where the snow piled higher than her house. She's also lived in Columbus, Mississippi, where the heat and humidity are so bad in the summer, you must run your errands before nine in the morning or you will be in a steam bath.

This may not seem remarkable on the surface, but think about it . . . Brenda, at the age of nineteen, when most kids are in college and going home on weekends to give their mom their laundry, decided to take a chance and marry a military man. She left her comfortable roots and not only had to start a new life with her husband (which ranks right up there on the stress charts), but she also had to adjust to a new culture, a dramatic job change (from waitress to flight attendant in Asia), and the other difficulties of military life. Amazingly enough, Brenda managed to do so well in her home-based business that she is now one of the top jewelers at Premier Designs, a large corporation. Through it all, Brenda has clung to two things: her faith and her family. She says, "I'm thankful to be a military spouse. The friends made, areas explored, and experiences gained have been well worth the sacrifice of leaving 'home'!"

Brenda is not alone . . . hundreds of military spouses like her, like you, leave what they know to follow someone they love. That's pretty remarkable. No wonder they call you a hero.

Brenda's Psalm

You who live in the shelter of the Most High,
who abide in the shadow of the Almighty,
will say to the Lord,
"My refuge and my fortress;
my God, in whom I trust."
For he will deliver you from
the snare of the fowler
and from the deadly pestilence;

he will cover you with his pinions,
and under his wings you will find refuge;
his faithfulness is a shield and buckler.
You will not fear the terror of the night.

—Psalm 91

CELEBRATING
LAUGHTER

★ 7 ★

THE YOUNG MARINES

Using Humor to Lighten the Load

Our two youngest sons, Joshua and Jonathan, had just finished earning a ribbon for marksmanship in their Young
Marines group. They spent dozens of hours over a period of four
months studying weapon safety and history and having their knowledge tested with written and oral tests. They also went to the range
multiple times, shooting at targets to improve their skill. Jonathan
graduated with the distinction of sharpshooter, and Joshua qualified
to receive marksman.

I knew Joshua had been spending a little too much time in this area
of interest, but I had no idea how it had impacted him until I got a
call from his fifth-grade teacher, Mrs. Drumheiser. Normally a very
patient woman, she felt she had to have a parent-teacher conference
after she read a creative writing project that Joshua wrote called
"Leprechaun Stories."

When I got to her classroom, she handed me a piece of paper.
Picture a take-home paper with "Leprechaun Stories" preprinted on
the top of the page and a cutesy little green guy with a pot of gold in
the corner. Here's Joshua's work (spelling included):

Once upon a time . . . there was a Leprechaun who stole a pot of
gold from the King. "King Evil of the dark ages."

A long name, you say. Yes you are right. But I made that up.

So he sent the secret police out, but they were actually terrists. So
they had a 12-gauge, a G-36, an assault rifle, and one guy had two P-99s.

So they found him and started shooting at him. So the Leprechaun pulled out two oozies and a long battle begun (about 4 hours long.)

Then, when they were out of ammo, they stood up and became a team. It's a long story how. But they became a team.

So with two oozies, an AK-47, a 12-gauge, an M-16 (with grenade attachments) and a G-36, they invaded the palace and killed the king.

And there was piece in the land.

The End. . . . by Joshua Kay

Life with children is usually interesting. Life in the military is always fascinating, and when the two meet in a partnership, of sorts, it can be interesting and fascinating—especially when viewed with a healthy sense of humor. Which is what I needed after talking to Joshua's teacher.

$$* \quad * \quad * \quad * \quad * \quad * \quad *$$

Jerry Lewis once said, "There are three things that are real: God, human folly, and laughter. Since the first two are beyond our comprehension, we must do what we can with the third." This lesson is a must for all families, military or civilian. Sometimes we have to step back and see the humor in the seriousness of life. In some cases, it may take months or years to crack a smile at an incident that happened while our loved one was away on deployment or even at war—as in my case above.

Humor isn't the only way to beat the stress; there are a wide variety of methods that individuals and families use to beat the heat. But humor is an easy and usually safe way to take the high road out of an argument, a bad mood, or a tension-filled room. Laughter is healthy for us. Studies show that those who laugh—last. Yes, they live longer.

Having an understanding of human beings and becoming a student of their behavior will always give us something to grin about. That's why understanding and humor often walk hand in hand. Some of the wisest guys I know are the ones who make me laugh the most. They're the ones I want beside me when Bob's flying across the country in a forty-year-old jet or when my writing deadlines are about to bury me.

As you read through the ways various people, families, and organizations cope using humor and understanding, try to think of the stories you would add to this list—and mail them to me. Or mail them to *Reader's Digest*'s "Humor in Uniform" for a $300 payment and the chance to be published! Who says humor doesn't pay?

Here are a few of my favorites, many of them submitted by people just like you!

How About Them Yankees?

Several years ago, Bob and I learned just how much humor can cut marital tension. We were in a marriage communication class and learned that when we find ourselves arguing about the issues of life, we could develop a code phrase that essentially means, "Are we making a mountain out of a molehill?" It's a reality check for both parties, and it's not meant to be a slam on our partner. We decided that our code phrase would be "How about them Yankees?" When one of us said this, we would realize that we were probably sweating the small stuff, and it would cut the tension. We chose the phrase because the Yankees were playing in the World Series at the time and doing some amazing things.

We have found it works surprisingly well. Here's an example:

Bob: "Hey, Beloved, did you notice I washed your Suburban?"

Ellie: "Really? Then why is it muddy; I noticed it when I dropped off the kids at school."

Bob: (Running out to the garage while Ellie follows) "WHAT? I just spent two hours detailing this YESTERDAY and it's all mud-splattered! Plus, you didn't even notice that it was clean right after I did all that work!"

Ellie: "Gosh! I'm running around after these kids; how COULD I notice? I wonder how it got muddy?"

Bob: "Did you take the construction route to school again this morning?"

Ellie: "Yeah, I did, and I guess it was kind of muddy where they hosed down the dirt they're working on. Hey! I can't help it if the road is muddy!"

Bob: "You could have taken it real slow, because the car WAS clean!"

Ellie: "How am I supposed to know the car is clean unless you tell me! Besides that, the speed limit in that area is only 15 miles per hour; how much slower am I supposed to go?!"

Bob: "How about them Yankees?"

Male/Female Differences

After the bestselling Mars/Venus phenomenon, a slew of books on the differences between men and women flooded the market. These issues can lead to great conflict unless we learn to celebrate the differences between men and women. One of the best ways to do this is to look at these relational dynamics in a lighthearted way.

One of the best books on male/female differences is by my friends Bill and Pam Farrel, entitled *Men Are Like Waffles—Women Are Like Spaghetti* (Harvest House, 2007). As they travel to bases around the globe, the Farrels have helped military couples improve their marriage. Here is an excerpt from that bestselling book:

If She Says	She Really Means
We need.	I want.
It's your decision.	The correct decision should be obvious.
Do what you want.	You'll pay for this later.
You're . . . so manly.	You need a shave and you sweat a lot.
This kitchen is so inconvenient.	I want a new house.
You have to learn to communicate.	Just agree with me.
I'm sorry.	You'll be sorry.
You're certainly attentive tonight.	Is sex all you ever think about?

If He Says	He Really Means
I'm hungry.	I'm hungry.
I'm sleepy.	I'm sleepy.
I'm tired.	I'm tired.
Do you want to go to a movie?	I'd eventually like to have sex with you.
Can I take you out to dinner?	I'd eventually like to have sex with you.
What's wrong? (first time)	I don't see why you're making such a big deal about this.
What's wrong? (second time)	What meaningless, self-inflicted psychological trauma are you going through now?
What's wrong? (third time)	I guess sex tonight is out of the question.

The point of this section and books that deal with these issues is that men and women communicate differently. We have a basic choice: We can learn the other person's language and celebrate the difference, or we can continue to fight World War III.

That's Not Funny!

Rodney Dangerfield was famous for his one-liners about how he could never get any respect. His wife was the primary target of many of those "lack of respect" jokes. For example: "I call my wife to tell her

I got hit by a bus on the way home from work, and she says, 'I guess this means I'll have to walk the dog.' "

There are certain things that are funny, and others just aren't. No matter how many years pass by and no matter what new spin you put on a problem, some things will never be funny. A good rule of thumb regarding what is worth joking about and what is not, is this: Does it violate the other person's line of respect?

A line of respect is a boundary that leaves the other person's self-esteem intact. If your humor attacks the *person* rather than the *action*, it will usually violate a line of respect. Men and women don't seem to merely *want* respect from their spouse, we actually *need* it to feel that we are important and that what we do matters. This isn't the same as feeding each other's ego. We are talking about genuine praise for actions, attitudes, and character traits that you admire in your mate. *Tell him* about the things you appreciate. This means that when friends at a Christmas party start to "joke" about their spouses by ridiculing them verbally and publicly, you will refrain. Some jokes just aren't funny—they're hurtful and are really daggers cloaked in "humor."

Bob and I made a commitment to each other the first month we were married: We would never make a joke at the other's expense, either in public or private. It's been hard to keep that commitment, especially among fighter pilots who delight in making themselves feel important by cutting the other guy down. One of their favorite lines was "You are so pretty; how did you get stuck with a guy like Bob?" Then they would laugh at their wit and be very pleased with themselves. If I laughed and said nothing, it would seem as if I agreed. So I said, "Are you kidding? I got the better end of the deal: I married the World's Greatest Fighter Pilot!" Not only did it shut those guys up, it gave me my favorite saying that I still use today.

Humor From All Branches of the Service

Oh, My! Semper Fi!

Military families aren't the only ones who benefit from lightening up in appropriate settings; active duty members are notorious for their antics—some are legendary. It's so much fun to recount these stories to each other and to find laughter and release each time we hear them. Tom Neven, a former Marine, is currently an author and freelance writer. He tells the story of when he was stationed in Okinawa at Camp Hansen with the First Battalion, Fourth Marines. Someone broke into the provost marshal's office, where they had an audiotape player that broadcast the national anthem and "Marines' Hymn" at 0800 every morning. The "criminal" substituted a Led Zeppelin tape. At 0800 the next morning, as each unit was waiting to raise the morning colors, a raucous "Whole Lotta Love" blasted across the base instead!

McRivalries—Aim High!

After 9/11, when military units were awaiting orders to deploy, tensions were understandably high. At Holloman Air Force Base, two rival squadrons found an acceptable (if unconventional) way to cut the pressure through a series of practical jokes. It started when the 8th Fighter Squadron "borrowed" the mascot of the 9th Fighter Squadron—the Knight. They took it all around town and took pictures of it in front of "The Tin Man Smoke Shop," in the toy train at the zoo, at the grocery store, and even in front of a sign for an adult bookstore. Then they sent a ransom note and the photos to the squadron.

As if that weren't enough, a few months later the 8th Fighter Squadron was at it again. They stole the 9th Fighter Squadron's flag. In its place, in broad daylight, they managed to sneak in and raise none other than—the McDonald's flag. They took a digital photo of the flag flying proudly in front of the 9th Fighter Squadron and emailed the operations desk with an attachment of the photo. It was their way of alerting their rival to their treachery—the photo had text superimposed over it that read: "You want fries with that?"

Parade Colors—The Army Keeps Rolling Along

When Lieutenant General Bill Caldwell was a Colonel, he had his change of command ceremony, in which he gave up his brigade to his successor. This commander was much loved by his men and women in the 10th Mountain Division in Fort Drum, New York. They would follow him into any battle anytime, anyplace, anywhere. During the customary parade in which the marching band performed, we noticed a tuba player in the back that was marching a little irregularly. Whispers started like waves among the crowd; finally the ripple met our ears and mixed with waves of laughter as we realized that the colonel's personnel officer, Lt. Col. Marty Klein, had confiscated a tuba and was marching with the band as a tribute to his commander. Afterward he said, "I wanted to do something special for a special man, and I thought this would make it memorable and fun for everyone." He didn't know how to play the tuba, but he never missed a beat.

Navy Sea Bats

Tom Neven, a former Marine, tells the story of his first time aboard a Navy ship. The sailors told the new Marines that they had just captured a sea bat—a rare find. It was contained in an upside-down fifty-gallon drum. In order for the Marines to see the bat, the sailors had them get down on their hands and knees while another sailor gently tipped the barrel. They were cautioned not to let the sea bat fly out the bottom when the drum was tipped. In this position, the Marine's posterior was elevated, and when the timing was just right—WHAM! A sailor walloped the man on his backside.

Tom said it took one of his fellow Marines *three times* to finally catch on to the prank. The Marine got down on his hands and knees, and each time he got hit with the broom, he'd turn and say in a frustrated voice, "Hey! Stop it! I'm trying to see the sea bat!"

★ ★ ★ ★ ★ ★ ★

So the next time you've just been told you're moving in two weeks, or any variety of stressors that are unique to the military, think about ways you can help your family lighten up through the use of appropriate humor. It's a healing balm with amazing power.

☆ 8 ☆

QUEEN OF EVERYTHING

Stress Busters

Every year at Holloman Air Force Base, two flying squadrons bring out a dozen sleek black F-117A fighters and set them out on the flight line ramp. The area between two sets of specially designed hangars that house the F-117s is called "The Canyon." The pilots' wives were going to have their annual photo shoot in front of these awesome jets—and it was no laughing matter. These women took this photo-op very seriously, and I was about to discover just how serious. We were instructed to wear white T-shirts, blue jeans, black boots, and brown bomber jackets (borrowed from our hubbies). We dubbed ourselves the Blue-Jeaned Stealth Queens as we strutted our stuff in front of the jets. Never mind the fact that all together we had 48 kids, 187 loads of laundry, and 67 dogs waiting for us at home. We were proud that we still had "it." The only problem was—most of us couldn't remember where we put it.

I was excited about being a Stealth Queen. Hey, I'd been called the "Coupon Queen" and the "Savings Queen" for years—why couldn't I just be Queen of Everything? So I thought royalty could slide on the dress code a bit: Instead of the mandatory white T-shirt, I had an ecru-colored shirt on. I thought the jacket would cover it and no one would notice. I was wrong.

When we were ready to walk out with the photographer, a mean-eyed mama thrust a white T-shirt under my nose and hissed, "Quick, put this on; that ecru-colored shirt will ruin the overall effect."

☆ Hidden Hero Profile ☆

Name: Bobbie Kennedy

Spouse's Name: Commander John Kennedy

Branch of Service: United States Coast Guard

Kids: Olivia, Marissa, and Jack

Number of Moves: eight (14,500 miles so far and no overseas orders)

Years in Service: fifteen since Bobbie "joined," seventeen since John's commissioning.

Work/Employer: I am a homeschool mom.

Hobbies: Volunteering, music: playing my clarinet and singing in choir, and exercising in any form that meets my busy schedule.

How many times have you deployed in the last six years and where?

The Coast Guard is always deployed, and while they aren't gone as long, they are gone frequently. A frustrating factor with our deployments is that the schedule frequently changes! John was gone 270 out of 365 days in a year that called for only 180 deployment days. I'm not trying to complain . . . we still have it far better than many other Service members!

Do you have any military family stories you can share?

We were delighted to be chosen as the National Military Family Association's "2010 Coast Guard Family of the Year." We were excited to see John's ship, the ELM, featured on national television during the Gulf oil spill.

We live the life God has called us to . . . I suppose it's the standard military lifestyle, with the above highlights thrown in as blessings from above.

Least Favorite Aspect of Military Life:

Being far away from extended family and missing out on cousins and grandparents.

Favorite Aspect of Military Life:

ADVENTURE! Seeing new places and meeting new friends.

Favorite Quote:

Psalm 37:23: "The steps of a good man are ordered by the Lord, and He delights in his way."

Any other comments you would like to make:

In the first seven years we were married, we moved five times . . . mostly cross country. I learned how to be very independent! And I also learned that you have to jump in with both feet wherever you are and make the most out of every move (which is also a good way to make friends!). Live a life of no regrets.

Support your spouse, no matter what. Keep your family together. The "hero at home" serves too, by serving her/his spouse, and we serve our country together. I doubt there is any higher calling or any greater honor than that.

Now is a good time to mention an important fact about a certain limitation I have. You see, when God passed out common sense, he gave my friend Myra a double portion and reduced my part to a morsel.

So I stood there looking at the guys on the flight line. The entire crew was resting in the shade by the jets. There were no bathrooms nearby, and the mean-eyed mama was staring at me with her lips tensed, tapping her foot. How in the world was I going to take off my ecru shirt and change into the white T-shirt in front of God and country and mechanics?

My thoughts were interrupted by a tap on my shoulder. It was common-sensed Myra. "Ellie, you could just slip the white T-shirt over the shirt you're wearing now," she said.

"Uh, yes, uh, of course," I stammered, wondering why I hadn't thought of the obvious.

I quickly pulled on the white T-shirt and then found myself faced with yet another problem. You see, when a woman has had a basketball team's worth of children, there's a basic problem. I was wearing "Great Shapes" No Nonsense panty hose (they guarantee to take five pounds off any figure). In fact, I was wearing two pair to remove that extra ten pounds.

There was no way I could leave that shirt untucked, or the added bulk would make me look like a buffalo in that there canyon. Once again my hero, Myra, came to my rescue. "Here, Ellie, Marcie and I will hold up our jackets while you tuck your shirt in."

What a relief!

The two women held up their jackets, shielding the view from the flight-crew members by the jets.

I quickly dropped my pants low enough to neatly tuck in my shirt and pulled them up again. With a sigh of relief, I zipped the jeans and turned around to pick up my jacket from the pavement. At that moment I saw an awful sight.

To my utter embarrassment, I noticed, for the first time, a row of twelve men sitting in the shade of the hangar about two hundred yards behind me. The girls shielded the view of the guys in front of us, but no one saw the crowd behind us.

Myra noticed the Peeping Toms at the same time I did and was quick to comfort me with "Hey, Ellie, don't worry about it; I don't think they even noticed."

Momentary relief accompanied my hope that maybe Myra was right and they hadn't noticed. I slowly stole a side-glance at the group sitting in the shade.

They were waving at me, slapping each other on the back—and laughing.

★ ★ ★ ★ ★ ★ ★

Sometimes I create my own stress. As if it weren't enough that Uncle Sam was constantly trying to check my fortitude with unexpected deployments, bizarre moving scenarios, and remote locations, I contributed to the mix in ignorance or vanity. Yep, I'm "Queen of Scream" when I get caught doing foolish things. It was months before I could think of the Stealth Queen incident without turning beet red. It took even longer for me to actually laugh at it. It's an incident that keeps me humble when the "Superwoman Syndrome" beckons me to succumb to its impossible standards.

But even if we can't laugh at ourselves, there are scores of other stress-relieving activities that help us in our journey toward joy. Here are a few ideas from the experts:

A Matter of Perspective

De-stressing can, on occasion, be as easy as changing the way you view a challenge. For example: moving. When we've moved to a new area, sometimes it is hard to even think of the positive aspects of a move. Here are some advantages to being the new family on the block. Some of these tips have been adapted from Susan Miller's wonderful book on moving, *After the Boxes Are Unpacked* (Tyndale, 1998).

- You have a completely clean house before you move in.
- You have the opportunity to share some of the stuff you don't need with others who do need it (why not give that high chair to Goodwill?).
- You'll unpack items you can use but forgot you had—thus saving you the expense of buying them again.
- Maybe some of the old clothes you've held on to for twenty years have come back in style! (They probably won't fit you, but they may fit your teenager.)
- You have more control over time, because you don't have old commitments.
- No one in your new neighborhood has seen your wardrobe; it's like getting a new one every time you move!
- You have the opportunity to reprioritize your life.
- Moving will give you a better education by broadening your perspective along with your horizons.

- As Anne of Avonlea said, "Tomorrow is always new, with no mistakes in it." You have a chance to be known for who you are today and not who you were yesterday.
- All the same old, same old—those things that are old to you about yourself and your family—will be new and exciting to others.

Exercise Your Body—The Natural Stress Buster

For years medical experts have told us that regular exercise helps lower our cholesterol, increases our metabolism, and helps fight heart disease. Not only can you join an aerobics class, find a walking partner, or swim laps in the base pool, in addition to *individual* exercise, you can encourage your *family* to do some of these things together. The Galvin family, from Fort Leavenworth, organized family soccer events and got most of the neighborhood to participate.

Army spouse Jody Dale says, "Our family walks a lot and enjoys hiking together for exercise. It really has a calming effect when someone is out of sorts or otherwise stressed. We also play tennis, even though none of us are really that good at it. But that's what makes it fun. We laugh at ourselves and at each other. We have table tennis contests too. We film a lot of these contests, and the kids always have fun watching these old home movies. It helps us to remember how time flies, and what really matters is each other and not the stressful circumstances that often surround us."

According to MetLife's consumer education center pamphlet, there are ways to make exercise a habit that works with amazing effectiveness. Here are a few of them:

- Choose an activity you enjoy.
- Tailor your program to your own fitness level.
- Set realistic goals.
- Choose an exercise that fits your lifestyle.
- Give your body a chance to adjust to your new routine.
- Don't get discouraged if you don't see immediate results.
- Don't give up if you miss a day; just get back on track the next day.
- Find a partner for a little motivation and socialization.
- Build some rest days into your exercise schedule.
- Listen to your body. If you have difficulty breathing or experience faintness or prolonged weakness during or after exercise, consult your physician.

Exercise Your Brain

A real key in the lives of those who are the most productive, even into their later years, is the ability to keep their brain cells working. Here is a list of seven ways to accomplish this, taken from *Lists to Live By* (Multnomah, 2004):

- Play complex puzzles and games such as Scrabble or chess.
- Learn a foreign language.
- Study music.
- Solve math problems without using a calculator.
- Write letters or poetry.
- Engage in thought-provoking discussions.
- Study and memorize Scripture.
- Sleep it off.

If you're sleeping all the time, it could be a sign of depression, but how do you know if you're getting enough sleep? The right amount of rest is key to your ability to manage and handle stress. Patricia Anstett wrote the following quiz in *The Oregonian* to help readers know if they're getting enough sleep. If you answer yes to three or more of the fifteen items listed, you are like thousands of Americans who are probably not getting enough sleep.

1. I need an alarm to wake up at the appropriate time.
2. It's a struggle for me to get out of bed in the morning.
3. Weekday mornings I hit the snooze button several times to get more sleep.
4. I feel tired, irritable, and stressed out during the week.
5. I have trouble concentrating and remembering.
6. I feel slow in critical thinking, problem solving, and being creative.
7. I often fall asleep watching TV.
8. I often fall asleep in meetings, in lectures, or in warm rooms.
9. I often fall asleep after heavy meals or after a low dose of alcohol.
10. I often fall asleep while relaxing after dinner.
11. I often fall asleep within five minutes of getting into bed.
12. I often feel drowsy while driving.
13. I often sleep extra hours on weekend mornings.
14. I often need a nap to get through the day.
15. I have dark circles around my eyes.

The answer to sleep problems seems simple: "Get more sleep." But it goes a little further than that. It's important to keep regular hours, get to bed and wake up at the same time each day, and prioritize your schedule to accommodate this much-needed, stress-relieving practice of sleep therapy.

Professional Help

Part of the human condition is that there are times when no method, activity, or technique will fix the stress we're under, and that's when it's time to see a counselor. If you are experiencing the majority of the following danger signals, consider seeing a Marriage and Family Life Counselor (MFLC) at the Airmen and Family Readiness Center or mental health facility on base/post:

- frequent headaches or stomach pains;
- more negative talk than usual;
- more difficult to laugh than before;
- procrastinating the important to accomplish the unimportant;
- less patient and more irritable than normal;
- feeling one step away from falling apart;
- sleeping problems;
- abuse of non-prescription drugs, alcohol, or food to relax;
- feeling exhausted when awake;
- trouble concentrating;
- easily distracted;
- being forgetful and absentminded.

If the last three items on the list are the only ones that count, any preschool mom would qualify as "dangerously stressed." But if eight or more items listed above describe you and your life, then it's time to consult a trained professional.

Stress Busters for Kids at Special Times

Sometimes the stress of military life (especially a parent's absence) hits our kids hardest, and they deal with it in not-so-special ways. If you have kids in your military family, you can count on at least a few times when their feelings are manifested in a negative way. Here are some tips that can apply to our kids when they come home with a bad grade, get in a fight at school, or develop a mouth that gives new meaning to "back talk."

Be Kind. The first inclination is to return evil for evil, but extra patience is needed; just as we need time to adjust, so do they. This is in no way an excuse to condone negative behavior, but we must refrain from returning it in kind.

Pray. According to a recent survey, 90 percent of Americans admit to praying every day, so you are in good company (*Washington Times,* Dec. 2008, Brandeis University). Now might be a good time to call the local military chaplain and make an appointment to talk through and pray through this stormy season with your child. But *you* can also pray with your child as you pass along your personal faith.

No Excuses. We don't have to explain our child's behavior to everyone. Only talk to those directly involved in the problem. Don't give your child an excuse to believe that you are gossiping about their behavior. They hear and see more than we give them credit for.

Concentrate on Today. Don't look too far forward or backward, and encourage your child to do the same.

Be Honest. There's a difference between being painfully honest and patiently honest. Let your child know how you feel and stress the "I felt hurt when you said that" rather than "You hurt me when you said that." Teach your children how to express themselves in this way and it will help them get the tension out in constructive, productive ways that will enhance their communication skills in the future.

Don't Fear. When our kids go through transitions, and when we are committed to their growth and to helping them in productive ways, we need to teach them not to fear. For example, Anne Alde, wife of a retired general, said: "When my children were afraid of lightning storms, I told them 'God is taking our picture and the angels are bowling.'"

Get Help. If your children's needs are greater than your capacity to help them, go to your base's chaplain program and ask them to direct you to the people and youth programs designed to help you and your child through this challenging time. Or go to your Marriage and Family Life Counselor (MFLC) on base; they are there for times like these.

De-Stressing on the Run

If you think you can't slow down enough to take the time away from work and activity to rest, then you need to read a book that Debi Stack wrote called *Martha to the Max* (Moody Press, 2000). She writes, "The key is to make breaks as different from work as possible. Vary the location, the body position, the activity level, the senses used—everything!

Whether we're constantly on our feet or trapped behind a desk, there's something from the list below to help us to relax."

Here are a few of Debi's relaxing-on-the-run tips:

- Toss a Frisbee.
- Power nap.
- Listen to soothing music.
- Listen to an audiobook.
- Get a massage. (I need to do more research on this tip!)
- People-watch on a bench.
- Sit in a library.
- Sit in a church and talk to God.
- Buy yourself flowers.
- Take a long lunch and see a matinee.
- Spritz your work area with a delightful fragrance.
- Arrange lunch with a friend at a park and swap the sack lunches you've packed.

Friendships

Thoreau said, "My friend shall ever be my friend and reflect a ray of God to me." Friends can cut our stress in half or multiply it by two—depending upon the kind of friend they are. Here are the different kinds of friendships I have found in our military career. As you'll see from the descriptions, some are worth having and others are not.

Regulation Friendships. These are the professional friendships we make with other spouses in the unit, the neighborhood, or at work. While some may develop into lasting friendships, many of these are little more than acquaintances. Still, it's nice to have one of these special kinds of friends to attend a unit coffee with, take the kids to the park, or ask to help out with a school fund-raiser.

High-Maintenance Friendships. Life is too short for high-maintenance friendships. Let's face it, some people drain all the life from a party just by walking through the front door! We are usually drawn into these before we know what they're about. A good rule of thumb is: Listen to the way your new acquaintance talks about her other friends, because she'll soon be talking about you in the same way! If she's negative, complaining, and constantly giving you tips on whom and what to avoid for gossipy reasons—then hightail it in the opposite direction as fast as you can!

Physical Conditioning Friendships. These are the people with whom you go running, attend aerobics class, power walk, play tennis, or swim laps. Some of these activities are more conducive to talking than others. For example, if you power walk, you have tons of talk time. With that in mind, be sure these are friends that don't drain you with negativity, ones that can listen as well as talk, and people who can keep confidences.

Temporary Duty Assignments. These are friends who come into your life for a week, a month, or a year—a very short time for a specific purpose and function. It may be that you will be the one encouraging them or vice versa. If we keep in mind that it's all right for some friends to be temporary, and the connection can still be real, then these people can be God's well-placed secret agents—helping us even as we help them in times of stress and need.

Deployment Friendships. It is amazing how a major deployment or war will bring people together. Sometimes I look at these as EMT friends, those who get us through an emergency-type situation. I've even been that kind of friend at times. We usually connect with these kinds of friends and bond deeply, only to have the connection fade after the conflict is over.

Permanent Duty Station. These friends are few and far between. We may have met these people during one of the above-mentioned activities or time periods, but these friendships stand the test of time, stress, distance, and bad hair days. When triumph is ours, these friends share the excitement—and don't get jealous. When tragedy happens—they are the first ones we call. Count yourself blessed if you find a couple of these friendships in a lifetime.

Dangerous Friendships. One of my favorite sayings is, "Life is too short for high-maintenance relationships." So now is a good time to distance yourself from friends who suck the life out of you, have a negative disposition, are of the opposite sex and could be a threat to your marriage, or gossip about others (because they are likely gossiping about YOU too).

* * * * * * *

If I had my entire life to live over again, I don't think I'd have the strength.

—Flip Wilson

Let's Fly Our Service Flags Again!

In recent years there has been a resurgence of the display of the Service Flag, an official banner authorized by the Department of Defense (DOD) for display by families who have members serving in the Armed Forces during any period of war or hostilities the United States may be engaged in and for the duration of such.

The Service Flag (also known as Blue Star Banner) was designed by World War I Army Captain Robert L. Queissner of the 5th Ohio Infantry, who had two sons serving on the front lines. President Wilson became part of its history when, in 1918, he approved a suggestion made by the Women's Committee of the Council of National Defense that mothers who had lost a child serving in the war wear a gold gilt star on the traditional black mourning armband.

This led to the tradition of covering the blue star with a gold star on the Service Flag, indicating the service member had died or been killed. The blue star represents hope and pride; the gold star represents sacrifice to the cause of liberty and freedom.

During World War II, virtually every home and organization displayed banners to indicate members serving in the Armed Forces.

In 1966, the DOD revised the specifications for the design, manufacture, and display of the Service Flag. Family members authorized to display the flag include the wife, husband, mother, father, stepfather, parent through adoption, foster parent in place of parent, children, stepchildren, children through adoption, brothers, sisters, half brothers, and half sisters of a member of the Armed Forces of the United States. The flag should be displayed in a window of the residence of those immediate family members. (Adapted from http://usflag.org/history/serviceflag.html.)

☆ 9 ☆

HIDDEN HERO PORTRAIT—
PAQUITA RAWLEIGH

A Military Bride Charms America

Forty years ago Paquita Rawleigh was a new military bride who married a Navy third-class petty officer while he was stationed in her home country of Spain. They arrived in the States and had to in-process in New York City for a week. Fresh off the boat, the slender, pretty brunette got tired of sitting in her room looking at the four walls, so she decided to wait in the hotel lobby and watch the "foreign" Americans as they interacted. On the third day of her "lobby watch," she was approached by a man who spoke Spanish. She was excited to finally be able to speak to someone in her native tongue. They discussed a wide variety of topics, including American food, culture, and traditions. After several hours of visiting, the man leaned in closely and said, "Do you love your husband?"

She looked him in the eye and caught the full meaning of the inappropriate question he was really asking.

"Do I love my husband? Indeed!" she started yelling in Spanish, and then she showed that man just how much she loved her husband by hitting him over the head with her purse!

* * * * * * *

☆ *Profile* ☆

Name: Paquita Rawleigh

Birthplace: Jerez de la Frontera, Spain

Spouse's Name: Chief MSgt. Rodger Rawleigh (Retired)

Kids: Three adult children, nine grandchildren

Branch of Service: U.S. Navy and U.S. Air Force

Years in Service: twenty-seven

Work: "Retired from Everything"

Hobbies: International Poet Society Award winner, published in *Seasons of a Woman's Heart* and *Treasures of a Woman's Heart*; sewing; telling jokes, and having a good time with friends

Least Favorite Aspect of Military Life: when my husband went away and I had to be alone with three kids

Favorite Aspect of Military Life: when he got back

Paquita is an amazing example of the foreign military spouse, but she's also a role model for all military families in her ability to be spunky, tell a funny story, and stand up for what she believes. Most military brides who immigrate to the United States face a double whammy: They must learn the military lifestyle, *plus* they must also learn a new culture, complete with different customs and often a new language.

But Paquita says she "loves to tell stories and make people laugh." She coped with the difficulties of a new life by learning to look at the world through plastic glasses with a fake mustache and a funny nose. This upbeat outlook can be an incredible gift to those around you who are struggling—an amazing gift, in fact. Few do it as well as Paquita Rawleigh. This ability to create pools of laughter starts and ends with her brilliant ability to laugh at herself. She's had lots of fun recounting those days when her Spanish was far better than her English. Here are a few more stories from the "Queen of Fun."

When the Rawleighs attended their first military social function, she was embarrassed by the fact that she didn't know very much English, and her husband, Rodger Rawleigh, said that in order to learn the language she should "Mingle with people; just walk around and mingle."

She stood in the same place for several minutes wondering what in the world *mingle* meant. Then she looked around at the sea of faces and decided she needed to go to the ladies' room. As she was politely working her way to the other side of the crowded hall, she needed to get past a sailor, and said, "Kiss me!"

He stared at her, looking a bit baffled, to which she repeated herself firmly and politely, "Kiss me!"

So he did.

She was shocked and reacted by slapping him across the face. Paquita's husband quickly came to her side and explained to the sailor, who was still rubbing his stinging cheek, "Uh, she doesn't know English very well, and she thought she was saying, 'Excuse me.'"

Recently Paquita decided she wanted to do something in her sixties to make her look younger. While her daughter has big bushy eyebrows, Paquita was not "blessed" in such a way. In fact, about thirty years ago someone told her that if she plucked out all her eyebrows, they would come back in fuller and thicker. So she did. But they never grew back—at all. So all these years she's had to pencil them in with an eyebrow pencil.

She says, "When I was junger, it was okay. I could see just fine. But now I no see so good. It is hard with my bifocals to see what I doing."

"Some days I look very surprised!" (Her eyebrows are upraised.)

"Other days, I look *very* angry!" (Narrow, furrowed brows.)

"And some days I just look confused!" (One eyebrow is up, the other down.)

So she went to an upscale beauty salon in her neighborhood to see what they would charge for permanent cosmetics that would give her a "happy" look. She entered the salon, went to the front desk, and boldly said, "Hell-o? Can chew make me loook ten jears junger?"

The receptionist looked baffled and went to get the cosmetic technician, who took an instant liking to Paquita and quoted her such a good price that this feisty woman replied, "Oooh, that eeese a verrry goood price! Tell me, is eeet for one eyebrow—or two?"

The tech laughed out loud and replied, "Well, for you, Paquita, it's 'buy one/get one free'!"

When Chief Rawleigh retired from the Air Force Reserves, the Rawleighs moved from California back to their roots in Texas. They covered a lot of open territory as they caravanned down the road. Paquita was in her Mercedes 280SL sports car and got pulled over by the highway police on a lonely desert stretch in New Mexico. The officer stuck his head in the window of her car and asked, "Excuse me, ma'am, do you know how fast you were going?"

Paquita replied emphatically, "Jes, I go eightee-five."

The officer was solemn. "Yes, ma'am, and that's twenty miles over the speed limit."

The little woman was incensed. "No! It is NOT! I saw sign. It say eightee-five, and I no go more than eightee-five! I no should get ticket because I go what the sign say."

The policeman's face flushed. "Ma'am, that's *Highway* 85; the *speed limit* is still sixty-five miles per hour."

Paquita suddenly became quiet and replied, "Oh." She paused a moment. "It has been many jears since I drive deeze highways. I thought it fast, but maybe, I say to myself, maybe these people in New Mexico, they like to go eightee-five."

She peered at him under her surprised-looking eyebrows. "Are chew going to give me a ticket?"

The officer, whose mood had gone from solemn to trying to stifle his laughter, smiled and answered, "No, ma'am, I'm not; just slow down to sixty-five. You're the best thing that has happened to me today!"

Whether she's telling stories to her girl friends or trying to escape her latest brush with the law, Paquita Rawleigh is a delight to everyone who meets her. Wouldn't you like that to be said of you? When she was being interviewed on the phone for the profile at the beginning of this chapter, she suddenly started to giggle and scream!

"Dere is a mockingbird who try to attack me every time I come onto my patio." (More shrieks and screams.) "She think I try to hurt her babies, and she chase me when I walk outside with de phone!" (Screaming and laughter as she hands the phone to her husband. You can hear her shrieking in the background as the killer bird attacks her hair.) Her husband patiently answers my questions about his time in the service, and then he hands the phone back to her. This time she's back inside the house. "I dun't know why that bird get so angry! I no want her babies, I already have my dinner today!"

Paquita has given the gift of laughter to her children, her grand-children, and everyone who reads this book. The only thing she loves more than laughing is her husband. Her devotion to him, through all his military adventures and separations, has been one worthy of emulating. She's more than a hidden hero—she's my mom.

I Pledge Allegiance . . .

One of the things my mom did when she became a United States citizen was to proudly recite the Pledge of Allegiance. But what do the words really mean? In 1892, the first pledge was created for a group of schoolchildren to recite to commemorate the 400th anniversary of Columbus's discovery of America. The words were revised three times, in the years 1923, 1924, and 1954. Let's look at the meaning of the pledge.

I Pledge Allegiance	I Promise to be faithful and true (Promise my loyalty)
to the Flag	to the emblem that stands for and represents
of the United States	all 50 states, each of them individual, and individually represented on the flag
of America,	yet formed into a UNION of one Nation.
and to the Republic	I also pledge my loyalty to the Government that is itself a Republic, a form of government where the PEOPLE are sovereign,
for which it stands:	this government also being represented by the Flag to which I promise loyalty.
one Nation under God,	These 50 individual states are united as a single Republic under the Divine providence of God, "our most powerful resource" (according to the words of President Eisenhower)
indivisible,	and cannot be separated. (This part of the original version of the pledge was written just 30 years after the beginning of the Civil War and demonstrates the unity sought in the years after that divisive period in our history.)
with Liberty	The people of this Nation being afforded the freedom to pursue "life, liberty, and happiness,"
and Justice	and each person entitled to be treated justly, fairly, and according to proper law and principle,
for all.	and these principles afforded to EVERY AMERICAN, regardless of race, religion, color, creed, or any other criteria. Just as the flag represents 50 individual states that cannot be divided or separated, this Nation represents millions of people who cannot be separated or divided.

(From http://homeofheroes.com/hallofheroes/1st_floor/flag/1bfc_pledge.html)

☆ 10 ☆

HIDDEN HERO PORTRAIT—
KARA SIERT

A Courageous Child Prodigy

Not all heroes at home are spouses; sometimes they are children of military members. The fact is that everyone associated with loved ones in the military makes some kind of sacrifice in their service as a hero at home. Kara Siert is one of these quiet heroes—and so are her parents. Ward and Linda, from England, call their daughter, Kara, a gift from God. They went through the lengthy process of adopting their little girl from China, and Linda says, "It was our plan from the beginning for me to stay home and homeschool our child. The years go by too fast for me to miss even one of them."

It was soon evident that this beautiful little girl with dark hair and porcelain-like skin was not only destined to be with Ward and Linda, but Kara was also a prodigy with a special gift for writing. But this family has not been without its share of heartache.

At the age of nine and a half, Kara started experiencing some pain in her arm, and a large bone cyst was discovered. The family went through several steps and consulted many doctors before they got the devastating diagnosis: cancer. Linda wrote: "Osteosarcoma is a very deadly bone cancer. It takes intensive chemo (at least eighteen weeks of inpatient chemo, and several weeks more for any complications) and a major surgery to give her a chance."

☆ **Profile** ☆

Name Kara Siert (age twelve)/dependent daughter

Parents' Names: Ward and Linda Siert

Branch of Service: Father in Air Force (Medical Group)

Place of Birth: Nanning, China

Work: Student, professional writer, and author, *Tales of Cunburra*. For more information, go to www.karasiert.com.

Number of Moves: Have lived in four places in eleven years.

Years in Service: Father has served for sixteen years.

Hobbies: Reading, writing, drawing, arts and crafts

★ ★ ★ ★ ★ ★ ★

Here is twelve-year-old Kara's story in her own words:

A little ten-month-old baby in Nanning, China, just north of Vietnam, was living with her foster parents. In the Chinese tradition of first birthdays, they presented this little baby who had a full head of black, shiny hair, a tray full of various objects to see which one she would choose. Whatever she chose would signify her future. As they hovered around her, they wondered what her decision would be. The only thing she wanted was a pen.

I was that baby.

When I was eleven months old, my parents flew to China to adopt me and make me part of their family forever. That was when I became a Siert and came to live in the United States.

I don't know if my choosing a pen at ten months old was a coincidence or not, but from as long as I can remember I have always loved to write stories. Being homeschooled has allowed me the time to write. When my family was preparing to move to England in the spring of 2005, I finished school early and had lots of time to read and write for several weeks. I was nine and a half at the time. My mom and I had been reading *The Chronicles of Narnia* together, which inspired me to work on a series of stories about my own fantasy world. I wrote a whole bunch of stories in about a four-month period.

In July, after we had been in England for about a month, we were getting settled into our house and starting to see a few sights in the area. The fact that my right arm was hurting was something I didn't want to think about. I was afraid my parents might take me to the doctor. The last time I went was for my kindergarten shots, and I didn't want to go back. But the pain became worse, and soon I couldn't hide it from my parents anymore. They took me in for an X-ray. We were shocked to find out I had a huge tumor in my upper-arm bone.

Seven weeks later, a biopsy revealed that I had bone cancer. My parents were devastated. They knew how serious my cancer was and that I could die from it. At the time I didn't realize how serious my situation was but trusted my parents to do the best thing for me. They didn't try to hide the fact that I might lose my arm or that I might even die. Although I prepared myself for the possibility of losing my arm, I guess I didn't really think that I would die from the cancer. So I wasn't as worried as my parents, although I did start to practice writing left-handed.

I had to get treatment right away to give me the best chance to beat the cancer, so we stayed in England. I had to have ten months of chemotherapy, which required my being in the hospital most of the time. The people here, our military "family," really rallied around us to help while I was in treatment those ten months. My mom explained to me that the chemotherapy would make me nauseated. I didn't know what that was because I'd never thrown up before. It didn't take long to find out! My mom also told me that my hair would fall out. At first I was a little worried about it, but once it happened, I didn't really mind because I knew it would grow back.

After my third month of chemotherapy, I had major surgery to remove my cancerous bone. I now have a titanium rod in my arm. My shoulder tendons were removed so I can no longer raise up my arm, but I'm grateful that I still have an arm. Life would have been much more difficult with only one arm, especially since I'm right-handed.

Ironically, cancer is what allowed me to get my first book published. Those stories I had written about my own fantasy world the months just prior to my cancer diagnosis became my book *Tales of Cunburra and Other Stories*. Being a published author at the age of ten was a dream come true for me! I never imagined how God would bless me through this experience.

My treatment was completed in July 2006, my hair has grown back, and I've been cancer-free for sixteen months now. Being treated in British hospitals is an experience I will never forget. Although the treatment was horrible, it saved my life, and I have made friendships that will last a lifetime. I will continue to have regular checkups to make sure the cancer doesn't come back. I'm thankful to God and for modern medicine, which has allowed me to continue writing stories and playing with my friends. I always knew I wanted to share God's love through my writing, and now since my cancer, people want to listen even more to what I have to say. Now He has given me an even more important message than ever by showing me that even at my young age, life is extremely fragile and is not to be taken for granted.

Ward and Linda Siert faced every parent's worst nightmare—the fact that their child might not live to see her next birthday. But the added challenge was the fact that they are a military family and had to decide if they would go through this life-and-death battle with their military family in a land far from home or with their natural family back in the States. They chose to stay at their assignment, knowing that between God and friends, they would survive—somehow.

Kara has not only recovered from her cancer and published a book, but she is also traveling and speaking to groups of children and adults, inspiring them to pursue their dreams and have courage in the midst of difficulty. Her parents are also an inspiration to those other military families who face unthinkable challenges and manage to live through the difficulty to the promise of hope on the other side of the trial.

When our *Heroes at Home* team went to England on tour, we had the privilege of seeing Kara and her family. We shared a book table, and while I signed copies of *Heroes at Home,* this precious twelve-year-old signed copies of her book, *Tales of Cunburra.* It just goes to show that courage comes in all sizes and shapes. Sometimes the courage comes from within and sometimes we are encouraged—our courage comes from others. With friends and family by our side, we can choose to rise above the challenges faced in this life we proudly call the military.

CELEBRATING
COMMUNITY

☆ 11 ☆

A TIME FOR HEROES

A Grounded Pilot and a Flying Wife

Being married to "The World's Greatest Fighter Pilot" has its ups and downs (so to speak), and one of the things I discovered about my man is: *His feet are restless while on the ground.*

He flew fighters for a decade before I even met him and eventually accumulated 4,500 flight hours in seven different jets. There's one phone call that a pilot's wife always waits for but hopes will never happen. I got that call when I was in New York City on business and at a Broadway show. The five minutes it took to check my voicemail during intermission forever changed our lives:

Bob has been in an accident and broken his back.

He punctured his lung and broke four vertebrae and four ribs. He had just flown his last sortie. It was a fluke accident that happened during a routine delivery of a jet.

You see, even though Bob was retired, he was still flying the F-4 Phantom as a production test pilot and civilian contractor. His company put avionics in the jet that turned it into a drone (meaning it could fly by itself), and he tested it to make sure it worked in the air. Then he delivered the jet 2,000 miles from California to Florida. The fifty-plus-year-old aircraft were well maintained but old and risky to fly. When he stopped for a gas-and-go in Abilene, they didn't have a ladder to fit the F-4, and instead of waiting for a metal staircase ramp, he intended to do what he had done several times before. He would walk from the top of the wing to the bottom, sit on his bo-hiney and jump the other five feet off the wing.

The only problem was he was tired, and when he got out of the jet, he stood up at the top of the wing . . . and then he doesn't remember anything but falling ten feet onto eighteen inches of tarmac. He bloodied his head and busted his dreams.

Our son Daniel and his wife, Jenn, drove from Dallas to Abilene to see Bob, and I flew in from New York City to take him home. He was in a wheelchair and in a world of pain. The trip home was the longest flight of his life. My pilot's wings were permanently clipped. My hero would never be able to fly in a fighter jet again.

After a lot of prayer and hard work, Bob recovered his health and is able to maintain a pilot's license, but his back will not sustain an ejection-seat aircraft. While he enjoys "flying" the Global Hawk as a civilian contractor and Cessnas as a pilot, he always gets a sad look in his eye when a fighter flies by.

I didn't understand the depth of his loss until something amazing happened to me.

I got to fly in a fighter.

After bringing the Heroes at Home message to military families in seven countries, at 100 venues, and traveling 300,000 miles to do this, with 500,000 military families reading my work and 1,000,000 military families having seen my presentations . . . the Air Force rewarded me with an incentive ride.

Bob and Joshua were also invited to Seymour Johnson Air Force Base, home of the 4th Fighter Wing and the world's most lethal tactical fighter, the F-15E Strike Eagle. They flew the simulator, but I was to fly the real deal.

Flying in a fighter for the first time is a lot like having your first baby. Everyone likes to tell you how painful it's going to be when you lose your cookies. Everyone talks about getting sick. Bob piloted a lot of incentive rides in his day and said almost every person he flew got rip-roaring sick. He advised me to go 100 percent oxygen if I started to feel bad, and then said I should ask the pilot if I could fly the jet. The distraction of trying to fly would help me not get ill.

I decided to do the same thing I did when I had my first child and everyone told me how horribly painful it would be: I would displace that negative thought with a positive one, such as: That may be your experience, but it doesn't have to be mine. If I could birth five children without drugs, IVs, or pain, I could also displace the discomfort of an upset tummy and keep my breakfast down.

Speaking of breakfast, the day started out with the best breakfast I've ever eaten. It was prepared by Dee Dee Doherty, the Wing Commander's wife. No wonder she runs half marathons: She has to work off her own cooking! As I daintily chowed down on two kinds of egg casserole, home-made cinnamon buns, fresh fruit, and an absolutely to-die-for French toast casserole, it suddenly occurred to me that I was flying that day. As good as it was, I really hoped that was the last I saw of my breakfast.

The next step was to see the flight surgeon, where I got a flight physical. The physiologist came in and told me how to breathe when I experienced g-forces, and then how to avoid getting queasy by trying not to move my head around a lot and just look straight ahead at the clouds. At egress training, I learned how to bail out of the jet safely and what to do if my parachute wouldn't open (besides praying hard and preparing for heaven). They also had tips on how to get sick in a bag and how to turn off the intercom to save my dignity. Then they said to look at the instruments and try to read the gauges, so I wouldn't succumb to a green-in-the-gills feeling.

The chaplain told me he would pray for me and that while I was up there, if I started to feel bad, I could pray for all my kids—after all, I was going to "touch the face of God," as the poem "High Flight" said.

Captain Chris "Wyatt" Koeltzow (he wouldn't tell us how he got the name Wyatt), the wing executive officer, told me that I could let the vents in the jet blow into the open arms of my flight suit, and that would cool me off and make me feel better.

At the 333rd FS Lancers squadron, we were met by LTC "Rosie" O'Donnell, who took me to the squadron bar and offered me jala-peno popcorn. But then someone else said maybe I shouldn't eat any because of you-know-what.

In the briefing that was led by Captain Ryan "Goat" Roper, he told me to think about the mission and not about getting sick, and to dwell on the fact that I'd fly over Kitty Hawk at 1,000 feet and view it from the back seat of an F-15E. His Weapons Systems Officer, Captain Sriram "Fuze" Krishnan, told me to drink a bottle of water after I asked my pilot if I could take off my air mask.

Then the big man himself, Colonel Pat "Moon" Doherty, the 4th Fighter Wing Commander, and my very own pilot, ordered me not to get sick. Well, maybe it was more of a "willing" than "commanding" me to not become ill. Actually, his call sign could have been "Cool Hand Luke," because his demeanor was both calming and compelling. He said he knew I'd be fine and I believed him. I had watched this man who had so much responsibility for billions of dollars of assets on his base, and he was intense, professional, and highly capable.

But when we got ready to step to the jet, I noticed something that surprised me about Moon. In fact, I noticed it in all the air crew for our two-ship sortie—there was an excited gleam in their eyes. It was as if they were little boys, and instead of being excited about playing baseball, their collective countenance said, "We get to go fly jets today!" It was the same look I'd seen on Bob's face when I watched him launch out into the wild blue yonder.

I put on my g-suit and harness, grabbed my helmet and air mask, tucked in those pesky air sickness bags into my flight suit, and we were ready. Excitement overtook me as I realized I was truly going to do this thing—I was going to fly in a no-kidding, real world, operational fighter with the second-best fighter pilot in the world (Bob always has to be the first).

We signed out the jet, stepped to the hangar, met the amazing maintenance crew, preflighted the aircraft, strapped on thirty tons of sheer power, and taxied down the runway. At the end of the runway, while we waited for clearance to takeoff, Bob and Joshua met us in a truck and took a gazillion pictures. There was a wistful look on the World's Greatest Fighter Pilot's face. He never would have dreamed that his wife would fly in the one fighter he had always wanted to pilot but never did.

Moon and I were cleared for takeoff, and we watched Goat and Fuze roar down the runway and head into a vertical climb. Then it was our turn; no going back now! As we blasted down the runway, the afterburner screaming, we took off on the wildest ride I'll ever have this side of eternity. We pulled about five g's in a straight vertical climb and then a sharp turn out to sea. The one-hour drive to the coastline took eight minutes. It gave a whole new meaning to the bumper sticker "If I were in my F-15E, I'd be there by now."

Fuze snapped photos of us airborne as we rose above the clouds. Moon asked what I wanted to do, as he didn't want to push me. But I was game for low levels, aileron rolls, and what I call the loop-de-loop. About twenty minutes into the ride, I started to feel my skin get cold and prickly—a sure sign I was going to get airsick.

I didn't say anything to Moon about feeling nauseous, but I did get quiet. As if sensing my predicament (if a great fighter pilot has anything, he has instincts), he asked me if I wanted to fly the jet. That was one of the "tips" in my training, so I took it. I didn't crash it, and that made me feel good, but I still wasn't that chipper, so I went 100 percent oxygen. Step-by-step I went through the tips in my training on how to avoid illness. I let the cool air blow into the arms of my flight suit, I prayed for my kids, I studied the gauges, I didn't move my head too much, I asked to take off my mask during a low level and drank the entire bottle of water. I began to feel better and really enjoyed the rest of the flight. It was just stone cold cool.

We flew a formation approach (ten feet from the other airplane), then flew back out in the traffic pattern for a couple more approaches. After 1.7 hours of flight time, we could say, "The Eagle has landed." I was beyond euphoric to have flown in this premier jet with a big-time pilot and not get sick. We taxied back to a cheering crowd, and when Bob learned that I held my own, he gave me the highest praise that could ever come from a fighter pilot when he declared in all serious-ness, "Beloved, I am as proud of you today as I was every day that you gave birth."

★　★　★　★　★　★　★

I learned some things on the hot tarmac on that humid North Carolina day. For one thing, we have the finest team of military pro-fessionals in the world. Each team member I met that day was very secure in their place on the team and performed their duties with pride and professionalism.

I learned that big boys still act like little boys when they get to do what they love.

I learned that as much as my man suffered from clipped wings, his love for his wife and excitement over her living out a bucket list dream was greater than any detraction he may have felt.

I also learned why Bob loved his work for thirty years and how hard it was for him to have his feet on the ground.

But one of the main things I learned from the F-15E Strike Eagle adventure was: When you start to get overwhelmed, fall back on your training. One day you may find that the moves, the single parenting during deployments, operations tempo, broken-down appliances, or sick children may make your skin start to prickle. You may begin to feel that military life is going to overwhelm you. This is the time to fall back on your training and your team: Go talk to an MFLC counselor, visit the chaplain, call your key spouse, get helpful resources from MilitaryOneSource.com, stop by the Family or Community Services Center, or take a class that will increase your brainpower. All of this "spouse training" can take your mind off the discomfort of challeng-ing circumstances and help deliver a happy landing that you can be proud of in the future.

When we were stationed with the Army, I met many families who were brand-new to the military, and many did not know how to tap in to the community that surrounded them. Others were intimidated by the brave new world they'd stepped into. But the Army had a great volunteer program called Army Family Team Building (AFTB) that taught both new and seasoned spouses about the military way of life. Now the Marine Corps, Navy, and Air Force have similar courses.

I took the course and then received training to become an instructor at our post. I so believed in the program that I was selected by the Army to go to Florida for a week of intensive master training. Once certified, I learned how to train the trainer. Much of the information in this chapter was acquired through this program, and I've selected the terms that are common to all four branches of the service. A list follows to better acquaint you with the terms, acronyms, and abbreviations that are common to the military lifestyle.

Acronyms and Abbreviations

AAFES	Army and Air Force Exchange Service
ACS	Army Community Services
AD	Active duty
A&FRC	Airman and Family Readiness Center
AFN	Armed Forces Network
ASAP	As soon as possible
AWOL	Absent without leave
BAQ	Basic allowance for quarters
BAS	Basic allowance for subsistence
CDR	Commander
CDS	Child Development Services
CG	Commanding General
CINC	Commander in Chief
CO/OIC	Commanding Officer/Officer in Charge
COLA	Cost of living allowance
CONUS	Continental United States
CY	Calendar year
DECA	Defense Commissary Agency
DEERS	Defense Enrollment Eligibility Reporting System
DEROS	Date of estimated return from overseas
DITY	Do-it-yourself move
DOB	Date of birth
DOD	Department of Defense
DOR	Date of rank
EE	Emergency essential
ETS	Estimated time of separation

FOUO	For official use only
FY	Fiscal year
FYI	For your information
GED	General Education Diploma
GO	General Officer
HOR	Home of record
HQ	Headquarters
IG	Inspector General
JAG	Judge Advocate General
KIA	Killed in action
KISS	Keep it simple stupid/sweetie
KP	Kitchen patrol
LES	Leave and earning statement
LOD	Line of duty
MI	Military intelligence
MIA	Missing in action
MP/SF	Military police/security forces
MRE	Meals ready to eat
MWR	Morale, Welfare, and Recreation
NA	Not applicable
NATO	North Atlantic Treaty Organization
NCO	Noncommissioned officer
NLT	Not later than
OCONUS	Outside continental United States
OIC	Officer-in-charge
OJT	On-the-job training
PAO/PA	Public Affairs Office
PCA	Permanent change of assignment
PCS	Permanent change of station
PDQ	Pretty darn quick
POA	Power of attorney
POC	Point of contact
POV	Privately owned vehicle
PT	Physical training
REG	Regulation
ROTC	Reserve Officer Training Corps
RSVP	Reply whether or not you can attend (*repondez s'il vous plait*)
SA	Situational Awareness
SBP	Survivor benefit plan
SGLI	Servicemen's Group Life Insurance
SOP	Standard Operating Procedure
SSN	Social Security Number
TDY	Temporary duty
TLA	Temporary living allowance
TSP	Thrift Savings Plan
USO	United Service Organization
VA	Department of Veterans Affairs

	Military Speak	Spouse Speak
Accompanied Tour	Tour of duty with family members	Lasts from a month (usually Hawaii) to ten years (in Minot, ND)
Active Duty	Military members actively serving and deployable	This means your address is written in pencil in address books.
Alert	Emergency call to be ready	What you're on when your spouse asks, "Are you in a good mood, honey?"
Allowance	Special pay and compensation	The amount you give your spouse from his/her paycheck
Article 15	Non-judicial disciplinary action	Their military career is over.
Benefits	Medical, dental, commissary, PX, etc.	Civilians see these as abundance, while the military family sees them as barely adequate.
Chain of Command	Leadership structure	Who you should be nice to whether you feel like it or not
Chaplain	Military minister, priest, rabbi, or pastor	Lifeline when life isn't in line
Colors	National and unit/ organization flags	Found on a dress uniform shirt when Junior's crayons end up in the dryer
Commissary	Grocery store for military members and their families	Where baggers work for tips, payday lines are longer than opening day for the latest blockbuster movie, and you usually can't find at least one thing you desperately need for dinner—like rice
Deployment	A mission without family members	When the washer breaks down, the kids get a stomach virus, you lose your car keys, and your in-laws come to visit the grandbabies (and cook, clean, fix the garage door, and remodel your home, if you can get them to do it)
Detail	Job or assignment	What your spouse leaves out of the conversation, as in: "Uh, my TDY is actually to *Italy,* but I guess I forgot to mention that part!"
Dining In	Formal social gathering for military members only	You'll always wonder what *really* goes on at one of these, since spouses aren't allowed to attend.
Dining Out	Formal social gathering for military and spouses	Don't *ever* throw a roll during one of these or it could end up in a formal food fight. (No, I promise I wasn't the one who threw it, and yes, it really ended in a fight!)

	Military Speak	Spouse Speak
Discharge	Departure from active duty	Your life may finally become "normal"—whatever that is. (But you're probably going to miss the military just a wee bit.)
DITY Move	Do-it-yourself move	The goal is to get through one of these and remain married.
Dog Tags	Identification tags worn by military members	Good for prying open cans of paint—but be careful you don't get the paint on the dog tag, because it's *very* hard to get off!
Duty Assignment	Job/place while on active duty	We made it our motto to "Never have a bad duty assignment." They are what you choose to make them.
Esprit de Corps	Morale within unit or organization	Another phrase for "I'm coming home late from work"
Airmen and Family Readiness Center/Army Community Services	A military organization that meets the needs of family members	You'd be a fool not to tap in to this source of help—it's there for *you*.
Formation	Prescribed gathering of military members	A volcano-shaped structure that your eight-year-old makes with Dad's helmet in his sandbox, using water and mud
Frock	Assume the next higher grade without pay	More work. Same money
Gear	Equipment used by military members or civilian employees	Somehow you or the kids are held responsible when your spouse misplaces the "little thingy" part of the gear.
GI Bill	Education entitlement	Working four years for a "free" education
GI Party	Clean-up duty	What he gets to do when you cook dinner
Guard	Members of the National Guard	Before 9/11, these were called Weekend Warriors, but now they are Essential Warriors, as they serve long stretches at a time.
Hardship Tour or Remote	Unaccompanied tour of duty	When you're tempted to go home to Mama for the year or hire a full-time nanny (yeah, right)
Hazardous Duty Pay	Extra pay for duty in hostile area	When you realize that even though they squeeze the toothpaste in the middle, put the toilet paper on the roll backward, and work too many hours, you'd rather have them home safe than the additional pay for this duty

	Military Speak	Spouse Speak
ID Card	Military-issued identification card	Make great cookie sheet scrapers, but you can't locate yours when you have to take your child to the emergency room in the middle of the night—and your spouse is TDY. (Hint: Look in the kitchen.)
Jungle Boots	Special boots for tropical climates	What you wear in your backyard when Dad is on a two-month summer trip. (Tip: Hire the neighbor boy to cut it.)
Klick	Slang for kilometer	The sound the garbage disposal makes just before you smell smoke
Latrine	Toilet	The name of the ugly witch in the movie *Robin Hood: Men in Tights* (rent it for laughs)
Leave	Approved time away from duty	What gets canceled to improve morale
Orders	Spoken or written instructions to military members	These start arriving at the door when your spouse is gone and you've spent too much time watching the Home Shopping Network.
Power of Attorney	Legal permission for a person to act on behalf of another	A good way to get that new SUV the next time your spouse goes TDY to Hawaii (and all three kids have the chicken pox)
Protocol	Customs and courtesies	If you *forget* this at a military ball, it could *feel* like one of those scary childhood dreams where you're walking to school in your underwear.
Quarters	Government housing	What the *military* calls five kids in two rooms and *we* make it "home"
Rank	Official title of military member	The way your spouse smells after coming in from survival training
Regrets Only	Respond only if not attending	What will happen if you forget to go to the General's little party
Reserve Component	Army and Air National Guard and U.S. Army Reserve	Fun for one weekend a month that has frequently stretched to fifty-two weeks per year—or longer
Retreat	Bugle/flag ceremony at the end of the day	What your husband should do if he doesn't know the correct answer to: "How do you really think I look in this dress?" (And the correct answer is: an *IMMEDIATE* "You look great!")
Reveille	Bugle call/ceremony at the beginning of the day	A pipe cleaner your kids use to make paper butterflies for the military member's homecoming decorations
Roster	List of members	An excellent resource for finding people to invite to your Pampered Chef party

	Military Speak	Spouse Speak
Short Tour	Unaccompanied tour, usually twelve months long	What it's called when it's *not* and you are left behind (There ain't nothing short about it!)
SA	Situational Awareness	Their ability to multitask with twenty variables in a real world combat situation and yet they can't see that the kids just got into the can of chocolate icing
Space A	Space available	Never available in Florida in the summer, but usually wide open in Fort Drum in the winter
Taps	Last call of the day	The saddest song in the world
TDY	Temporary duty (off the installation)	Usually happens around birthdays, anniversaries, and holidays

In concluding this chapter, keep in mind that when a family is new to the service, all these terms, acronyms, and customs can be overwhelming—kind of like taking a sip from a fire hose or even crawling into the back seat of an F-15E Strike Eagle. Even military time is different: it starts counting at 1:00 A.M. with 0100 and continues until midnight (2400). If you're new, be patient with yourself and don't expect to learn it all overnight—Rome wasn't built in a day and neither is a military spouse.

Realize that there is an entire team of people out there who are willing to help you adjust. This new training is what is going to see you through the ups and downs of military life. If you're not new, have an extra amount of patience with those who are new to the service. We're in this community together, and often the kindness of a veteran hidden hero to a novice inductee will make all the difference in his/her perspective. Just strap in and get ready for the loop de loop of your life.

☆ 12 ☆

OPERATION
HOSPITALITY CHECK

I Volunteer to Have a Ball at the Ball

I was hosting my first coffee for the spouses of my husband's new unit. I wanted to keep the evening simple and decided to forego the traditional crystal, silver, and china. Since we were new to the area, I decided to center the coffee around a common military theme. So I decided to host a "moving coffee." The invitations were printed on packing paper glued to small pieces of moving boxes. We thought the entertainment could be assessing the damage of our household goods. (The latter is a joke, the former was not!)

Everything had to be nice, and several days were spent in preparing the food, house, and agenda. The table was decorated with boxes, packing paper, and claim forms. The cake arrived from the baker, depicting the Kays in front of our new house, with a moving van in the background. The evening of the coffee, I put the finishing touches on the table, while Bob watched our youngest two, Jonathan and Joshua, aka Señor Mischief and his protégé.

Then their apprentice, Courtney, arrived. She was a two-year-old bit of feminine fluff that lived across the street. She was also the self-proclaimed president of the tricycle gang on Ft. Drum Circle. Her petite frame, blue eyes, and blond curls belied the fact that she could hold her own against my then three- and four-year-old boys.

☆ *Hidden Hero Profile* ☆

Name: Jocelyn Green

Spouse's Name: Lieutenant Rob Green

Branch of Service: Coast Guard

Kids: Elsa, five years old, and Ethan, three years old

Number of Moves: two

Years in Service: six active duty, two Reserves

Work/Employer: I'm self-employed as a freelance writer and author.

Hobbies: Scrapbooking, baking, reading, gardening, playing with my kids

Describe your military service before you became a spouse and after:

I had no connection to the military before I married my Coast Guard husband. Two days after we married, in Washington, D.C., we left for our next duty station in Homer, Alaska. In addition to all the adjustments newlyweds need to make, I experienced the typical culture shock that comes with moving from a large city to a small one, from one side of the country to the other, from being a civilian to joining the military community, and from having a career to being unemployed. I learned firsthand that military spouses need spiritual support to weather their own storms as we try to support our military member husbands.

As a Coast Guard wife living in Alaska, I had been haunted by the sense that I was just tagging along with my husband, following his orders for the next move, with no apparent life purpose of my own. Frankly, I felt like my identity was eclipsed by his military title. But when I discovered all that God had to say to me personally in His Word about what I was going through as a military wife, I was amazed at how relevant the Bible was to my situation.

That experience led me to recruit fourteen other Christian military wives from all branches of service to put together a book of devotions squarely addressing from a biblical perspective all the issues the military wife faces. *Faith Deployed: Daily Encouragement for Military Wives* was released by Moody Press in 2008. The sequel, *Faith Deployed . . . Again,* was released by Moody in 2011.

I continue to be compelled by the home front heroes I know and consider it a privilege to both encourage them and to help tell their stories through the *Faith Deployed* books and through *Battlefields and Blessings: Stories of Faith and Courage from the Home Front.* The most inspirational people I know belong to the military family.

Least Favorite Aspect of Military Life:
The time it takes to reconnect with a spouse after a separation.

Favorite Aspect of Military Life:
Being able to serve my country with pride—living a life of passion, honor, and duty. But even more important, the way the military life-style shows me truths in God's Word in a new light.

Bob's temporary duty mission was to watch the little ones, which he did while he chatted with Courtney's father, our Army friend Trace, in our garage. They were discussing the finer points of artillery warfare when they were interrupted by a series of piercing screams. The shrieks, coming from inside the house, sounded like those of a woman who had just seen a mouse. The fact was, she hadn't seen one mouse, but three. Their names were Joshua, Jonathan, and Courtney, ages three, four, and two, respectively.

As Bob ran toward the house, the front door burst open, and he was run over by three blind mice scrambling out of the house. Their paws were covered with a gooey mess, their eyes shut tightly in fear. Behind them ran the farmer's wife, carrying a broom and shouting incoherently (thankfully, she left her carving knife on the kitchen counter). Inside, Bob saw the reason for his wife's wrath. While he was supposed to be watching the mice, they added another item to the Kays' list of damaged household goods: the cake.

* * * * * * *

Unit coffees are just one way military families celebrate community, such as the one I just wrote about. Another way is through the customs and courtesies that give our families a sense of purpose, heritage, and pride. From the early camp followers to the diverse group of professionals and family members that we now have, our military is rich with tradition. These elements of community, for the military spouse, are always *voluntary*—you are not forced to participate in any of these conventions. As a matter of fact, most of the military awards for family members' volunteerism are tied up in the various aspects of military customs and courtesies, alongside other volunteer organizations.

These aspects of community can become a burden if we're not sure what they mean and how to participate in them. Not only does the military family need to balance its available time with volunteer commitments, but it also needs to understand what the various customs and courtesies mean so it can rank order its priorities and participation in these events accordingly. For example, if a husband thinks the event of his wife's getting an award and decoration at an awards ceremony is about the same thing as an office hail and farewell, he may miss a very important part of his wife's life. I've seen a few promotions where the service member pinned on a new rank and his wife didn't feel it was worth the effort to get a baby-sitter—so she missed a once-in-a-lifetime event because of a lack of understanding.

One of the most intimidating aspects of military life for a new spouse or a family who has recently joined the military is the "who, what, where, why, and how" of the various customs, courtesies, and traditions.

This section is designed to give you a better working knowledge of this part of military life. But it's more than mere definitions and terms. It is also chock-full of ideas as to how you can participate in a fun yet meaningful way in your own community—within your own comfort zone.

Here is a list of the most common traditions found in the military:[1]

A Note About Children

You should never assume that your children are invited to any of the functions listed below unless specified in the invitation or announcement. If they are allowed to attend certain ceremonies, such as your spouse's award, promotion, or change of command, they should be well behaved. (At the time of this writing, our youngest, Joshua, could not attend any of these functions—we practically funded our baby-sitter's college education while working on his behavior at public events.)

Reveille

The installation's American flag is raised daily, usually at 6:00 A.M., while the bugle call "Reveille" is played. Everyone should stand quietly during this ceremony, unless you're still in bed, like most sane people.

---

1. Portions of this material have been adapted from AFTB handouts 1.01.

Retreat

The retreat ceremony is held at the same time each evening, usually around 5:00 P.M., but the exact time varies from one installation to another. Unit formations, often including promotion or award ceremonies, may be held in conjunction with retreat. Then the flag is folded and retired for the day.

If you hear reveille or retreat being played, and you are in a moving vehicle, you must stop. (It is not mandatory for civilians to get out of their cars once they stop.) If you are outside, you should stand quietly, facing the direction of the flag.

Honors

Rendering honors means to stand quietly and respectfully. When required, a salute is given by military persons in uniform. If you are in civilian clothing, you should place your right hand over your heart. Honors are given to the nation, to certain individuals, or to the uniformed services; these are often represented by a flag or a song, such as the national anthem. When in doubt, follow the lead of the senior people present, unless you *are* the senior person present; in which case, be aware that everyone will be watching *you*!

Parades

Official marches and reviews may include soldiers, vehicles, and a band, and may be included as part of a change of command, an honors ceremony, a retreat ceremony, a retirement, or to observe a special holiday. Certain areas will be reserved for invited guests, and additional seating may not be available for everyone. These parades are official functions, and appropriate dress and behavior are expected (which means I have to leave my rhinestone-studded cat's-eye sunglasses in the car).

Receiving Lines

At official functions ranging from a change of command to a unit social, you may be invited to greet the host, hostess, or guest of honor in a receiving line. Your name(s) will be given to the aide or adjutant at the beginning of the line. From there your name will be passed down the receiving line, but be sure to reintroduce yourself if there is a problem, without "correcting" the previous person in line. I've been in lines where it's like a game of "telephone gossip": I started out as Ellie Kay and ended up as Kelly May! Here are some more points to keep in mind:

- *Punctuality.* Arrive on time, because your unit will likely go through the line together. At larger events, guest arrival times are staggered so as to avoid congestion going through the receiving line.
- *Don't shake hands.* You will never shake the aide or adjutant's hand.
- *Keep it moving.* Receiving lines are for introductions only, not conversations.
- *No drinking!* Never eat, drink, or smoke in a receiving line. Often there are small tables provided by the line for leaving food, drinks, and purses.
- *Move along.* Do your part to keep the line moving.
- *Name, please?* When making introductions, be mindful of hyphenated names and spouses with different last names.
- *Ladies first.* Except for receiving lines at the White House, diplomatic corps, and Air Force functions, the lady precedes the gentleman in the line, even if the lady is the active duty member and the gentleman is a civilian spouse.

Teas

A tea is the most formal activity held during the day. It usually takes place between two and four in the afternoon. An appropriate dressy dress or suit is usually worn, unless the invitation specifies otherwise. It's considered an honor to be asked to pour tea, and a formal pouring schedule is often used.

Coffees

A coffee is a more informal or casual function and may be held any time during the day or evening. Dresses, slacks, skirts, and sweaters are acceptable attire, unless otherwise specified. I once went to a "sweatshirt and socks" coffee hosted by the commanding general's wife. Her desire was to be approachable and have a less formal function. We had to tell why we chose our particular sweatshirt, and the best "reason" won a prize. I couldn't decide which of two I wanted to wear, so I put my feet through the arms of a very large sweatshirt, and it looked like sweat bottoms when I pulled the hood up under my other sweatshirt—securing the hood with a belt. When I stood up to share, I told them I couldn't decide between the two, so I wore both. Then I released the hood of the sweatshirt around my legs, and it dangled between my knees like a tail. It was so funny, they gave me the grand prize!

Hail and Farewells

These are parties to welcome newcomers and to say good-bye to those who are leaving. They can range from office get-togethers to formal events. Spouses (and sometimes families) are invited.

Awards

The military presents many awards in recognition of service, achievement, or valor. The ceremony can range from an officer gathering to a unit formation. The award is read from the official orders, followed by the pinning on or presentation of the award. Spouses also may receive volunteer and service recognition awards.

Promotion

The military promotes individuals as they show an ability to perform at a higher level. At a promotion, the orders are read, and the new rank is pinned on. Family and friends are invited, and oftentimes the spouse will help the officiating officer pin on the rank. Promotion parties are at the discretion of the person who is promoted. Sometimes there is a reception on site or a party in a home, or the honoree buys a round of drinks for the O Club or NCO Club.

Change of Command

The change of command ceremony is a clear, legal, and symbolic passing of authority and responsibility from one commander to the next. The official orders are read while the unit guidon (or colors) is passed from the outgoing commander to the incoming commander. The senior noncommissioned officer also participates in the passing of the colors. Spouses of incoming and outgoing commanders are usually presented with flowers, and they should rise from their seat when accepting this honor. Both of the commanders represented usually make speeches, after which there is appropriate applause. At the conclusion of the ceremony, the new commander normally goes to the reception area, while the outgoing commander does not usually attend the reception. There is a receiving line at the reception for the commander and his spouse, and sometimes their children will stand in the line with them.

Retirement

This ceremony recognizes a person's years of service to his or her country and includes an official reading of the orders and presentations of certificates and awards. Attendance at a retirement ceremony is a thoughtful way to show appreciation for the person who is retiring. The spouse is usually presented with a certificate signed by the president of the United States. These are some of the most emotional events I've ever attended in the military, as one chapter ends and another begins.

Ideas for Community Coffees/Socials

General Comments

Coffees and socials, just like everything else in the military, are *voluntary* for spouses. The key to a healthy, vibrant, organized social group is to make these events a place where people want to be! It's got to be fun, brief, and serve a purpose. You can make it fun with the following ideas and a general attitude of thankfulness that your guests have made it a priority to attend (rather than the attitude that they are *expected* to be there and are only doing their duty). It can be kept brief by keeping announcements to two or three minutes each (if someone else is making announcements, be sure they understand there is a time limitation). Too often the business part of the coffee drags on forever because the person in charge feels they have to state the same thing five different ways.

Finally, a coffee needs to serve a purpose. Sometimes it has a dual function: fund-raising and social interaction; event planning and unit bonding; welcoming newcomers and volunteer recruiting. Be sure the attendees know the purpose of the coffee or social so that their expectations can be directed accordingly.

You never get a second chance to make a first impression, or so the saying goes. Remember that the very first coffee you or your unit host is likely to set the tone for the year, the tour of duty, or the group. As much as is possible on your part, put enough thought and preplanning into making sure that every person feels valued and welcomed and will want to come back next month.

Meeting People[2]

Life as a military family is too short to be shy about meeting new people. With a few tips and experiences under your belt, even the most reserved personality can learn to work a room with ease. Anne Abel, a retired general's wife, says: "Be genuinely interested in others. Everybody has a story and very few people will ask about you. Be yourself. At social functions my husband, Dick, will have met everyone in the room, but I will know two to three people well." Here are a few of my favorite tips for first impressions, learning names, and how to meet people:

- *Eye Contact.* When you introduce yourself, remember to smile and make eye contact.
- *Handshakes.* Offer your hand, and give a nice, firm handshake, putting your thumb in the V of the other person's hand.
- *Remembering Names.* Repeat the name upon meeting the person and try to draw a verbal association with the name.
- *Pronunciation.* If the person is wearing a name tag, visualize the name as you read it. Be sure you get the correct pronunciation.
- *Party Pal.* If you're going to a party, ask someone to come with you who will know which people you will feel most comfortable with, and ask them to introduce you to those people.
- *Be Bold, Not Brash.* There's a difference between taking the initiative to introduce yourself and interrupting a conversation to do so. If you wait for a break in the chatter, you'll find a natural opportunity to meet the others in the circle. You will likely be doing someone else in that circle a favor by helping them remember other people's names. It could be that they've had a fifteen-minute conversation without introducing themselves!
- *Be Confident.* One of the most common mistakes in conversing is to lack self-confidence and to act rejected by a perceived slight when there was none intended.
- *Body Language.* If you cross your arms, turn your back on someone, or keep your hands in your pockets, you are putting up a barrier. If you smile, keep your hands free at your sides, and look directly at the person talking with you, you will communicate positive body language.
- *Drilling.* Don't ask the other person a series of brief questions as if you were fact finding. It will appear as if you are invading their privacy. Keep the initial comments general and non-intrusive.

2. Some portions of this material have been adapted from AFTB course 2.01.1.

- *Monosyllabic Language.* Another common error in conversing is keeping your answer to one- or two-word responses, as if you have nothing to say or your thoughts are limited. The remedy is to try to answer in complete sentences; this will give you a chance to think of something else to say. For example, if the question is "Are you Colonel Kay's wife?" my answer would be, "Yes, I'm the wife of 'The World's Greatest Fighter Pilot.' "

- *Interaction.* An important element of a pleasant conversation is listening. Make it a habit to truly *listen* and to ask interactive questions based on the other person's responses.

Themed Coffees

Pick an idea, such as my "Moving Theme," and get creative! Below is a list of ideas to get you thinking. Remember to tie in as many elements to the theme as possible—everything from the invitation, to decorations, food, and even take-home souvenirs!

International Delight. Because so many military families are world travelers, you could pick this theme and have everyone bring food and a souvenir from another county. During the icebreaker, when you want to help people get to know each other, each person could show and tell a little about their souvenir. If you have a fun bunch of people, you could even ask them to come dressed in a costume from that country!

Give Yourself a Coffee. This idea came from Anne Abel, who used to give a coffee for herself, shortly after they moved to a new location. She invited all her neighbors in order to meet them. She also gave an annual "Love Tea" at Valentine's Day to show her friends and neighbors how much they are loved.

Tacky Coffee. Rather than stress and fret about a formal coffee, try giving a tacky coffee instead. I did this at my house and pulled stuff out of my "garage sale" box to decorate with. I even put Elvis on Velvet for display by the front door. We gave prizes for the tackiest costumes and refreshments.

The snacks included Cheese Whiz on saltines, and one woman even brought a tray of vanilla wafers with cool whip and a peanut on each. You don't even have to dust your house for this one!

Restaurant Theme. If you don't have time to host a monthly event at your home, check out a local restaurant that can handle the arrangements. Your group may meet for dinner at a different restaurant each time. You might even try to have it at lunchtime to accommodate those spouses that work outside the home. More and more coffees are being moved to central locations due to working spouses and busy schedules.

Wedding Theme. Have everyone bring their wedding photos; number them and place them on a poster board. Have everyone guess who's who; the one who gets the most right receives a prize (such as a marriage book or a bouquet of flowers). It's easy to plan the menu around a wedding cake purchased from the local bakery, nuts, dinner mints, and other wedding reception goodies. The decorations could follow the same theme; you may even want to have a few of the bolder women share their favorite or funniest honeymoon memory.

Baby Shower. I've been to some coffees that have a dual function, serving as a baby shower for the women in the unit who are expecting. Group gifts seem to work best for this type of event, but keep in mind that not every member of your unit will appreciate a function that serves as a baby shower. These are best reserved for the focus on the mom-to-be rather than a focus on unit business or announcements. That way if a member declines to attend, she won't miss any official news.

Ask the honoree if she wants games played on her big day and honor her request or decline. Be sure to have her fill out a very detailed list of items she needs or have her register online at the local Wal-Mart or Target. That way there won't be duplicate gifts. Include this information on the invitation and indicate to whom checks should be mailed for group gifts.

You could have women send their baby pictures and have the same kind of game as was suggested for the wedding theme, or they could each bring their favorite stuffed animal or doll and tell the rest of the group why it's their fave.

Book Fest. One way to keep to a theme and keep it simple is to have everyone bring their favorite book and/or the book they are currently reading. It gets people talking, and you get to know something about them that you would not normally know. Plus, it's a good way to get a tip on a great book that you may have overlooked in the past.

Craft Fair. Some people are incredibly gifted when it comes to creating something out of nothing. If you are one of these people, I envy you. A craft-fair coffee is where the hostess provides the supplies and know-how to create a simple yet elegant craft that the attendees can take home. The hostess should have a completed version, and it should be simple enough for her to assemble in front of the guests. Have a couple of other crafty friends available to help the creatively impaired people finish their works of art. You could even have each guest bring her favorite homemade or purchased craft for show-and-tell.

Sweatshirt and Socks. When we were welcomed to the 10th Mountain Division at Fort Drum, New York, the general's wife, Gloria Magruder, hosted this kind of a coffee, and it was so much fun (as previously mentioned). Everyone wore their fave sweatshirt and had to explain why they chose that particular shirt. We all took off our shoes at the door and remained casual and relaxed throughout the evening.

Mug and Muffin. If your coffee is in the cold of winter or even on a Saturday morning, a mug and muffin coffee could be just the thing. Ask each guest to bring her favorite mug and share why it is her fave. Have some unusual mugs to give as door prizes, and provide a variety of common and unusual muffins for the food table. Or you could have the guests bring a half dozen of their favorite muffins along with the recipe (or the muffin mix box!). You might even want to have your guests bring along their slippers and have a large fire roaring in the fireplace to create a cozy and warm environment.

Pamper Night. One of the best coffees I ever attended was held at a local upscale beauty salon. The staff let us have our meeting there and also provided catered munchies. Then they gave brief self-introductions with a list of their area of expertise and offered their services at no charge. They set a time limit so they wouldn't be there all night. We got free manicures, haircuts, facials, hand waxing, and eyebrow shaping! The salon picked up several good regular customers, and it was a win/win situation for everyone involved. They even brought in a licensed massage therapist and her chair to give mini massages. Ah . . . I think I need to go back to her for more "research."

Keeping It Simple. Army spouse Jody Dale says, "I'm not very good at coffees, but what works for me is simplify, simplify, simplify. Having just desserts makes the cooking time a breeze because you can start making these days in advance and put them in your freezer. I use outside branches, nuts, seeds, flowers, and weeds to decorate my table. If appropriate, I have icebreaker games, because it helps the walls come down and has people laughing and opening up."

Volunteering

The military depends on volunteers to keep programs running and to allow for a better quality of life for the community. Each year the installation volunteer coordinator presents a check to the installation commander with the equivalent of volunteer hours paid out at minimum wage. One year our wing commander was presented with a check for the amount of $229,968.10 or the equivalent of 44,654 volunteer hours at minimum wage.

It's evident that the community greatly benefits from volunteers, but the volunteers benefit greatly as well. Here are five reasons for volunteering:

1. *Contribute to Community.* Your volunteer efforts often make the difference between allowing a program to continue and letting it fall to the wayside. That translates into areas such as your kids getting to compete in soccer games (volunteer coaches), young troops getting cookies at Christmas (annual cookie drive), families being able to buy household goods and clothing at reduced prices (thrift shops), and college scholarships (spouses' organizations). These are only a small sampling of programs that exist because of volunteers.

2. *Meet People.* Volunteering alongside others of like vision forges some of the best and most lasting friendships. Whether it's working with the Red Cross or helping out at the chapel—these are great opportunities to meet people.

3. *Support Children's Activities.* Our kids have outside interests that spark community service within them when they see us volunteering for their groups. Scouting programs, Vacation Bible School, children's unit parties, and sporting teams are some of the ways to keep our kids involved and healthy emotionally, physically, and spiritually.

4. *On-the-Job Training/Enhance Résumé.* The volunteer hours you spend in certain areas come with training. Whether it's with the Red Cross in a hospital or on a computer at the Family Support Center, you are learning new and marketable skills while gaining valuable experience in a variety of fields. Your volunteer hours and awards on your résumé provide continuity for future employers as you move from place to place.

5. *Volunteer's Bill of Rights.* If you volunteer long enough, you'll find that as long as people are working in these different areas, there are likely to be some people problems. We don't live in a perfect world, and abuses do occur. I've seen a few people who volunteer at their children's expense, play the power game, and run off anyone else who is a threat to their position. In order

to keep the volunteer's perspective where it should be, Army Family Team Building (AFTB) (Course 2.02.1 handout 4) has developed what I have found to be the best guideline for what you should seek out as a volunteer:

(1) The right to be treated as a co-worker—not as free help, but neither as a prima donna.

(2) The right to a suitable assignment with consideration for personal preference, temperament, life experience, education, and employment background.

(3) The right to know as much about the organization as possible: its policies, its people, and its programs.

(4) The right to training for the job—thoughtfully planned and effectively presented.

(5) The right to continuing education on the job—as a follow-up to initial training, to learn about new developments, and to train for greater responsibility.

(6) The right to sound guidance and direction from someone who is experienced, well-informed, patient, and thoughtful, and who has the time to invest in giving guidance.

(7) The right to a place for your work—an orderly, designated area that is conducive to working and worthy of the work to be done.

(8) The right to promotion and a variety of experiences—through advancement, transfer from one activity to another, and special assignments.

(9) The right to be heard, to have a part in planning, to feel free to make suggestions, and to have respect shown for an honest opinion.

(10) The right to recognition through promotion, awards, and day-to-day expressions of appreciation, and by being treated as a bona fide co-worker.

(11) The right to fun—a pleasant as well as a productive atmosphere for volunteering.

Recruiting Volunteers[3]

There are a few key steps to getting people to help your volunteer efforts, and most of them center on how specific and committed you

---

3. Portions of this material have been adapted from AFTB course 2.02.1.

are to your own goals! Here are a few things to keep in mind the next time your face is on the recruiting poster:

- *Be committed.* If you've lost faith in the project, you'll never get anyone else to value the assignment you're recruiting for.
- *Be descriptive.* Know exactly what you're asking the volunteer to do, how much time it will take to do it, and how this job fits into the organization as a whole.
- *Brainstorm.* This is a good way to explore sources of potential volunteers that could fit the requirement.
- *Matching.* Use a recruiting technique that will fit sources of potential volunteers. For example, if you're looking for public speakers for your group, approach Toastmasters; if you're looking for soccer team assistant coaches, approach the youth center; if you are looking for baked goods for the airman cookie drive, send a note to the wives in your unit.
- *Benefits.* Be prepared with the knowledge of what benefits this volunteer job has to offer the volunteer and present them clearly.
- *Objections.* Listen carefully to the objections of involvement and do not proceed if it's not a good match. On the other hand, clarify any misconceptions that could be standing in the way of a potential volunteer.
- *Materials.* If it is an ongoing job, have some printed materials available for candidates to take with them.
- *Follow-up.* Be sure you check back with the person and also that you have their contact information. It is often in the follow-up that you are able to recruit the volunteer.

* * * * * * *

If you've been a military family for long, volunteering in your community becomes a part of life. Your kids can earn college tuition scholarships as a result of their volunteer efforts as you teach by practicing what you preach about community involvement. With time, attending social functions can be something you look forward to and participate in with ease and grace as you carefully pick and choose which events to attend and which to decline. You will find the balance that works best for you and your family.

Finally, the patriotic traditions of the customs and courtesies of this lasting piece of Americana can really get in your blood and be something you take everywhere with you. For example, one year I was at the world's largest honky-tonk, Billy Bob's in Fort Worth, Texas, for a post-event gathering of writers and publishers. Our little group was experiencing the Texas culture, complete with mechanical bull riding (which I'd done before), live bull riding, and a band called Nighthawk. The group I was with thought I was a real jokester—and I was! At the end of their set, the band played "The Star-Spangled Banner," and my mood quickly changed to something more serious. I stood up and put my hand over my heart, while the people at my table just stared. A couple of them began to laugh, thinking that I was once again cutting up. But I looked at them and said, "Hey, fun is fun, but this is serious. This flag is why my husband flies and fights."

None of them were military, and they had never seen someone stand up inside a building when the national anthem was being played. One by one, each of them stood up and put their hand over their heart in respect for our flag.

* * * * * * *

Peace is that brief period of time when everyone stands around reloading.

—Lloyd Cory
Quote Unquote

☆ 13 ☆

THE CITIZEN SOLDIER

The Guard and Reserve Component—A Volunteer Force

Prior to the attacks against the United States on September 11, 2001, the National Guard's general policy regarding mobilization was that Guardsmen would be required to serve no more than one year cumulative on active duty (with no more than six months overseas) for each five years of regular drill. Due to the strains placed on active duty units following the attacks, the possible mobilization time was increased to eighteen months (with no more than one year overseas). Additional strains placed on military units as a result of the activity in Iraq further increased the amount of time a Guardsman could be mobilized to twenty-four months. The current Department of Defense policy is that Guardsman will be given twenty-four months between deployments of no more than twenty-four months (individual states have differing policies).

Traditionally, most National Guard personnel served one weekend per month, two weeks per year, although a significant number served in a full-time capacity in a role called Active Guard and Reserve (AGR). This title has lost most of its relevance since the Iraq War, when up to 40 percent of total U.S. forces in Iraq and Afghanistan consisted of mobilized personnel of the Reserve components. Furthermore, most National Guardsmen have now served at least one combat tour in support of the Global War on Terrorism (source: National Guard Bureau website *and* Wikipedia.org).

☆ Hidden Hero Profile ☆

Name: Stephanie Theis

Spouse's Name: SFC Timothy Theis

Branch of Service: Kansas Army National Guard

Kids: Four, three who live at home: Andrew, thirteen; Zachary, eleven; Morgan (part-time), eight

Number of Moves: None

Years of Service: My husband has been in the Army National Guard for twenty-one years. I have been with him almost five years.

Work/Employer: My husband's civilian job is as a laborer. I am a teacher in the Park Hill School District in the Kansas City area.

Hobbies: I enjoy reading and working with projects at my church or the Family Readiness Group (FRG).

Describe your military experience before 9/11 and after:

My association with the military was witnessing my sister-in-law and her family. Her husband served in the Army, and when he retired at twenty-two years, he was a CW4. During the time I was in that family situation (eight years), her husband was gone for probably five of those years. I saw how she relied on other families as well as her own for support as she tried to raise her three children on her own and far from home.

The events of 9/11 led to one of the reasons I met my husband. He was deployed for a one-year mission to Ft. Leavenworth, Kansas. We met while he was on deployment. I remember him asking me if I could support him, since he knew that the Guard was being deployed more and more because of 9/11. I told him that because of my experience with my former sister- and brother-in-law, I highly respected the military and would fully support his decision to serve our country, no matter what. Since that time, I have taken on the role of FRG leader and have helped families through two previous deployments and am currently working with our third major deployment in as many years. This last deployment is different for me personally, because my husband has been activated to be part of it.

How many times have you deployed in the last six years and where?

My husband has dealt with two deployments. One during 2002–2003, and he is currently activated. This is the third deployment for his battalion in three years.

Do you suffer a loss of income when you serve on deployments?

My husband and I have not dealt with a loss of income, but from my work as an FRG volunteer, I know many families have recently dealt with financial issues due to how orders were written and pay drops occurred.

How does this loss of income impact your life?

I know that for many of the families I work with, they have to rely on the Family Readiness Group (FRG) and Family Assistance Centers (FAC) for assistance. We are helping to set up a network with our families and community members to help alleviate the financial burdens that are occurring. Right now, we have a few families that are being connected with local VFWs and American Legions. These families will be "adopted" for the holiday season.

Do you have any war stories you care to share?

The biggest war stories I have are the ones of the connections and friendships that have been made because of the deployments and working with the families. It is so nice to network with others and to help each other out during difficult times. Our group really tries to work with the families to give them an outlet, but also a safe place to go when they are having a hard time. In the National Guard, we are separated by as few as five miles or as many as three hundred or more. Even though those miles may separate, it is comforting to know that there are other families who are willing to share a phone call of support or advice. It is also nice to get together at FRG and volunteer events to connect with those families. We are like one big family trying to help take care of one another.

Least Favorite Aspect of Military Life:

The least favorite aspect is related to the separation from our spouse and the problems that come with pay drops and the unknown with timing of deployments.

Favorite Aspect of Military Life:

My favorite aspect is the connections and families that become your friends.

Favorite Quote:

From a Mark Schultz song titled "Letters from War," a mother writes to her son, "You are strong, you are brave, what a father you will be someday." It goes on to say, "Bring him home!" My husband is already a father, but I think of him and tell him this when I write him.

Any other comments you would like to make:

My husband and I see our work with the military as a gift from God. Although it is hard sometimes and can be lonely, we believe that we will be a stronger couple and a better family because of our service to our country.

In addition to the National Guard Bureau changes since 2001, the Reserve component of the military (Army, Air, and Navy), has also undergone some radical changes. According to Lt. Gen. Jack C. Stultz, the Commanding General of the U.S. Army Reserve Command, "Since September 11, 2001, more than 180,000 Army Reserve soldiers have mobilized and deployed to Operation Enduring Freedom and Operation Iraqi Freedom."

The United States Army, Air Force, Navy Reserve, and Coast Guard Reserve comprise the Federal Reserve Force of the United States military, and they comprise around 46 percent of total military manpower (esgr.org). Together, the Reserves and National Guard constitute the Reserve components of the United States military. It was initially formed in 1908, to provide a reserve of medical officers. But in today's military, it is a vital element of national and international security.

Reserve military members perform only part-time duties as opposed to full-time ("active duty") soldiers, but may be called upon to do full-time duty. At the bare minimum, they generally perform training or service one weekend per month and for two continuous weeks at some time during the year (annual training). Many Reserve soldiers are organized into Reserve units, while others serve to augment active duty units.

All United States Army, Air Force, Navy, and Coast Guard military members sign an initial eight-year service contract upon entry into the military. Typically, the contract specifies that some of the service will be served in the regular military or "active component" (two, three, or four years), with the rest of the service to be served in the Reserve component. However, some soldiers elect to sign a contract specifying that all eight years be served in the Reserve component. The soldier entering directly into the military Reserve component is only required to be on active duty for basic training and some sort of advanced training. Those soldiers who serve a period of years in the active component and choose not to reenlist in the active component are automatically transferred afterward to the Reserve component to complete their initial eight-year service obligation. After the expiration of the initial eight-year service contract, soldiers who elect to continue their service may sign subsequent contracts consecutively until they finally leave the service; however, officers may have the option of an "indefinite" contract, in which case the soldier remains a part of the military until they retire, are removed from the service for cause, or elect to leave the service. (Military.com, GoArmy.com, NavyReserve.com, and AFReserve.com).

New Challenges for the Reserve Component

With heightened demands on the Reserve component, longer deployments, more time away from their civilian jobs, and heightened stress on families, there is a greater need than ever for these families to be integrated into the support available through their civilian and military communities. A lot of the information in this book applies across the board to the Reserve as well as the active duty component of the military, but there are unique demands placed upon Guard and Reserve families as well. For example, a lot of these families do not live on base or even near their main base or post. Consequently, it is harder for them to plug in to support groups in order to get information about services and benefits for which they qualify, as well as information about the status of their military member while they are deployed.

These heightened challenges are making Family Support Groups (FSGs) and Key Spouses more important than ever. Usually these positions are filled by volunteers who want to help other military families get the information and help they need during deployments. It is crucial to plug in to your FSG in your part of the state. If there is not one within a one-hundred-mile radius (which would be unusual, since there are chapters all over the state), then you might consider becoming an FSG leader and working with your Reserve or National Guard unit to help the other reserve component families in your area.

On our Heroes at Home World Tour we've met dozens of these FSG leaders, and they are to be commended for their service to the families, the military members, and our country. They are heroes at home that are doing their part to make life in the military better. There are also other organizations that are helping the Guard and Reserves, and they are found at the Employer Support of Guard and Reserve site: www.ESGR.org.

The ESGR is a Department of Defense organization. It is a staff group within the Office of the Assistant Secretary of Defense for Reserve Affairs (OASD/RA), which is in itself a part of the Office of the Secretary of Defense.

The nation's Reserve components (referring to the total for all National Guard members and Reserve forces from all branches of the military) comprise approximately 46 percent of our total available military manpower. The current National Defense Strategy indicates that the National Guard and Reserves will be full partners in the fully integrated Total Force. Our Reserve forces will spend more time away from the workplace defending the nation, supporting a demanding operations temp, and training to maintain their mission readiness.

In this environment, civilian employers play a critical role in the defense of the nation by complying with existing employment laws protecting the rights of workers who serve in the Reserve component. Organizations like the ESGR are helping promote cooperation and understanding between Reserve component members and their civilian employers, and they are critical in assisting in conflicts that arise from an employee's military commitment.

All About the Guard—Q&A With an Expert: Major General Robert Knauff

The Army and Air National Guard has changed so much since 9/11, I wanted to hear from those highly involved about how they are coping with the changes and what those challenges entail. The following is from a Q&A session I had with Maj. Gen. Robert Knauff, the Deputy Adjutant General for the state of New York. His answers were thoughtful, insightful, and highly favorable of the men and women who are serving in Guard units throughout the United States and in all parts of the world.

What are some of the greatest needs, in your opinion, among Guard families?

It's hard to say, because there are a number of challenges for the Guard that differ from active-duty challenges. Some of the unique needs include the fact that Guard families are not part of nearby geographical units. The Army National Guard is especially widely dispersed, with many small units and detachments located in cities and towns a long way from any active duty facilities. While the Air Guard facilities may look like AF bases, they are without the support facilities for members and families.

In addition, some people may have the convenience of a local armory or airbase, but many Guard members commute. The Army Guard frequently has organizations with subordinate elements that might be hundreds of miles apart. Their families will not be close to a mobilization point, where orders are processed and troops are trained. People are scattered all over the state and may have no physical link to other members of the organization that are deployed. There are minimal social networks available.

Sometimes it can be as simple as trying to get TriCare problems solved after they've been dropped from the Defense Enrollment

Eligibility Reporting System (DEERS). They have to go through a military installation to fix the problem and reprocess the paper work. The nearest place may literally be hundreds of miles away. Active duty members and their families do not deal with these types of geographical challenges.

Are there Family Support Groups (FSG)?

In the National Guard, we have dedicated family support organizations in both the ARNG and the ANG. For the Army Guard we have Military Family Assistance Centers (MFAC). In the Air Guard there are Family Program Coordinators (FPC) at the ANG airbases responsible for family support at the individual base but who also work with the MFACs. Although funded separately, both organizations work together to provide assistance wherever needed. They help to keep families informed and channel concerns to the state and national levels. The MFACs and FPCs do amazing things for the military members and their families; however, they are over-tasked and undermanned. For example, in the state of New York, there are ten thousand Army Guard members and six thousand Air National Guard members, and yet there are less than twenty family readiness employees to service the needs of this many military members and their families.

While the full-time staff keeps things moving on a daily basis, the real power behind these organizations is their volunteers. When notified of pending deployments, volunteers swing into action and provide the muscle necessary to pull together the many activities people come to appreciate. Whether running children's activities, keeping the lines of communication open before, during, and after deployments, or simply providing a friendly and concerned ear, these folks make the whole family support business work. They become a lifeline to the families of deployed Guard members.

How has life changed for the Guard since 9/11?

Prior to 9/11, the Air Guard was a force performing routine operations for flying rotations through the AEF system at a basic operations tempo. Since 9/11, their ops tempo has increased exponentially. Security Forces have had mobilizations that last a year with multiple deployments. Civil engineers are heavily engaged, supporting bases worldwide. Numerous other non-flying disciplines are finding themselves mobilized in support of "in lieu of" taskings with the Army. The Air units are in a continuous state of deployment and redeployment that has never been seen in the Guard in recent history. But the overwhelming challenge has been the increasing length of the deployments.

For the Army Guard, it was a major culture shift. For years they provided support for peacekeeping missions in the Sinai, Bosnia, and Kosovo. These support missions were few and far between, and while they were challenging for the individual soldiers and units involved, they did not demand a lot of the Guard as a whole.

Post 9/11, the Army Guard is now deploying far more than most active duty units did *before* 9/11. The ops tempo never stops. They stand up, go through training, deploy, come home, and then go through post deployment. Some deployments now last as long as twenty months for Guard members. They now face second rotations for another twenty months, something no one ever anticipated. This is hard on equipment, employers, military members, and families.

Does Employer Support for the Guard and Reserve (ESGR) help most Guard and Reserve families?

This is one of the more effective volunteer organizations out there. They have a dual charter to be advocates for both military members *and* employers. They have to have an even approach to understand the employer issues as well as the military members' issues.

It can be something as simple as needing a set of orders for the company to be able to process the employees' documents for the company. But the employer cannot get orders for their records to prove that the employee has been mobilized. The ESGR steps in and tries to help expedite and facilitate the process. Organizations like ESGR are critical during times like this—for both sides. There is a need for balance, and they do this very well. One of the challenges of ESGR is that they are made up largely of volunteers, a fact that makes it hard to train and sustain the organization. Some states may have highly effective chapters, while others have inexperienced volunteers that hinder their effectiveness.

What is one aspect of Guard military service that is unique?

Most Americans do not understand the dual responsibilities and services that the Guard provides for the public. The National Guard is both a federal combat force that serves the president of the United States through the Army and the Air Force and also serves the governors of the states as the Constitution-directed militia force. There are times that a governor will call out the Guard as a means of responding to a crisis at home, and the very act of calling out the Guard sends the message that the governor considers the event serious. And while the Guard is a state force, there are also more than 106,000 Air and over 320,000 Army military members fighting the Global War on Terror. Mobilization and support of wartime operations tells only *part* of the story because the National Guard also shows up for snowstorms, ice storms, hurricanes, tornadoes, earthquakes, and floods at home.

The Yellow Ribbon Program (YRP) for the National Guard and Reserve Service Members

I recently brought the Heroes at Home conference to our Guardsmen, Reservists, and their families at a wonderful program called The Yellow Ribbon. I highly recommend that you run, not walk, to the nearest YRP conference near you. These programs are designed to keep costs minimal for the military member or their family members, and they have programs for youth as well. For specific cost information, you would need to contact your unit's Yellow Ribbon manager.

It's a fabulous way to gain useful information that will help you prosper as a Guard or Reserve family, and it's also a really nice treat to get a break in a beautiful conference center courtesy of the YRP! Here are some questions and answers about this program that will help familiarize you with the services they offer. For more information, go to YellowRibbon.mil.

What is the Department of Defense (DOD) Yellow Ribbon Program?

The Yellow Ribbon Program (YRP) is a DOD-wide effort to help National Guard and Reserve Service members and their families connect with local resources before, during, and after deployments, especially during the reintegration phase that occurs months after Service members return home. Commanders and leaders play a critical role in assuring that Reserve Service members and their families attend Yellow Ribbon events, where they can access information on health care, education/training opportunities, financial, and legal benefits. The DOD works in conjunction with Federal partners, including the Small Business Administration and Departments of Labor and Veterans Affairs, to provide up-to-date and relevant information to the members of the all-volunteer force and their families.

What's the difference between DOD and the VA Yellow Ribbon Programs?

The Yellow Ribbon Program is a Department of Defense program that falls under the Office of the Assistant Secretary of Defense for Reserve Affairs. The Veterans Affairs (VA) Yellow Ribbon Program is part of the Post–9/11 GI Bill and focuses mostly on partnerships with institutes of higher learning.

Is the Yellow Ribbon Program specifically intended for National Guard and Reserve members?

Yes, the Yellow Ribbon Program is dedicated to addressing the unique needs of National Guard and Reserve members during the deployment cycle. The National Guard and Reserve differ from the active duty component in the way they prepare for deployments and reintegrate after returning. Many Service members are geographically separated from other members of their units. Recognizing that the National Guard, the Reserves, and their families face unique challenges, Congress mandated the Yellow Ribbon Program be established to respond to those challenges.

Is the Yellow Ribbon Program only for Service members after they return from deployment?

No. The Yellow Ribbon Program spans the pre-, during, and post-phases of deployment. It helps Service members and their families prepare for deployment, cope with the challenges during deployment, and at the 30-, 60-, and 90-day post-deployment points.

Where can I find more information on my Service's Yellow Ribbon Program?

For more information, contact your chain of command, or your unit Yellow Ribbon Program Manager.

Why should I attend a Yellow Ribbon Event?

Regardless of the number of deployments you may have experienced or the information you've already received, the Yellow Ribbon Program offers the newest and most current information to participants, such as current eligibility for certain benefits or available resources. Yellow Ribbon events give many Service members the opportunity to see fellow unit members or talk to professionals about deployment-related topics such as employment, finances, and health care.

☆ 14 ☆

THE HEROIC PARENTS OF SERVICE MEMBERS

Dawn and Erv Trilles

☆ *Profile* ☆

Name: Cadet 3rd Class, Alec P. Trilles, United States Air Force Academy

Parents Names: Dawn and Erv Trilles

Siblings: Melyssa, sixteen; Tanner, thirteen

Our Story:

Just over a year ago we delivered our son Alec to USAFA with smiles, a few tears, and great anticipation of the amazing experience he was about to embark upon. This is all he ever wanted to do since he was nine years old and had prepared himself in every way possible. It was his dream.

- **BCT I**—The first few days of Basic Cadet Training (BCT) were difficult, and we waited with such anticipation for that first letter. It didn't come for almost two weeks, and I almost wished it hadn't. As a mom I felt helpless for the first time, panic spreading at my inability to help my son. I was so out of the loop and had no way to reach him except by "snail mail." Still, we sent letters and cards daily and waited patiently for *the* phone call on Doolie Day In. When the first call of the day came (there were many), my heart sank. He was so unhappy. His faith had been tested and he wanted to come home. As a mom and

155

as a professional used to being in control, I was devastated and at a loss for what to do.

- **BCT II**—The next day began another very trying period for him—the march to Jack's Valley. He broke his nose in a training mishap and came down with the dreaded "Jack's Hack." When it got worse, he was treated for pneumonia and given one day of bed rest.

- **Back to the Hill**—Upon returning to the Hill, Alec was diagnosed with torn abdominal muscles and rib cage connective tissues from the two weeks of violent coughing. He went on a bed rest/no training schedule for two months, and then depression set in.

- **Acceptance Day Parade**—We were determined to make the journey to watch the Acceptance Day Parade. If I could give Alec one shred of hope and instill in him the will to keep fighting, I was going to do it. The parade was beautiful and pride filled my heart as I watched our cadet march through the stadium. We had a great lunch with his high school friends. Then Alec looked at me sternly and said, "I'm giving it one semester and then I'm coming home." He felt he had nothing left to give.

- **Setbacks**—Our family became consumed with seeing Alec through this. Emails went out daily along with Scripture quotes and anything we could think of to keep him going. Then another call came. Alec had broken his foot and was in a cast. He was just beginning to be able to work out with his squadron, and now this. He felt the others saw him as a weak link, and he began to pull away, becoming depressed again.

- **Parents Weekend**—We all made the trek to USAFA for Parents Weekend with great anticipation. Alec had become a different person. Having to wear the uniform 24/7 with a cast on had done him in. He had missed out on the glory of marching in with the wing at the first game and didn't get to do push-ups after their many touchdowns.

- **Desperate News**—The next few days were quiet with few emails. Then I received a call from Alec while I was in an important meeting. Knowing he wasn't allowed his phone at this time, I panicked. He was calling to tell me he was getting two F's in his core classes. He'd not had a problem with scholastics before. THEN he explained. Over the past six weeks he had been progressively losing his vision. He'd not been able to read a book or see a board in five weeks. Now he was seeing only shadows. I needed to get him to a doctor immediately, but how?

- **Help From an Academy Liaison Officer**—I quickly hung up, said a prayer, and called Bill Preston, Alec's ALO and one of the wisest men I know. He quickly helped me put things in perspective, and I went about contacting Alec's Air Officer Commanding (AOC) and told her what Alec had been too fearful to reveal. In twelve hours he was seeing the eye doctor. Then the most heartbreaking call came. The Air Force Flight Doctor told me my son was going blind! He was unsure if he could reverse the process, but he began aggressive treatment.

- **Devastating News**—Two days later, I received a call that Alec was en route to Denver, now legally blind. Such a downward spiral in just two days! I'd had enough. As he arrived from his emergent trip to Denver, I was arriving at the Denver airport. In fact, I was on a plane less than two hours after getting the phone call. I spent almost two weeks in Colorado, taking Alec to all of his appointments and treatments. The busywork was a blessing. It kept both of us from falling apart.

- **Amazing Hope**—Upon returning to the Academy, the dreaded meeting with his AOC was upon us. But with kindness and immeasurable compassion she asked, "What can we do?" Instead of sending him home, they were determined to see him through this. Alec had at least three appointments weekly and ended up on academic probation. He still had no vision, but he was learning outside the classroom through verbal teaching from a group of amazing and dedicated teachers.

- **Perseverance**—The next three months were difficult. Alec was blind, unable to study, and unable to visit his sponsor family. But energy and attention were constantly flowing his way from our family, each of us trying to find ways to distract him from the devastation his life had become.

- **A Miracle Day!**—Two weeks before finals, Alec began getting his vision back. In about a week's time it was almost completely back. This allowed him to participate in his academics and finish the semester. Christmas was a blur of happy emotions, and for the first time since arriving at USAFA, Alec appeared relaxed and content.

- **A Brotherhood to the Rescue**—During the next three months, he would lose a portion of his vision several times, making a very aggressive course of chemotherapy his only choice: faith. He continued to feel his squadron was not with him, but what none of us knew was that he had told no one about his difficulty other than his AOC. We worked to get the word out in an appropriate manner, and the next thing we knew upperclassmen were typing papers, classmates quizzing him verbally, and he was beginning to feel the brotherhood he so craved.

- **Recognition and Legacy**—The forty days of recognition were upon him, and Alec felt like he would fail. And then it was the night of recognition. Would he be recognized? Or would this be the end. Then the call came. He had been recognized, and in no small way! Not only had he received his one set of prop and wings, but he had received twenty others, several of them legacy pins. That meant many people saw him being there the next year to pass on the legacy pins to another deserving cadet. He was having his first real taste of success. Our whole family felt like we had overcome a huge hurdle. Alec had gained the respect of his peers, and that could never be taken away, regardless of his physical challenges.

- **Going the Distance**—The remainder of the school year saw several battles with lost vision and more aggressive treatment. But for the first time, I saw a determined young man, ready to stay the course. He is no longer the fearful basic cadet, but now a more confident cadet determined to throw his hat in Falcon stadium in 2014.

CELEBRATING A BALANCED BUDGET

☆ 15 ☆

BUDGET WARS

Painless Budgeting (and Other Myths!)

I get more mileage out of a quarter than a Hyundai gets out of a gas can. You see, I'm a born saver. I started saving money so early in life that by the time I was twelve years old, I'd saved enough money to fund a trip to Spain to visit my cousins. I took three rolls of film with me and only took six pictures, thereby "saving" two and a half rolls! Okay, I guess I used to be a little compulsive about saving. I know how to save money so well that I built a career around teaching others how to do things like feed a family of seven for only $250 a month, pay down debt, and establish a workable family budget.

On the other hand, my husband, Bob, is a born spender. When he was a kid, his paper route money never even saw the inside of his pocket. This pattern continued into his adult years, and when he became a fighter pilot in the Air Force, he could still spend money faster than his Stealth F-117 could go from zero to 500 mph. For you Air Force novices, that's pretty fast!

So what happened when this spender landed in the life of a saver, and she was swept off her feet? Well, I'll put it this way: Bob decided that he'd rather dodge flying missiles in Baghdad than come home and tell me he forgot to use the coupon for the pizza he brought home for dinner. Early in our marriage, Bob unceremoniously deemed budget the B word. The unmentionable sent him scrambling.

Now, don't get me wrong! Bob and I have a lot in common—we both enjoy gourmet coffee and dark chocolate, and we like moving often with the military. When we fly, both of us also like to rate the airline pilot's landing on a scale of one to ten. Amazingly, we always rate the landings the same. I've even been tempted to bring along markers and Post-it Notes so we can each write our rating secretly and then hold them up to each other upon landing. It could be our own version of Mini Olympics for Pilots. As a matter of fact, we agreed on just about everything when we got married—except money. And yet we wanted to manage our finances as well as we rated a pilot's landing.

Bob and I are not the only couple with contrasting viewpoints when it comes to money—finances is mentioned as the number one topic couples argue about in marriage and is also cited for the most divorces. Money matters can be a real problem, even if two savers are married to each other, because they still have to decide on their financial goals and priorities. We found that an effective tool for working out our financial differences was that dreaded B word: budget.

Bob and I knew that if we didn't get a firm grip on our extreme approaches to money, we'd have to face some ugly consequences someday. Our spending consequences would include juggling bills and nasty calls from bill collectors, while an overemphasis on saving would only cause stress on our marriage. As the saver, I had to adjust my expectations for Bob: Was it really reasonable for me to demand that he lunch at McDonald's only on Tuesdays, when they give free super-sizing? Was it reasonable for Bob not to expect me to get upset when he came home with a $200 power sander he bought on credit? Yes, we both needed to get a grip.

It wasn't easy for the spender in our relationship to get into the budget habit. We had some harrowing takeoffs and hit turbulence while in flight. Initially, we went off and on our budget, straying one month and staying on target the next. I'd blow up when he came home with a used VCR that worked great and only cost $25—because he didn't check the Consumer Guide first! No, it certainly wasn't clear skies, but eventually, with prayer and perseverance, both of us found balance, and peace once again reigned in our home. That is, until we had five children in seven years, but that's another very long story.

* * * * * * *

Couples have cited financial problems as the number one issue in the majority of divorces. Therefore, getting a grip on your family budget could be one of the best divorce busters you implement for the sake of your marriage and family. Here are some financial statistics from a recent study[4] about debt and savings among members of our armed forces:

4. Jim Fishback, *Defending the Military Marriage* (Family Life Publications, 2008).

- Fifty-two percent of active-duty personnel carry a balance from month to month on three or more credit cards.
- Twenty-four percent had personal unsecured debt payments of more than $600 per month.
- Twenty-four percent have monthly payments that are one fourth or more of their monthly income (the national average is 15–20 percent).
- Twenty-eight percent report that they have fallen behind in paying credit card accounts.
- Twenty-four percent have no savings, and 29 percent have savings of less than $1,000.

Military families especially need to make their dollars stretch because of the hidden costs often associated with moves, TDYs, and deployments. Not to mention the meager pay of enlisted men and women in our armed forces.

Here's a sampling of nonreimbursable expenses to give you an idea how quickly things can add up:

Moves

- Child care during a move
- Cost to have a military house cleaned for inspection
- Airfare and mileage to visit extended family members due to geographical separation
- Internet service and smartphone plans to stay in touch with family and friends
- More meals eaten out before and after the move and while unpacking
- Replacing lost and damaged household and personal items that missed getting on the movers' log or that cost more than the reimbursable allotment
- New blinds, curtains, rugs, carpet, drapes (because those you already have do not fit in your new home)
- Increased insurance premiums on home or auto due to higher-cost area
- Increased rent beyond the COLA allowance

TDYs and Deployments

- Increased child-care costs
- More meals eaten away from home

- Airfare or mileage to visit family while spouse is absent
- Increased spending on entertainment as diversions
- A tendency to spend more on "guilt gifts" for the children
- Increased long-distance bills
- Impulse "pamper" purchases that rack up credit card debt
- Clothing purchases and "welcome home" gifts to surprise spouse upon return home

All of these costs are factored into a military family's budget, so there is a greater need to know where the money is going and to plan for the events that are a normal part of the lifestyle. There are services available within the military community, such as Military Fleet and Family Support Center, Marine Corps Community Services Center, Army Family Services and the Airman and Family Readiness Center, and Personnel Service and Support Units that can also help your family develop a workable budget. With a little creativity and some hard work, you can aim high and fly with the best.

Hey, Where Did All the Dough Go?!

Remember to make an appointment with your financial adviser on base or post to go over your budget. This would cost $300 if you had to pay a CPA or CFP to help you. There are also some great software programs available through your finance person on post. For example, Payoff Strategies software shows you which debts to pay off first in order to save money on interest. Delores Faye Jenkins, a financial expert at Airman and Family Readiness Center at Seymour Johnson AFB, said, "We helped several families save $1,000 or more in interest and pay down their debt five months sooner."

When you discuss your budget at home with your spouse, begin your discussion when you are both relaxed. Breathe in, breathe out. Drink some warm milk. Have an Oreo. Have another one. Feeling relaxed now? No? Then try lighting an aromatherapy candle called "Tranquility," and put on some Frank Sinatra or James Taylor mood music. Better? Good. Now you can take your serene mood right into the budgeting process with you.

Now that you're relaxed, you can create your own budget worksheet by writing out the following categories, or for an online budget tool, go to www.elliekay.com.

Tithe—10 percent
Savings—10 percent
Clothing/Dry Cleaning—5 percent
Education/Miscellaneous—5 percent
Food—10 percent
Housing/Utilities/Taxes—30 percent
Insurance—5 percent
Medical/Dental—4 percent
Recreation/Vacation/Gifts—6 percent
Transportation—15 percent.

The percentages and categories offered here are only guidelines.

Make three vertical columns beside the categories and title them: (1) Current Spending; (2) Spending Percentages Recommended; and (3) Actual Budget. Fill in the first column by figuring the average for each category for the last six months. Establish your total monthly income and fill out the second column based on the percentages given in the guideline. Leave the third column blank for now.

They're Singing Our Song

Families usually have favorite restaurants, movies, and even special songs that reflect the character and tastes of the family. Your budget will be just as unique as your family. It will be based on variable factors, such as your family's size, geographical location, debt load, and income. For example, housing can be a big variable due to your geographic location and whether or not you live in base housing. There are plenty of great resources to help you cut back painlessly on household expenses. As near as your base library, Barnes and Noble, or at www.elliekay.com, you'll find my books: *The 60-Minute Money Workout; Living Rich for Less; The Little Book of Big Savings; Half-Price Living: Secrets to Living Well on One Income;* and *A Tip a Day With Ellie Kay: 12 Months' Worth of Money-Saving Ideas.*

Stay on the Same Sheet of Music

We realized that *both* of us wanted to try to have healthy finances, even though we approached money *differently*. As the two of you go through the sometimes painful process of establishing and sticking to a family budget, it is important to make a real commitment to these important issues.

We also realized that we didn't need to get carried away with the idea of putting our budget to work. We found that living on an austerity program strained our relationship, and we didn't want to become so detail-conscious that the budget controlled our entire life. So we allowed an occasional indulgence, implemented budget-cutting techniques slowly, and modified the budget as needed. As time went on, we fine-tuned some aspects of our budget and then had an annual checkup to keep it running smoothly.

Thrift Savings Plan—TSP

As Federal employee or member of the uniformed services, you have the opportunity to participate in the Thrift Savings Plan (TSP). You can go to www.tsp.gov and request an explanations booklet or download it as a PDF file. This booklet provides an overview of the TSP. The TSP is a retirement benefit that is offered to employees of the U.S. Government. It is similar to 401(k) plans available to many private-sector employees. The purpose of the TSP is to give you the ability to participate in a long-term savings and investment plan.

Saving for your retirement through the TSP provides numerous advantages, including:

- before-tax contributions and tax-deferred investment earnings
- automatic payroll deductions
- low administrative and investment expenses
- a diversified choice of investment options, including professionally designed Lifecycle funds
- agency contributions, if you are an employee covered by the Federal Employees' Retirement System (FERS)
- access to your money while you are still employed by the Federal Government (under certain circumstances)
- a portable retirement account that can move with you when you retire or leave Federal service
- a beneficiary participant account established for your spouse in the event of your death
- a variety of withdrawal options

If you are covered by FERS, the TSP is one part of a three-part retirement package that also includes your FERS basic annuity and Social Security. If you are covered by the Civil Service Retirement System (CSRS) or are a member of the uniformed services, the TSP is a supplement to your CSRS annuity or military retired pay.

TSP benefits differ depending upon your retirement system (FERS, CSRS, or uniformed services). Therefore, if you are not certain which retirement system you belong to, you should check with your personnel or benefits office.

Regardless of your retirement system, participating in the TSP can significantly increase your retirement income, but starting early is important. Contributing early gives the money in your account more time to increase in value through the compounding of earnings

Budget Busters

Since finances are so important in a military family, they probably deserve one more peek. There are a few problem areas that can throw a budget off course in a matter of seconds—sending it reeling toward disaster. Here are a few tips to avoid these pitfalls:

Debt or Credit. Some people have a policy of paying cash only. Some couples set up an envelope system for cash. Every two weeks they place the budgeted amount of cash in envelopes marked *food, entertainment, gas,* etc. When the money runs out, they stop spending until the end of the two-week period. A regular peek at the amount of cash left in each envelope is a vivid reminder of your budget commitment. If credit has become a habit, then you might even do something dramatic, like cut up your credit cards.

Impulse Buying. Nothing busts a budget like impulse buying. If you don't have the cash to splurge by going to your favorite Italian restaurant, then don't go. If you buy compulsively at the mall, do your marriage a favor and stay out of that place! If you're an online buyer, spending money you don't have over the Internet, pull the plug.

Thirty-Day Rule. A good way to short-circuit impulse buying is the thirty-day plan. If it's not in your budget, wait thirty days, thereby delaying the purchase. During that month, find two other items that are similar and compare prices. If it's still available at a good price and it fits the next month's budget, then buy it. You will likely find that you're buying less stuff, because this delay gives you the opportunity to get beyond the impulse.

"Comfort" Spending. Many couples find themselves indulging in comfort spending on clothes, sports equipment, expensive restaurants, and excessive entertainment, to name a few. But this is another budget buster you can't afford. Even cutting back on *some* of this kind of spending can add up positively. For example, if you really can't afford to go out to eat four times a month, then go only twice.

Gifts. Think about the gifts you buy for relatives, teachers, baby showers, weddings, birthdays, Valentine's Day, Mother's Day, Father's Day, kids' birthdays, and anniversaries. This doesn't even cover the biggie: Christmas. The first thing we should do is evaluate the "why" of gift-giving. Do we really have to give a material gift in each circumstance? Wouldn't a card work just as well in some cases? What about baked goods instead? Occasionally, giving a gift may even put the receiver under a sense of obligation. Think through each of these gifts to put them into perspective and save your budget at the same time.

Vacations. A nice romantic getaway can seem like a dream and turn into a nightmare for your budget when you get the credit card statement. Some advance planning can keep this from becoming a budget buster. Consider all travel costs, including tickets for the theater or amusement park, tips, meals, and souvenirs. If you have to sink further into debt to accommodate your vacation, then simplify your plans until they fit your financial limits.

The Ultimate Budget Buster: Red, White, and Scammed

What is the use of making the sacrifices to stay on budget if you get scammed? Thousands of service members engaged in fighting America's battles overseas are now encountering a foe here at home. Young and sometimes inexperienced in the ways of the financial world, these military members are often drawing their first paychecks. Consequently, enlisted men and women are easy marks for sleazy car dealers, insurance scammers, predatory lenders, and identity thieves. So pervasive are the rip-offs and so troubling is the debt incurred by military personnel that U.S. Department of Defense officials recently labeled the situation a threat to national security.

The following is part of a Q&A held on the ABC News "Good Money" Show, and also at an open forum with military members and their spouses at a DOD-sponsored Yellow Ribbon event.

Q. The DOD has labeled the fraud situation among the military as a threat to national security. How does getting scammed impact lives overseas?

ELLIE: It's all about distraction. When military members are distracted, whether it's worry over identity theft or wondering if their spouse is able to deal with messy finances at home—that's when accidents happen. Distraction leads to worry which leads to accidents. And when accidents happen, then there is loss of life. So if we want to help save lives overseas, then we can all do our part to protect our military members by exposing rip-offs and scams whenever possible.

Q. What kind of paycheck does a typical recruit make and what are some of the questionable ways local businesses try to get a piece of that paycheck?

ELLIE: They earn about $1,800 per month, and these paychecks can be carved to bits by bad deals. For example, a computer store outside of Great Lakes Naval Training Center in Illinois employs attractive women to troll for new sailors. Once they get them inside the store, they are pressured into buying a very basic laptop for more than $4,000, which is three times what the computer is worth. Then they finance the deal, and the computer ends up costing even more, with the store also making money on the financing.

Q. What are some other common ways the military is ripped off that people should be aware of?

ELLIE: There was recently a multistate investigation launched into life insurance scams that were being perpetrated against military members just before they took off for the Middle East. These scamsters sold soldiers extremely overpriced or misrepresented policies, taking advantage of the emotional situation of leaving their families and going into harm's way. This investigation ended with the unethical companies offering more than 70 million dollars in refunds to thousands of service members. When it comes to life insurance, military members are offered SGLI or Service Members Group Life Insurance, which is a sanctioned and legitimate source for high coverage and low premiums, so there's really no need to secure other private insurance.

Q. Tell us about the "Red Cross" scam that is getting a lot of attention among military families.

ELLIE: This is fairly despicable, as it preys on the emotions of families of service members. A con artist claiming to be with the Red Cross will call a parent or spouse of a service member, telling them their loved one has been injured and they need their social security number to authorize help for them. In some cases, they ask for an initial cash payment. Military members need to clear any report of injury through the chain of command or by contacting the base family community services.

Q. It seems that our military is very young. What is the average age of a service member, and do they receive any kind of personal finance education as part of their training?

ELLIE: Yes, they are young. In fact, the average age range of military members is between twenty-two and twenty-eight. Of the groups I routinely speak to around the world, I'd say the average twenty-two-year-old has an even younger wife and a baby as well—so it is a lot of responsibility for someone so young. The good news is that since 2004, service members learn about personal finance as part of their early training. When I give my Heroes at Home message, I teach about finances and also encourage them to use the resources they have available to them on base. Army Community Services, Airman and Family Readiness Centers, Fleet and Family Support Centers—all of these have personal finance counselors there who are ready and willing to give free financial counseling to service members and their families. It's what I call my $300 tip, because a couple hours with the caliber of financial professional at any of these centers is equivalent to paying $300 to a CFP or CPA.

Q. Is Congress doing anything to try and help prevent this kind of fraud that is being perpetrated against our service members?

ELLIE: Fortunately, yes, they are. This is, essentially, war profiteering, and it requires congressional action. They are in the process of creating a new federal Consumer Financial Protection Agency (CFPA) that would guard all Americans, including the military, against scams. Although Pentagon officials specifically requested that the CFPA oversee auto sales, car dealers argue that they should be exempt from such oversight. They say that they're not responsible for bad loans—bad lenders are. But consumer advocates counter that dealers are often involved in financing and sometimes work directly with loan providers. The issue is currently under debate, but there will be some kind of regulation to expose and prosecute scammers.

Q. Ellie, you came to our Army base to speak last November, and I think your message really helped me get through my husband's deployment. Thank you for the work you are doing with military families. I did have a question about ordering items online. You showed us how to pay 40 percent less by using some websites, but how do I know if the website is legitimate?

Steph, Germany

ELLIE: Steph, thanks for writing and thank you for what you do as a military family member. I admire you so much and know it's a hard job! To avoid getting scammed online, make sure that you never respond to an email inquiry, but you find the site yourself on your own search. Then, go to BBB.org to make sure they aren't listed and also check out the FTC.gov, plus the Internet Crime Complaint Center at IC3.gov, to investigate complaints against the company.

Q. I'm nineteen and have been a soldier for eighteen months. There are quite a few of my friends who regularly go to the payday loan business that is right outside our base. I keep telling them that they are losing a lot of money by getting a pay advance, but they say the interest rates are low and it's no big deal. What do you think?

Pvt. Benjamin, Fort Bragg

ELLIE: Private Benjamin, thanks for your service, and you're the smart one. Tell your friends that some of these payday loan companies are charging as much as 500 percent interest. Even though the Defense Authorization Act of 2007 put a cap of 36 percent on interest loans to military members, many of these companies skirt the law by added exorbitant fees and calling the loans "revolving lines of credit" instead of payday loans in order to bypass the law.

Q. My husband's hazardous duty pay was backlogged by red tape and didn't arrive early enough for us to pay our bills. How am I supposed to pay things like our car loans while he is in the Middle East if I shouldn't go to a payday loan center?

Justine, Fort Drum

ELLIE: In situations like yours, there are resources as near as your Army Community Services center where they can offer free financial advice. In extenuating circumstances, such as yours, you might even qualify for special programs offered by the Army's charity, Army Emergency Relief (AER). By going to these legitimate resources, you can avoid getting ripped off.

Q. Our community here in Alamogordo, New Mexico, is very supportive of the military, and so is Las Cruces, which is a little farther down the road. Many businesses carry banners that say, "We support our military." Even so, a friend of ours bought a car from one of these places and it turns out that the dealership didn't own the title

and then went out of business. Now our friend has a $12,000 loan to pay and no car to show for it! How can we avoid being "taken" and who can we trust?

Heidi, Holloman Air Force Base

ELLIE: Heidi, I'm so sorry to hear of that situation, especially from a business that advertises its support of the military. Unfortunately, auto vendors are a huge source of complaints. In most cases, the salesperson will offer you "easy credit" but you pay jacked-up prices, hidden fees, and interest rates of 15 to 20 percent. Military financial counselors have files full of horror stories. Bad dealers have taken cars in trade, promising to pay them off and then they go out of business, leaving service members with two payments. Go to BBB certified dealers, and if the deal sounds too good to be true, just walk away, because it usually is.

Q. My daughter just got commissioned with the Marine Corps, and I'm concerned about the possibility of someone taking advantage of her financially. Are military members a bigger target for fraud than civilians?

Sue, Stillwater, OK

ELLIE: Military members have guaranteed paychecks and won't ever get laid off. This makes them good credit risks. But it also makes them targets. Some people see the military as cash cows, and they want to get their cut. One of the greatest evidence of this fact is that outside of any large military installation, you'll see businesses that offer payday loans, pawn shops, and check cashers. These are the kinds of businesses that prey on unsuspecting military.

* * * * * * *

There is no reason for a military family to suffer financially because of a lack of resources. If there is an extenuating circumstance in your family's financial resources, you may qualify for programs offered by your branch of the service's aid programs. For example, the Army Emergency Relief Fund regularly helps families with unexpected medical bills or those associated with hardship moves. The Air Force Aid Society helps families who have special financial needs as well. Plus, there are programs at your Family Support Center equivalent that will teach you and your spouse about everything from how to buy a car to investing and budgeting.

There's still a huge need for pay increases, and articulate, experienced voices like yours might be needed with your congressmen to speak out on behalf of the military family. But things have gotten a little better with the recent pay increase and a couple of other changes. Congress passed the Military Family Supplemental Subsistence Allowance (FSSA) Act, which has effectively eliminated the need for military families to be dependent on food stamps. If you qualify for food stamps, you qualify for the FSSA, which is included in your pay. Once you receive the FSSA, you're no longer eligible for food stamps. WIC is another story, since it's a combination of factors, and while income is a primary factor, it isn't the only factor. That is another program to look into at your Family Support Center equivalent.

Financial sacrifices are another way that many military families contribute to our nation's freedoms. Most technical jobs in the military have a considerably higher pay counterpart in the civilian sector. And yet many of these families remain in the military. This indicates that financial compensation, while greatly appreciated, is not the primary reason military members serve their country. In this way, the family members, by accepting a lower standard of living, are contributing to a higher good—the freedom that our nation enjoys. So when you are tempted to grumble about the low pay and long hours or how the compensation is greater in the civilian sector, just remember that the work your spouse does is not measured in dollars and cents—it is measured in commitment to God and country.

☆ 16 ☆

A PENNY SAVED IS MORE THAN A PENNY EARNED

Easy Ways to Save Money on Everything

When I married my husband, Bob, I got a "three-for-one" deal—which I thought was a wonderful bargain. Bob brought two precious daughters, Missy and Mandy, into our family, and they were a delightful addition! But our finances were not quite so charming. We had $40,000 in consumer debt and nothing to show for it. Bob was in the aerospace industry at the time and lived for the few days a month that he would fly in the California Air National Guard. He longed to get back into the Air Force and fly full time. That's exactly what he did six months after our marriage, and I supported his dream.

As mentioned in the previous chapter, the civilian sector often pays better than the military, so we took a $15,000 a year pay cut to come back in. We ended up paying one-third of his income to Uncle Sam in various taxes, one-third toward the girls' child support, and 10 percent toward our tithe to our local church. This left us paying off that $40,000 debt while living on roughly 25 percent of Bob's income as a captain in the Air Force. We had five babies in the first seven years of marriage, plus Missy and Mandy, to make a total of seven children to support. And I wanted to stay home with my children, especially while they were young. If you do some quick mental math, you can easily understand why we didn't have money for groceries some weeks—even on an officer's wage. We supported

175

a family our size on the financial equivalent of a Senior Airman. We needed a miracle.

And we got one.

Our financial miracle resulted in our family's becoming completely debt free in two and a half years. What do you think happened?

An inheritance?

The lottery?

A lucky trip to Vegas?

The answer to our financial woes may surprise you, but it is the premise of this entire chapter. The answer was found in something that is very, very small and seemingly insignificant: coupons.

* * * * * * *

Before I married Bob, I learned how to "coupon." I didn't have a financial need; it was just a fun hobby for me. After we married, I used coupons to feed our family. I got so good at slashing the prices for groceries that I started giving modest seminars to teach others. Then we started slashing our monthly expenses in other areas as well: clothing, household goods, and our vehicle insurance. All of these "little" things added up to big bucks. Let's do the math together:

If you can save $5,000 a year on the items we mentioned (we saved $8,000 on groceries alone last year—not including the other savings areas), it would be equivalent to earning about $6,800 (by the time you pay taxes and Social Security). That is an additional $5,000 added to your family—free and clear! That is how a penny saved ends up being more than a penny earned.

We also did one other seemingly little thing that yielded big dividends—we prayed. We set up a budget, and we prayed for God's provision to help us stick to it and to get out of debt. Here's what's wrong with debt:

- Debt borrows on your future.
- Debt makes you a servant to the lender.
- Debt places financial stress on your marriage and family.
- Debt erodes resources through high-interest payments.
- Debt promotes impulse buying.
- Debt limits your ability to be generous.

But how do you get $40,000 out of debt and live on so little at the same time? One thing we did after we decided to get on a budget and get out of debt was to apply every bonus, unexpected check, or financial gift toward our debt. Here were just a few of the checks that came our way:

- USAA insurance premium refund
- GI Bill for Bob's master's program reimbursement (six years after he finished the program)
- Christmas checks from relatives
- *The Price Is Right* (I went on the show and won a prize that we sold for cash)
- Military bonus for signing a five-year commitment

All of these miracles, we believe, happened because we were finally committed to being good stewards of our financial resources and to tithing a percentage to our local church. But while these checks helped pay down our debt, they didn't pay the living expenses we had. That happened because we learned to stretch the value of a dollar. The old saying "Necessity is the mother of invention" was never more true than in the Kay household in those early years.

But the story doesn't stop there. I developed an uncanny ability to save on practically everything a family must buy. My seminars were mainly given to teach other families how to do the same thing, and I did it on a volunteer basis as my way of giving back to the community.

By the time we reached Holloman Air Force Base in 1997, my seminars came to the attention of Lenn Furrow, the director of the Family Support Center. She saw that the quality of life of hundreds of HAFB families was being positively impacted by my *Shop, Save, and Share* seminar, and she approached the Air Force Aid Society to fund a film project. They made this seminar into a video that was distributed to 120 Air Force bases around the world, and it began to make an international impact on military families.

But once again, the story doesn't stop there. The seminar came to the attention of a senior editor at Bethany House Publishers via an author friend, Becky Freeman. This editor, Steve Laube, was impressed with the distribution of the seminar and saw a potential to reach many more families with a book. So Bethany House published *Shop, Save, and Share* in 1998. Steve later told me that there was only a 1 percent chance that my book would get published (the percentage of unsolicited manuscripts that get published).

In addition, Crossings Book Club picked up the book, and it sold so many copies that it made their bestseller list. The success of the first book led to *fourteen books*. I've become a guest commentator on a national radio program, *Money Matters,* a regular expert on ABC News Now, *Good Money,* and a featured expert on Fox News, Neil Cavuto, MSNBC, CNBC, *Nightline,* and more than 600 radio or television interviews. But the best part of this success is the ability to give back by getting to visit YOU at various military venues around the world, having had the profound privilege of helping raise millions of dollars to feed hungry children in developing countries via *Life Today*'s annual nationally televised hunger campaign.

So why did this miracle happen to our family? Well, the answer can be found along the lines of The Little House That Jack Built:

1. We were committed to getting rid of $40,000 in debt.
2. Lenn Furrow had a desire to help Air Force families with my program.
3. Bestselling author and friend Becky Freeman had a vision not only for helping me but also for helping others through the message and methods God gave me, and gave the book to the right editor.
4. This editor, Steve Laube, caught the vision and saw to it that through this book, thousands of families in need of real-life tools to get them on solid financial ground would get the message.

But did it all really start with a commitment to get out of debt? No.
It started because we had a huge financial problem.
Sometimes a destiny is an opportunity wrapped up in a problem.

★ ★ ★ ★ ★ ★ ★

Whatever your challenges are, you can do more than live through them—you can rise above them! Furthermore, if you persevere beyond the problems of today, you will be in a position to be a source of hope to others.

Our financial problems became the opportunity to fulfill my destiny of helping others manage their money better. If you find yourself in similar circumstances, my books offer a detailed, realistic approach to putting debt behind you and your destiny before you. Even if you are not currently experiencing financial difficulties, you still may want to save a substantial amount each year in painless ways! Whether you *want* to save or you *have* to save, here are the best tips I've gleaned from my experience. While they are not exhaustive, they will get you started.

Insurance

I was an insurance broker for several years before I met and married Bob. This is one area where a few minor changes could yield big savings. There is a chart at the end of this section to help you navigate your way around standard life insurance policies, but one of the best options is offered by SGLI, Serviceman's Group Life Insurance.

SGLI Q&A

What is SGLI?

SGLI is a program of low-cost group life insurance for service members on active duty, ready Reservists, members of the National Guard, members of the Commissioned Corps of the National Oceanic and Atmospheric Administration and the Public Health Service, cadets and midshipmen of the four service academies, and members of the Reserve Officer Training Corps.

How much coverage is available?

SGLI coverage is available in $50,000 increments up to the maximum of $400,000.

How much does SGLI cost?

SGLI premiums are around seven cents per $1,000 of insurance, regardless of the member's age. To view premium rates at different coverage levels, go to www.insurance.va.gov.

What about life after the military?

Service members with SGLI coverage have two options available to them upon release from service. They can convert their full-time SGLI coverage to term insurance under the Veterans' Group Life Insurance program or convert to a permanent plan with one of the participating commercial insurance companies.

USAA

The first time I heard of USAA was when my minivan had a close encounter with a garage door. It was a sad day. We were moving with five kids, seven and under, and Bob went onto the base to fill out the out-processing paper work. My plan was to go to a friend's house and do laundry since all our household goods were en route to the new destination. These friends knew I hated the Laundromat, with five kiddos, so they offered theirs. She gave me the code for her garage door (they were at work). I was so distracted with the kids and the move, that I forgot Bob had put the travel pod on top of the van. I entered the code, got in the van, and drove into the garage. The pod tore off the door and glass came raining down on the van. Bad day.

But apparently, USAA is used to distracted military moms of many, because they took care of the van, the garage door, and my injured pride in one fell swoop. The adjustor was kind instead of being appalled—I got the feeling he had seen worse. Even if he hadn't, he was out to make me feel better. We were back on the road by the next day, and I wouldn't revisit USAA until two years later, when I had yet another close encounter with a garage door. This time it involved a partially opened door that is not visible in the rearview mirror of a Suburban when there are five screaming kids in tow—especially when one's hubby is on alert to fly in harm's way in his F-117A Stealth Fighter.

I was invited to a blogger conference at USAA and learned a lot about the company that serves military members and their families. USAA was formed in 1922, when twenty-five military officers joined together with a common vision. After being turned away for auto insurance due to his mobile military lifestyle, Maj. William Henry Garrison called a meeting with his peers to discuss a bold new idea: to organize an association of military members who would insure one another. At the end of the day, those individuals became the charter members and founders of the present-day USAA.

Nine decades later, that founding vision remains intact. Today, USAA is nearly 8.5 million members strong, offering a full range of insurance and financial services.

With more than 22,000 employees, USAA's mission has expanded beyond the initial offer of auto insurance to include a full range of highly competitive financial products and services with the goal of becoming the provider of choice for the military community.

USAA's commitment to its members is evident as they are routinely ranked number one with organizations like MSN Money Customer Service Hall of Fame and *Bloomberg BusinessWeek* magazine. *Military Spouse* magazine ranks them number one in their "Top Ten Military Spouse Friendly Employers" and *G.I. Jobs* magazine has regularly rated USAA in the top ten of military-friendly employers, proving that at USAA, they do know what it means to serve.

With products designed with the military member in mind, from a checking account with no minimum balance requirement, no monthly maintenance fee, and free paper checks to ten free ATM withdrawals per month and refunds up to $15 of what other banks charge you for using their ATMs, USAA's innovativeness does make military lives easier. Such innovation—USAA pioneered Internet banking in 1999 with usaa.com—allows members to safely conduct business online to include using Deposit@Home and Deposit@Mobile. USAA was the first to offer an iPhone application allowing members to deposit checks using their phone's camera.

Other benefits to military members include early payday, rate reduction on credit cards during a PCS or deployment, and access to USAA Certified Financial Planners. Their newest offerings to military lifestyle: Movers Advantage, Auto Circle, Home Circle, and USAA MemberShop.

Homeowners

Carry only the coverage you need. If your home is valued at $100,000, and you insure it for $120,000, and it burns down, they will only pay $100,000, and you've overpaid the premium. Keep in mind also that the insurance price of the home does not include the land. But be sure that you get replacement value on the home and contents.

Homeowner's Deductibles

Carry a $500, $1,000, or 1 percent deductible on your homeowner's policy.

Special Riders

Check with your insurance company to see their limitations on personal articles. Jewelry, collections, antiques, computers, and guns may all need to be added as riders to get the full coverage on these personal items. Insurance companies will only cover a minimum on these without a rider.

Flood Insurance

Remember that flood insurance is only sold by the state, and you are not covered unless you've purchased this policy from the government.

Tenant Policies

If you do not own your home or you live in military housing, you will need to get a tenant policy. Ask for a nonsmoker's discount if you qualify, and shop around. You will want to get replacement value and special riders if necessary.

Automobile—Mutual Risk Drivers

If you or your spouse has a less-than-perfect driving record, you are considered a greater risk to insure. The same applies to drivers under twenty-five years of age. Put these drivers as the principal driver on a vehicle that does not carry full coverage. You might have to put a car title in a teenage driver's name in order to be able to do this. Check with your agent, because the rules on this vary from state to state. Taking driver's education is another good way to get a ticket off your record or a discount on your policy.

Uninsured Motorists

If you are driving a car that does not carry full coverage (comprehensive and collision), the state requires that it carry at least liability coverage. Part of the basic auto coverage package is medical and uninsured motorists. These two portions of a liability package can be excluded with your signature on a form in some states. However, it is not advisable, because the savings are minimal. And more important, in the event of an accident in which the other person is at fault and they don't have insurance, your auto and medical expenses will be covered.

Discount City

There are often tons of discounts on your homeowner's policy—and especially your automobile policy—that are yours for the asking. Depending upon your state and insurance providers, homeowners can get discounts for a security system, tile roof, fenced yard, nonsmoking household, gated community, or enclosed garage. For automobile policies, ask for discounts for driver's education, safe driving records, security system on your car, an enclosed garage, nonsmoker's policy, drivers ages thirty to sixty, multi-car discounts, and military discounts. Purchasing auto and homeowner's insurance within the same company will also sometimes qualify you for special discounts.

Bonus Tip

Young Drivers—If you have a teenage driver, ask your insurance agent to give him/her an informative talk about driving safely and responsibly. Ask the agent to give your child examples of how much insurance can cost if they get one ticket or have an accident. We did this when I was an insurance broker, and it seemed that kids received counsel from a professional better than they would from their parents.

Everything You Wanted to Know About Life Insurance *(but Were Afraid to Ask)*

Term Life Insurance

The most common type of insurance is term insurance, which can otherwise be known as "temporary" insurance. Term life builds no cash value, and once either the term is up or you stop paying the insurance, the policy is over. If you die, your heirs will benefit from a tax-free payout of the face amount of the policy. Term insurance is very attractive for younger individuals, but still can find its place in a boomer's life insurance plan. There are four basic types of term life insurance:

- **Annually renewable term life insurance.** Annual Renewable and Convertible Term is term insurance that is automatically renewable at the end of each one-year term period, with generally increasing premiums.
- **Convertible term life insurance.** This allows you to convert your policy to a whole life insurance policy with no additional underwriting.
- **Guaranteed level term life insurance.** Guaranteed Level Term insurance offers term insurance protection for the term of the policy with guaranteed level premiums, and may be renewed thereafter without evidence of insurability at an annually increasing premium scale.
- **Return of premium term life insurance.** Return of premium term life insurance (ROP) is unique in that it allows the policy holder to get a full refund of all the premiums paid at the end of the contract. This type of term life insurance policy is a bit more expensive than regular term life insurance, but the premiums are designed to remain level.

Permanent Life Insurance

Permanent life insurance has the ability to provide coverage for your entire life and will stay in force as long as you continue to pay for the premium or the built-up cash value pays the premium for you. The cash value is the distinguishing factor between permanent life insurance and term life.

Whole Life Insurance

Whole life insurance is a type of insurance that remains in place for your entire lifetime. Unlike term life, it does not expire, never needs to be renewed, and cannot be revoked. When you take out a whole life policy, the premium will stay level. As you continue to pay your premium, the cash value should build up as your dividends are reinvested.

Universal Life Insurance

Another form of permanent life insurance is universal life. Universal life is similar to whole life except that it separates the three components of the policy: death benefit, expenses, and cash value. By doing so, it gives the insured more options as you age and your needs change. Having this type of flexibility, however, does make these policies more expensive than their insurance counterparts. Here are some of the characteristics of a universal life insurance policy:

- **Universal life insurance premiums are flexible.** At the beginning of the policy, you'll have to stay regular with your premium payments. As you keep paying those premiums, the cash value should accumulate and grow as long as the underlying investments grow. When this occurs, you won't be required to pay as much to keep the policy in force. **Warning:** If those investments decrease in value, your once "paid up" policy will require that you keep making payments.

- **Universal life insurance has cash value.** As you continue to make your premium payments, in time your policy will accumulate a cash value or what is called the accumulation fund.* The cash value is the amount you can borrow from as the policy ages. This amount is often called the investment portion of the policy.

- **Death benefit.** Universal life insurance is just like the rest of life insurance policies, in that your beneficiary receives a tax-free death benefit when you die. This and the features mentioned above make universal life an attractive option for estate planning purposes.

* Just like variable annuity contracts, the cash value of this life insurance policy initially has surrender charges if you try to touch the money too soon. As the policy ages, the surrender charge decreases until it is eventually nonexistent. If you do try to pull money out, the cash value that you are allowed to withdraw is the cash value minus the applicable surrender charges.

Survivorship or Second-to-Die Life Insurance

While universal life insurance is an effective estate planning tool, the premiums on two separate policies can get pretty expensive. In

walks the survivorship policy, otherwise called second-to-die life insurance. What makes second-to-die policies less expensive is that the
death benefit is not paid until the second owner of the two insurance
policies dies, which usually involves husband and wife. Aging boom-
ers that are looking to minimize their estate tax liability using trusts
will incorporate this type of policy in the estate planning process.

Comparison of Life Insurance Policies

Overwhelmed? When comparing the differences of your life insurance options, it's easy to be. Be sure to sit down with an insurance
specialist or an independent financial planner to help sort through
the life insurance maze.

Type of Insurance	Advantages	Disadvantages
Level term	Level payments over specific period, usually 5, 10, 15, or 20 years; may be convertible to a permanent policy.	More expensive than ART in early years; less expensive in later years.
Whole life (permanent)	Fixed premiums; cash value you can borrow against; possible dividends; tax-deferred earnings; guaranteed death benefit.	Initially higher premium than term insurance; little flexibility in premium payments.
Universal life (permanent)	Flexible premiums; tax-deferred earnings on cash value; access funds; different options allow cash buildup or insurance protection.	If interest rates fall, low cash value buildup may cause policy to lapse unless you add money.
Variable life (permanent)	Fixed, level premiums; guaranteed death benefit; choice of investment options.	You assume risk for policy's cash value; rate of return varies with investments chosen.
Annual renewable term (ART)	Most coverage for the least money; protection in increments of one year; can renew yearly up to specified age (usually 70); may be convertible to permanent policy.	Premiums start low but rise with each new term; nothing back if you outlive contract.
Variable universal life (permanent)	Similar to variable life but with flexible payments. You select the investment vehicle that generates your cash value growth (stocks, bonds, etc.).	Potentially higher earnings than other cash value policies, but also greater risk.

Buying a Car

The least expensive car for you to drive is probably the paid-for older vehicle you are now driving! People talk themselves into a car for a variety of reasons. Take, for example, gas mileage. When you actually calculate gas mileage and the money you "save" when compared to interest payments and depreciation on that new car, you will find that you do not even come close to saving money. The average new car depreciates roughly 30 percent within the first eighteen months, with an average loss of value of five thousand dollars as soon as you drive it out of the parking lot. So look for a used vehicle before you consider new.

However, when interest rates are incredibly low or a family needs the warranty (because of high mileage), it may be best to get a new car. Try to get an end-of-the-year clearance model, a demonstrator model, and, if possible, buy it in December or January—the leanest months in the industry. The following tips can apply to buying a car new or used.

Negotiate these three sales points separately:

Price

Negotiate the price of the car at a dealership apart from the value of the trade-in. Tell the salesperson you want to determine the price of the car without a trade-in. The reason you want to do this is because salespeople will often give you far more for your trade than you expected—thus hooking you on the deal. However, they discount the price accordingly—giving you less of a discount because of the additional amount they've put into your trade. Look up the value of the car at www.kbb.com or www.edmunds.com, print out the page, and bring it with you to the car lot.

Trade-ins

Now that you've determined the price of the car, ask what the dealer will give you for your trade-in. Most *honest* dealerships will tell you that you will get more for your car if you sell it yourself. A little elbow grease and some top-notch detailing can net you hundreds of dollars more than a dealer can give you. But military families don't always have the time to do this due to moves, TDY schedules, and courses. Again, to determine the value, go to www.edmunds.com. Not only does Edmunds' car-buying guide list new car prices, used car prices, car comparisons, and car-buying advice, but they also give car ratings, car values, and auto leasing prices. Remember to print out the page listing your car and bring it to the dealership with you. You could also try the Kelley Blue Book site at www.kbb.com.

Financing

The finance and insurance office is where the lion's share of a dealership's profit is made. In this office, you will have to navigate interest rates, payments, terms, and warranties. Unless you put miles on your car for business, the extended warranties are usually not a good value. Also, you can generally do better on interest by selecting your own creditor. Additionally, the credit life insurance they offer is more expensive than raising your regular insurance premium by $20,000 to cover this expense.

Food and Household Products

I calculated that over twenty years of using coupons, I saved $160,000 (based on the Cost of Food at Home chart provided by the USDA). I fed our five school-aged children (including six-foot-four and six-foot-five teenage sons) for $250 a month. This included toiletries, household cleaners, and medicines. It may sound amazing, but you don't have to look any further than reality TV to see the value of couponing. You'll find scores of people across the country that are now doing the same. Here are the main points to remember:

Make Sure the Price Is Right

Yours truly was actually on this game show—and won! But that's another story. This list will help you determine the right prices on groceries. So buy quality—but make sure the price is right.

Hungry? Stay at Home!

Never shop when you're hungry; you'll be tempted to buy products *you* don't need. Also, leave those babies with a neighbor or spouse. They're *always* hungry and will bully you into buying junk *they* don't need—take it from a busy mother of seven.

Try to Buy Only Items on Sale—and Stock Up

When you purchase a product on sale, you've usually paid the least price possible for that item. This buying method is different from menu planning. With a specific menu, you're obligated to buy the groceries on your menu. However, when you buy groceries on sale and stock up, you'll have a great selection from which to choose your meal. You will also have paid less. So make up your weekly menu according to what you have and save more.

The Coupon Mom

I saved our family of seven over $8,000 one year by using coupons—and I only spent one and a half hours a week doing it! It's easy, if you are organized. Go to my website at www.elliekay.com or link to /resources-links.php to see which grocery stores in your area offer double or triple coupons—and their advertised limitations. If you follow the previous tip, and *only* purchase items when they're on sale *and* you make it a policy to use a coupon on each of these items, then you've paid the least price possible. To simplify these matches of sales with coupons, go to www.couponmom.com. You're a super saver, and you've even paid less than you would at discount stores or warehouse clubs.

Clip Every Coupon—for a Swap Box!

If you don't use a particular product, you can donate a coupon for that product to a swap box. It's easy to organize a coupon swap box at your workplace, club, or church. Just keep a shoebox-size container in a central location. Use the plastic bag system. Donate your coupons in a plastic bag with a 3 x 5 card attached. Sign your name at the top of the card and you'll know you donated that bag of coupons. When you look through a bag of coupons, pull out the ones you need and sign your name. Only look through the bags without your name signed on the card. A coupon coordinator pulls expired coupons out of the bags at the end of each month and mails them to military units overseas. They're good for six months past the expiration date in commissaries outside the United States—so your friends and family members can help military families in the process, if they will send their expired coupons to you.

Sharing—the Gift That Keeps on Giving! And Get a Tax Deduction for Sharing!

If you follow the above tips, and clip every coupon, you'll get many items free. If an item goes on sale and you have a double coupon, you may get it at no cost or for a few pennies. If you can't use the item, then donate it to a nonprofit organization. For example, I've received many free trial-size bottles of shampoo, conditioner, and deodorant. I've donated these to the local homeless shelter.

On a $250 a month food budget, we were able to donate $1,000 worth of groceries to people and organizations in need. Ask the organization to which you're donating groceries for a tax-deductible receipt. Then you can deduct the value of the products as a charitable donation on your income tax. Besides the organization's receipt, I also keep my grocery receipts—with the donated items highlighted. Check out this deduction with your accountant on a year-to-year basis.

Do you see why sharing is the gift that keeps on giving?

Price Comps—Ask Your Store!

If you have a store that will match competitor's ads, then you can save time and money. Most Wal-Mart Supercenters offer this benefit to their consumers. Just take in all the local sale ads and have the store match the sale price from the circulars. There may be some restrictions, so be sure you ask for the details at the customer service desk. For example, Wal-Mart will not honor buy one/get one free (BOGO) sales, nor will they honor percentage-off sales. But they will substitute their brand for other store brands that are on sale, and it may even end up being a better deal!

Search High and Low for Bargains

In today's grocery store, many of the bargains are located on the top and lower shelves. The pricey, expensive items are at eye level. To those in marketing, the reason is obvious—you'll buy something that's in front of your nose! Also, avoid the fancy floral, deli, and bakery departments. They're usually overpriced and can bust your budget.

Use a List—Don't Leave Home Without It!

There was a credit card slogan years ago, encouraging us to "never leave home without it." A list is *definitely* something you should never leave home without. An organized list minimizes time spent in the store, keeps the "buy" on target, helps avoid impulse buying, and serves as a reminder of sale prices.

Coupon Apps

Coupon Sherpa and Yowza are great apps to help you find the values at your local store. Download these apps and use them regularly to save 30 percent or more in the store. Both of these apps use geolocation or ZIP code to bring you the good deals, show you the stores that accept coupons, and help you find the best values.

Garage Sales

These are a way of life for military families—it seems you're either having one or your neighbor is. But these can also be a great source of saving money if you do it the right way. Here are the top ten tips to garage sale success:

1. *Leave Them Home.* We love our kids, but if at all possible, leave them at home, and you'll do better at a garage sale. You'll leave at dawn or as soon as they open, and you'll need to concentrate.
2. *Bargain.* Don't pay more than you are comfortable with for a given item, but balance that with the fact that people have gone to a lot of work to make some extra money. I think the best rule of thumb is to say, "What am I willing to pay for this?" Then ask the seller if he'll take the lower amount you're willing to offer. If the price is reasonable, eight times out of ten they'll take your lower price offer.
3. *Strategize.* You'll need to develop a plan of action. First of all, think about the things you're looking for in a garage sale and make a list. Categorize your clothing, making a complete inventory. Determine the right sizes of the people in your family. If you buy things too small, you'll be wasting money. Do you need a new bike for Johnny? Could you really use a good snowblower? Determine the items you need to buy within the next two to three months and put them on your list.
4. *Plan.* Get a newspaper with the garage sales listed in it and get a good city map. Note the opening times and the items advertised in the notices. Prioritize the garage sales according to the advertised items you need most, and then plan your route accordingly. You may want to start in the area with the earliest openings. Visit all the sales in the same area to save time and money. Don't arrive sooner than the set opening time—sellers won't have all their things set up yet, and they won't be in a

negotiating mood that early in the day either. The sales you visit later in the day are more likely to yield a bargain, as anxious sellers will ask you to "make an offer."

5. *Friends.* If you go with a friend, agree on the same strategy. If you can't agree, then go alone. Brenda Taylor was one of my all-time best garage sale buddies—she and I think alike! I really miss Brenda. Sometimes this military life stinks; that is, when it takes you away from your friends. Ah, but I digress.

You probably won't have the time (or energy) to hit all the sales, so keep your trips to each house short and sweet. It might be a good idea to take along some coffee and snacks if you're going to be out for several hours.

6. *You Aren't Saving Anything If You Don't Need It!* Unlike grocery shopping, I don't buy things at yard sales unless there's a specific use for them. It isn't saving if you're just shopping. A good garage sale mindset is: Buy goods you will have to buy anyway. For example, if you find a pair of panty hose still in the package, in your size, for a quarter—buy them! You would pay at least $3 for them elsewhere, and you've just saved $2.75! If you'll never wear them, however, because they're two sizes too small, you've just wasted twenty-five cents.

7. *If It's Broken, Don't Buy It!* People have garage sales for different reasons. Everything on their tables and hanging in their awnings is there for a reason. Sometimes the reason is that it's broken. So if you can't plug it in, put a battery in it, or start it—then don't buy it, because it's probably broken. Life is too short to buy things you need to repair—unless you know what you're doing.

8. *If It's Stained, Leave It.* You can afford to be choosy at a garage sale. If it's dirty and can easily be washed, buy it. But if it's stained, or you can't tell, leave it on the table. There are quality products for sale at garage sales that are in great shape. You don't have to settle for second-rate goods. Look for clothing with sales tags still on them and products in their original packaging.

Check the zippers, buttons, and snaps on clothing. Pick and probe gadgets to make sure they work well. Count the accessories to a game to make sure all the pieces are there. Look pottery over carefully for nicks and dings. Check the knees on jeans to determine wear and tear. If you're looking at curtains, be sure you know the correct size for your window, and be sure you have the correct curtain rod for it. It's not a bargain to buy $5 curtains when you have to pay $25 for a custom curtain rod in order to hang them!

9. *Can This Marriage Be Saved?* People get rid of new things for all kinds of reasons. I love the *newlywed sales.* They have wedding gifts (they didn't like or cannot yet appreciate) still in boxes. Or they have duplicate toasters, microwaves, and coffeemakers. My garage sale buddy, Brenda, bought a new coffee grinder for $2 at one of these sales. Regularly, we pick up brand-new silver, crystal, and china at newlywed sales and keep them on hand for hospitality gifts, wedding gifts, or even a birthday gift here and there. There's absolutely no difference between paying $45 for a silver chafing dish at a department store and paying $8 for the same piece, still in the box, at a yard sale.

10. *Estate Sales.* These sales have many of the same bargains, especially on antiques. Check the appliances carefully at these sales, though, as they tend to be well-worn older units. But if you know what you're looking for, you can find a diamond among the coal.

If you live near a university that has family housing, you can find some great deals at yard sales. At the end of each semester, especially in May, families sell off household goods they can't take with them. It's worth a peek!

Hit the *wealthy neighborhoods.* Most of these people have never been to a yard sale and don't know how to price many items. If anything, they tend to price their items lower than other yard sales because they don't know common prices—or they don't care. If an item is overpriced in these sales, you can make a comment about its price: "I usually find shoes like these for $2 at most garage sales." They will often give it to you for the lesser amount. It's a great way to get name brands. I've even found a few Neiman Marcus labels at these sales!

Two Kinds of Garage Sales

I took our oldest son, Daniel, to a lot of garage sales with me—it was not like taking the whole herd. Daniel understood the ground rules of advance garage-saling. He learned the fine art of bargain hunting too.

He knew not to bother me when I was concentrating on the search or bargaining with the seller. He spent his own money, and he spent it judiciously. He did his own bartering and was rarely turned down when he asked for a lower price. Daniel learned there are basically two kinds of garage sales.

The first kind is where *they want to get rid of stuff* and the second is where *they want to make money.* In the military we see a lot of the first kind of garage sale—they're our favorite. They have things priced to sell or even give away. Military families move a lot and only have a certain weight allowance. They have to trim the extra fat and get rid of the things they can't take with them.

I don't like the second kind of garage sale as much, and I don't stay long. Most of the stuff at these sales is overpriced (for the average garage sale), and the folks get defensive if you ask them to take less. There are too many good sales out there to waste time on an overpriced garage sale. The irony of these two sales is that the first kind makes more money than the second because of the volume they sell.

Stay on Budget

Garage sales need to be a part of your monthly budget. We usually budget $50 a week. This covers even the major garage sale purchases in the long run. The garage sale benefit greatly diminishes if you go over budget to save money. It defeats the purpose of shopping these sales. If you're one who is given to impulse buying, leave your checkbook and wallet carefully hidden in the car. While you're walking back to your vehicle to get your money, you'll have time to think about your purchase and decide whether you really need it or not.

Cheap Thrills!

Garage-saling is fun! I go out for two or three hours and come back with $300 worth of merchandise for which I paid $30. Let's see, that's a savings of $270 divided by three hours for a total of $90 per hour. There's a psychological boost involved in the savings game and in seeing how we can save in the little ways; plus, you also get to relieve yourself of the urge to shop!

Bonus Tip: How to Have a Successful Garage Sale

If you're thinking of having a garage sale, look over this list before you commit. It does require a lot of work and time for the profit you will make. Some families may decide that donating their items to the Salvation Army for a $500 tax-deductible receipt is a better option for them than the effort of a garage sale.

However, if you decide that you have enough time and energy, follow these steps to garage sale success!

Collect

Throughout the year, throw stuff in a big box marked "Garage Sale." You'll be amazed at how much you collect. This also helps relieve clutter—thereby relieving stress. Once you see how much junk you have, you'll know whether you have enough for a garage sale or whether you need to buddy-up your sale with a neighbor or friend.

Locate

Choose your location carefully. The ideal place to have a garage sale is in a neighborhood where these sales are common. If you live in an out-of-the-way or hard-to-find location, you probably won't have a successful sale.

Advertise

If you live in an area where garage sales are common, you won't need to advertise—a good sign will suffice. Otherwise, take out a small ad in the local newspaper. Buddy-up this expense with a neighbor having a sale on the same weekend. You'll bring her business and vice versa, because people want to hit two or three garage sales in one stop.

The Sign

Make an attractive sign that is legible and catches the eye. Use red or blue permanent marker on a white poster board and attach a balloon to the sign. Yours will stand out among *common* signs, and people are more likely to remember your address. Have a sign at high-traffic areas in your neighborhood, at each end of your street, and in front of your house—each with a balloon attached.

Legalities

If your city or housing area requires a garage sale permit in order to conduct a sale, apply for one. There is usually a very small fee, if any. Some cities require only a completed registration form.

Price It

Mark everything ahead of time and categorize your wares as much as possible. Make sure prices are clearly visible. If you're having the sale with a friend, use different colored price stickers to keep the money straight. DO NOT throw everything out in the yard without a price sticker.

If you don't price your wares, you require people to ask how much each and every item costs. They'll either get tired of asking and leave or they'll buy less.

Generally speaking, you should mark things from 10 to 50 percent of the original price of the item, depending on its condition. People expect to negotiate at a yard sale, so be prepared. Usually there's not as much negotiation at the beginning of the day as there is at the end.

If you don't feel comfortable selling the item at a lower price, then hold firm on your price and ask the person to come back later in the day if he still wants to negotiate. Just as you have to feel good about the price you *pay* at someone else's garage sale, you have to feel good about the price you *get* at yours.

Cash

Have enough change on hand to get started. You should have at the very minimum $20 in coins, $20 in one-dollar bills, and $20 in five-dollar bills. Get a good container for your money and don't leave it unattended. Every $50 or so, take the bigger bills into a safe place in the house.

Unless you know the person, don't ever take a check. My parents once sold a set of bunk beds for $200 and helped the folks load them on the truck; the check bounced!

Hold It

Don't hold items for people—unless they've already paid for them. The most sincere-looking person may not come back, and you've lost the potential to sell it. Experienced garage-salers do not expect you to hold the item—but they may ask anyway.

If the person has paid for a large item and wants to come back at a later time, put a small *Sold* sign on it and leave it in the yard. It will continue to attract customers to the great bargains you have at your sale.

Clean It

You'll get twice the money if your things are clean. Run heavy plastic toys through the dishwasher, put products in their original boxes, hang up as many clothes as you can. I've heard of some folks who shop other garage sales, clean and repair the stuff, and sell it for two to three times as much at their own sales. That's not a garage sale—that's a business!

Marketing

Just as grocery and department stores use marketing strategies to sell their goods, you too should think about your marketing plan. Big items, like furniture and bikes, draw people to the sale. Put these items nearest the road or in a visible place.

Categorize clothing by size and, again, hang up as many items as possible. Group similar items together. A cardboard box of children's plastic hangers is junk. On the other hand, plastic hangers tied neatly together with a ribbon will sell. Rearrange your merchandise on the tables throughout the day, as shoppers usually end up moving things around (jeopardizing your well-planned marketing strategies in the process)!

On more expensive items, you might want to cut a copy of the item from a sale circular or catalog—with the price noted. It reminds customers of the original price of goods and helps move the items off your lawn!

Expand

You might want to consider broadening your sale: If local ordinances permit, you may want to let your children set up a lemonade stand or sell cookies, doughnuts, hot chocolate, and coffee in conjunction with your garage sale. In the morning the hot drinks will go well; at midmorning and afternoon the cookies and cold drinks will sell. Suggested prices: 25 cents for two medium-size cookies and 25 cents for a small cup of coffee or lemonade; hot cocoa or soda pop goes for 50 cents each, and doughnuts for 50 cents each.

Be sure the child is responsible enough to handle money. It's a wonderful opportunity to teach children financial principles. Make sure they have a money box, adequate change, extra cups and napkins, and an ample supply of product on hand. Put two to three cookies in plastic lunch bags. Set up a trash can by the stand for empties. One of our regular stops in the Fort Drum garage sales was a perpetual weekly sale with hot chocolate and Samoan donuts—greasy, but oh, so good.

Whatever your motivation for saving money, you've seen from this chapter that it doesn't have to be painful; in fact, it can be downright *fun*. It's a good idea to read some of this information with your spouse, so you'll be in agreement when you start doing things that may appear to be out of the norm—like coming home with twelve bottles of shampoo (that you got for free!). You'll create a brighter future for your family by paying attention to the little expenses in life. Otherwise, these "little" things can add up to big debt that will only bring stress and strife to you and your spouse.

Remember: A penny saved is *more* than a penny earned!

You spend a billion here and a billion there. Sooner or later it adds up to real money.

—Senator Everett Dirkson

Quoted in *Tale of the Tardy Oxcart* by Chuck Swindoll

☆ 17 ☆

FISCAL FITNESS FOR KIDS

How to Get a $450,000 Education for Free!

Following in a Father's Footsteps

In the military lifestyle, heroes beget heroes. There are so many families that have a history of military service, and oftentimes military "brats" will grow into adults who have the desire to serve as well. Here is a short essay that was written by a young man in his application to the United States Naval Academy. This young man just happens to be my son.

Growing up in a military home, I saw very little of my father at times. As an officer, he was often gone taking care of his troops, performing his duties, and faithfully serving his country. I never truly understood why he did what he did until his dream became mine. When I walked on the campus of the Naval Academy this past summer during the Summer Leadership Seminar, I saw greatness. I saw an institution that taught men and women to be leaders, thinkers, and people of character. But most important, I saw my cadet commanders as men of high leadership with a servant's heart. They put our comfort ahead of their own, as my father did with his men.

All my life I have dreamed of one day leading hundreds or possibly thousands of men and women. I have sacrificed much in the process of becoming a competitive candidate for the academy. It was not Summer Leadership School that made me want to be in the military, it was my father's integrity and service. However, it was the midshipmen that I met that made me determined to attend Annapolis. It was my goal to become an officer; now it is my goal to become a warrior and a gentleman, in the finest sense of the word. To learn "Integrity first, service before self, and excellence in all we do." I desire to carry on the legacy of the service academies and to achieve a sense of accomplishment that no other college or career can offer.

Many nights I would stay up late, wondering if my father would come home or be deployed. I wondered if he was okay, or if it was his life that had been taken in one of the plane accidents that occurred in his various Air Force squadrons. However, these experiences did not make me turn against the military—it was quite the opposite. I began to see my father as someone very different from my friends' fathers. I saw him as a warrior and a true hero. So many times I read about or see the actions of evil men. These are men who would not hesitate to strike down those whom I have come to love and cherish. I knew there was only one thing standing between me and those men—it was my dad. It was men like my father and those with whom he served that rose to stand up to people who seek to destroy everything we hold dear. I knew that I was called to be one of those men who took a stand, and I know it is the service academies that will teach me to stand, and to stand strong and proud.

"The ultimate measure of a man is not where he stands in moments of comfort, but where he stands at times of challenge and controversy."—Martin Luther King Jr.

* * * * * * *

Sometimes we take it for granted that we walk among greatness. In our community we have those who serve in quiet heroic ways, while others are called to make a more visible impact. Philip recognized Bob's commitment to duty and wanted to do the same. Not every military member will be called upon to make such sacrifices, but the vast majority of them stand ready to do so. So be sure to hug your spouse and kids today—the heroes in your home.

Speaking of those heroes in your home, as exciting as my bucket list item of riding in a strike Eagle was, there's nothing more adventurous than raising my kids and teaching them financial responsibility. It may be a challenge, but one that is well worth it. For some parents, the thought of teaching kids about money can be as much fun as potty training triplets. But it doesn't *have* to be a chore! In fact, it can be downright fun, *almost* as fun as riding in the backseat of an F-15E, if you approach it positively. A trip to the zoo or going out to eat can be great opportunities to learn about budgeting. The local ice-cream shop can become a classroom for saving. A routine visit to the local Stuff-Mart can be a golden opportunity to learn about delayed gratification. A trip to the food pantry to donate groceries can become a satisfying lesson in sharing. Why, even going online can be a fun way to explore an allowance.

"But why teach kids about money?" you may ask. There are three primary areas where people have financial problems—you may even recognize them. They are:

- the accumulation of debt
- failure to adhere to a budget
- living a consumptive lifestyle

On the other hand, if your kids grow into adults who can manage money well, they could:

- have a better marriage (the #1 cause for divorce is finances)
- have less stress and be more responsible
- not become a financial burden to others (you!)

Allowance

Some parents believe it's easier to give their kids money than it is to hassle with an allowance. I can see their point—administrating an allowance is hard work at times. But if we use an allowance as a teaching tool, our kids will learn basic money management skills such as:

- *Budgets*—Money has limits and everyone needs to budget.
- *Discernment*—If a child has her own money, she will learn how to spend it wisely.
- *Saving*—You can save for items you really want if you spend less.
- *Sharing*—Kids quickly learn how wonderful it feels to share with someone else.
- *Values*—We tend to take better care of items we have to buy for ourselves.
- *Delayed Gratification*—It takes a long time to save money and little time to spend it.

The administration of an allowance is up to the parents and the family situation. Here are some quick-start suggestions:

- *Amount*—The amount depends on the child's age and the family budget. For example, when our kids were young, we paid fifty cents/age/pay period to be paid every week or every other week. For example, a six-year-old would get $3 weekly or $3 every *other* week, depending on the family's ability to pay. Our five children got paid every other week because of our family size.

- *Consistency*—Pay the same amount on the same day of the week/month—just as you count on your paycheck, they are counting on theirs.
- *Responsibility*—Establish each child's responsibilities. If they don't fulfill them, pay someone else to do the work. For example, I once paid our daughter Bethany fifty cents from our son Daniel's allowance to make his bed when he left without making it. He faced the penalty of losing part of his allowance and had the double whammy of watching his sister get his money! He never "forgot" again! This ties responsibility and allowance together.

Saving With Kids

- *Long-Term Savings Account Goals*—Establish an account where money will not be removed to cover short-term goals. This may be an account for a car, college, or other big items.
- *Family 401(k)*—Offer to match a quarter on the dollar for long-term savings.
- *Looney Tunes Accounts*—Many banks have fun kid accounts for younger children that can be opened with as little as $5, and they offer freebies as incentives to save.
- *Short-Term Goals*—Saving for a bike, doll, or video game also teaches delayed gratification.
- *Matching Funds*—Consider matching funds for the short-term goals if it will take more than a year for your child to save for the desired item.

Sharing With Kids

- Teach them to give to nonprofit organizations or your church or synagogue and let them observe your example.
- Gather groceries from your pantry and take them to a local food pantry.
- Collect outgrown clothing and donate them to a nonprofit thrift shop.
- Sponsor a child from www.worldhunger.org or a similar organization and post the child's photo on the refrigerator.
- Bake and share goodies with their teachers, your neighbors, or a single-parent family.

Fun Kid Budgets

- *Restaurant Fun*—The next time you go out to eat, put your kids on a budget for their meal. Make it realistic with a little wiggle room. Have them budget for the entrée, drink, and dessert (you'll get the tip), and whatever they don't spend (e.g., drinking water instead of a soft drink or forgoing a dessert), they get to keep, but they have to eat *something*, not just keep the money!

- *School Supplies*—Figure the amount you would spend on these supplies (per semester), and allow your child to spend from this budget and keep whatever is left over. It's amazing how few pencils they'll lose with this fun budget.

- *Amusement Parks and Zoos Too!*—When you make a big family outing to one of these places, set up a budget for your child that will include admission fees, food, drinks, and souvenirs. They will be surprised at how quickly the money goes—especially with the admission fees!

Money Matters on the Go

- *For More Fun*—Go to www.aza.com and research an annual family membership zoo pass in your part of the country. Get your family into the zoo with this pass and let your child keep the admission fee—they'll learn that saving has a long-term benefit.

- *Kids and Savings*—Help your child start a fifty-state quarters coin collection from the U.S. Mint at www.usmint.gov.

- *Kids' Allowances*—For more facts, go to www.kidsmoney.org/index.htm.

- *Family Budgets*—If you don't currently have a family budget, visit this free online tool to help you get started at the tool section at elliekay.com.

Kids' Jobs

As long as you are willing to supervise your child's work, see to their safety when dealing with the public, and set the boundaries that are appropriate for them, allowing kids to earn money can be a fun and prosperous venture.

Here are some great ideas to help your kids raise their very own cash cow while enjoying the benefits of earning, saving, and sharing. While some of these are not new ideas, we've gone through the trouble (mental agony of trial and error) to list some tips on how to do the job well and to inform the areas of particular jobs that need special attention.

Let your kids read the following job descriptions and see which sound fun to them. We've written them with a child reader and adult supervisor in mind. We've also started out with some tips for parents to ensure that your child's job is safe and to maximize the teaching benefit of the work.

Parental Tips *Before* **the Kids Take the Job**—It may be the kids' job, but parental involvement is essential for a variety of reasons. For one thing, if your child doesn't follow through with his work or if he does a lousy job, then it reflects poorly on your family, and even you as parents. Safety is also another biggie—especially in today's culture. Here's a checklist for parents to review with their child before they accept a job.

- **Safety**—Do you know the people your child is working for? Will your child ever be in the employer's home? If your child is working for neighbors and you prefer that your child work outside, then you need to give them strict instructions that they are not to go into a stranger's home—even to go to the bathroom or get a drink. If you aren't familiar with that neighbor, then your child can come home to take care of the essentials. Or you might want to have him buddy up with a friend to do some of these jobs.

  When it comes to jobs that require special equipment, be sure your child understands safety issues for lawn mowers, edgers—even pool cleaning equipment. If your child breaks someone's equipment due to improper use, then you (or your child) will need to pay for repairs. So be sure they know how to operate the tools necessary for the job.

  If your child ever feels uncomfortable on a job, give him the freedom to come to you immediately with his concerns without fear of a scolding. It's far better to be safe than sorry when it comes to your child's well-being and the well-being of the employer's property.

- **Age-Appropriate Work**—Do you remember an incident in your life when you were given a task that was far beyond your ability? How did it make you feel? Were you frustrated or confused? Did you want to give up? Now, I'm *not* talking about the daily grind of parenting children or going through the "joys" of adolescence— I'm talking about the requirement to do a job that was not a good fit with your basic skills and abilities.

  It's important that we try to match up a child with a job that is appropriate for their age. A seven-year-old shouldn't be allowed to get a job walking a seventy-five-pound St. Bernard—unless your seven-year-old is about five-foot-four and weighs 130 pounds!

There's a difference between childish irresponsibility and a child's ability. It's your role to help determine the difference in your child and their ability to adequately perform the task at hand.

A mismatched job will only lead to frustration and a bad feeling about work. On the other hand, there are some jobs that we don't think our kids can do and they surprise us with their efficiency! The key is to supervise any of your child's work in which you're not sure of the age appropriateness of the job. Once the child shows you they can do it, then let them excel!

- **On-the-Job Training**—All the areas we've listed below come with job descriptions and the details on how to do the job well. But there's no substitute for experience. Before your child ventures out on a job for pay, have them practice at home. In exchange for the training you give them on how to do the job well, you will get the free fringe benefits of a clean car, a weed-free flower bed, a freshly mowed lawn, sparkling windows, free baby-sitting, a clean garage—you get the idea!

- **Follow-Through**—Don't allow your child to do any job that you are not committed to helping them follow through. Just as I ended up throwing the boys' paper route on occasion (with the help of two small assistants), you will need to be prepared to baby-sit or find a satisfactory substitute if your child gets sick at the last minute.

  If you have to finish a job due to your child's lack of responsibility or inappropriate behavior, then your child will pay you the FULL amount he receives for the job—even if he did half the work but didn't complete it. For example, when I had to throw Philip's paper route due to an after-school detention, he had to pay me twice the amount of a normal substitution. It's one of those "tough love" lessons that will be priceless in the long run (even if it's painful in the here and now).

- **Quality Work**—One boundary you might want to establish before your child starts to work is the standard required for the job. Quality work and excellence should be the standard for our work as parents, and it's a good standard for our kids' work too!

  Part of this work quality will be demonstrated in the on-the-job training sessions, while another large part of it will only develop as they work for other people.

  It's important to praise your children when they do a good job. It's also wise to stress how one good job leads to another referral, which leads to more work, which will culminate in a bottom line of more profits.

Fiscal Report Card

Where are you, as a parent, when it comes to teaching your child financial literacy at the right age? Here's a Fiscal Report Card that will help you look at what they need to know and when.

Youngsters

AGES TWO TO FOUR

- Picks up toys cheerfully
- Obeys parents most of the time
- Is on a schedule for sleep, play, and work (or school)

AGES FOUR TO SIX

- Makes bed in a basic way (not necessarily neat)
- Picks up room regularly
- Brings clothes to hamper
- Knows how to set and clear the table
- Hangs up clothes and puts them in drawers
- Knows how to take out the trash
- Gives away clothing or toys or money to those in need
- Does work without grumbling
- Does not throw "Wally-world" tantrums

Middlers

AGES SEVEN TO TEN

- Is a master bed maker
- Knows how to sort laundry into whites, colors, and darks
- Can fold laundry and put it in everyone's room
- Is given an allowance
- Has a savings account at home and at a bank
- Regularly tithes from their earnings
- Can load and clear the dishwasher
- Knows how to vacuum and dust
- Manages a fun kid budget (restaurant, zoo, amusement park, etc.)

AGES ELEVEN TO TWELVE

- Has advanced to "potty training" (they know how to clean a bathroom)

- Begins to do additional "jobs" for hire within the home and occasionally for friends or family
- Has a savings account with at least $200 to $250 in it
- Manages more advanced budgets such as a semester-long school supply budget
- Is learning the meaning of delayed gratification
- Can save up for half of a larger ticket item they want (bike, skates, video game, etc.)
- Can tell you how many hours it takes to work or save for goods and services
- Knows how to read a savings account statement
- Is *regularly* contributing to a community organization either through volunteer hours or donating goods (clothing, toys, money)

Teens_____

AGES THIRTEEN TO FIFTEEN

- Is regularly sponsoring a third-world child or mission
- Can manage and balance their own checkbook, with supervision
- Has enough in savings to take out $200 to $300 to start a mutual fund
- Is able to do outside jobs for hire among approved "employers" in the neighborhood and regular summer jobs (appropriate to age and ability)
- Realizes they will continue to do "twice the work" if they do not work with a good attitude
- Regularly pays for half of larger-ticket items
- Regularly pays for *non-family* outings (movies, theme parks, virtual game centers, restaurants, etc.)
- Is saving for a vehicle
- Is aware of the fact their grades in high school will impact their ability to get into college and earn scholarships for college
- Understands their primary job in school is to work hard and to get the best grades they are capable of making

AGES SIXTEEN TO EIGHTEEN

- Has opened a mutual fund and is contributing monthly to the fund
- Can tell you how much money they will earn in their mutual fund by the time they are forty-five, fifty-five, and sixty-five if they continue to contribute the minimal amount they are now
- Can balance a checkbook without supervision

- Has a debit card and can use it responsibly (follow-up supervision required)
- Has a prepaid credit card in their pocket as training for the temptation of plastic (close supervision required and minimal prepaid limits on the card come from the child's savings account or earnings—parents do not prepay the card)
- Can manage and balance a clothing budget and personal financial budget
- Regularly goes over their personal financial budget with parents
- Regularly works inside and outside the home during breaks from school
- Keeps a neat room and car
- Has paid for one-third to one-half the cost of their car
- Pays insurance if they have a ticket or accident (parents can pay if they keep their driving record spotless)
- Maintains a good GPA (or what they are capable of)
- Has a regular volunteer position (hospital, coaching, church involvement, etc.)
- Has a good grasp on delayed gratification
- Can use social media to learn ways to save money

The College Crunch

So far, all the Kay kids are going to graduate from college with at least a bachelor's degree, and a few are going on toward their master's as well, and we have no student loan debt. There are a number of ways they are doing this, but basically we tell them: Our love for you is unconditional, but our money is conditional. This means that they know they will earn a portion of their college experience themselves by applying for college scholarships, participating in work/study programs, and working in the summer; one child even took a year off between her sophomore and junior years and worked full time, then went back and graduated from Columbia University with honors.

It also means that they will not go to the best college they can get into. They go to the best college they can get into *that we can afford*. For example, one son got a $60,000 scholarship from Syracuse University and an $80,000 scholarship from Texas Christian University. He also got a $20,000/year scholarship to the University of Texas/Arlington. He chose UTA because he could graduate debt-free, whereas the other schools would still mean $50,000+ in student loan debt, even with the scholarships. His magna cum laude graduate status has garnered him gainful employment as a writer in Texas, and the fact that he has no student loan, consumer loan, or major debt takes a lot of pressure off of his marriage.

So here's the Kay College Philosophy summarized:

1. **Make the Right Choice**—Choose a school not because it's the best, but because it's the best value. Change the conversation from "I'll go to the best college that I can get into" to "I will go to the school where I can get the best education possible for the least amount of student loan debt."

2. **Save Big on Books by Renting**—The average student pays more than $600 for course materials[5]—the largest expense after tuition and room and board. By renting textbooks through Follett's Rent-A-Text program, students can cut costs by 50 percent or more. CafeScribe's digital textbooks are another great way to save, and both options are available to purchase in-store and online through efollett.com.

3. **Make Scholarships a Part-Time Job**—Millions of dollars of scholarship money go unclaimed every year. This is free money that parents or prospective students who are willing to do some detective work may find more quickly than they think. We ask our kids to invest five hours a week filling out college scholarships at www.collegeboard.com or www.salliemae.com. This year's high school graduate ended up getting over one million dollars in scholarship offers!

4. **Create a Budget, and Stick to It**—As a parent of a college student, your love for your student is unconditional, but your money is conditional. To ensure students are making the most of their money, set a budget for spending, and manage it by loading funds on a campus card to help track spending. Then determine which on-campus retailers take college dollars.

For a more detailed outline of debt-free college, email assistant@elliekay.com and request the "College Crunch" file. We'll send you a free twenty-page-plus document that will go into further depth on the topic.

5. Student Watch, NACS.org

Service Academies and Military-Funded Education

I mentioned earlier that our recent high school graduate garnered one million dollars in scholarship offers; two of those offers were from federal service academies. These are highly competitive and look at the whole person. So it's not enough to be a brainiac (super smart), they are also looking for students who are exceptional in the areas of athletics, community involvement, and leadership. In return for this amazing education valued at $450,000, your student will be required to serve in the military for their commitment period. The commitment is a minimum of five years of service and can be longer, depending on a number of factors with regard to additional training after graduation. A lot of the following recommendations will also work if your child is trying to get an ROTC scholarship, as the emphasis on the whole person is just as important and so are the academics. If you have a "hero at home" who wants to go to a service academy, there are several things to keep in mind.

One of the first places to visit is your service academy's admissions site:

USAFA—The United States Air Force Academy: www.academy admissions.com

USNA—The United States Naval Academy: www.usna.edu/ad missions

USMA—The United States Military Academy: http://admissions .usma.edu

USMMA (Merchant Marine): www.usmma.edu/admissions

Coast Guard Academy: www.cga.edu (does not require a congressional nomination)

From Prospect to Appointee

- **Prospect:** A student who has filled out the initial response form showing interest. This means they are essentially on an admissions mailing list. You can fill this out as early as middle school by going to the academy's website.
- **Applicant:** The individual has filled out a pre-candidate questionnaire and provided initial info on PSAT/SAT/ACT scores, grades, and extra-curricular activities. This is usually done NO LATER than the spring of their junior year. This is also the time to contact your congressman and senator with regard to a nomination. In addition, if the student's parent is qualified for a presidential nomination (see nominations and appointments below), the student can contact the academy directly to pursue this nomination as well.

- **Candidate:** To move from applicant to candidate indicates that you have cleared your first competitive hurdle. This step is decided by the academy's admissions staff in the early summer of a student's senior year. Not all students will get to this point, but this is when they will be interviewed by the Academy Liaison Officer (or the equivalent). It is from this list that appointments will be offered as early as the fall. For example, one of our sons was offered an USNA appointment by October.

- **Appointee:** This means the candidate has been offered an appointment into the academy. They can choose to accept it or turn it down, but it means they have not only received an official nomination, but they have also been approved by the Academy's admissions board and offered an actual appointment.

Basic Requirements

It's important to check the specific military academy website for updated information on your desired academy, but in general, here are the basics you will need before you even consider applying:

- United States citizenship
- unmarried with no dependents
- good moral character
- at least seventeen years of age, but not past twenty-third birthday by July 1 of the year entering

Recommendations

Because it is so incredibly competitive to gain entry into a service academy, the following high school courses will help make the applicant more competitive:

- four years of English
- four years of college-prep math
- four years of lab science
- three years of social studies
- two years of a foreign language
- one year of computer study

Character

One of the academies defines character as "One's moral compass, the sum of those qualities of moral excellence which compel a person to do the right thing despite pressure or temptations to the contrary" (USAFA). They also define leadership as "the process of influencing people and being responsible for the care of followers while accomplishing a common mission." These academies are looking for future leaders with the highest moral character possible.

Diversity

Academies are looking for people from a wide variety of life experiences, and the word *diversity* at these institutions no longer applies exclusively to race or cultural background. USAFA defines diversity as: "a composite of individual characteristics that includes personal life experiences (including having overcome adversity by personal efforts), geographic background (e.g., region, rural, suburban, urban), socioeconomic background, cultural knowledge, educational background (including academic excellence, and whether an individual would be a first-generation college student), work background (including prior enlisted service), language abilities (with particular emphasis on languages of strategic importance to the Air Force), physical abilities (including athletic prowess), philosophical/spiritual perspectives, age, race, ethnicity, and gender."

Nominations and Appointments

Admission to one of the service academies requires both a nomination from one of your nominating authorities and an appointment from the academy the child wishes to attend. I would strongly suggest that the child also contact your congressman and senators to request a nomination and contact the academies to express their interest. There are also vice-presidential and presidential nominations available. If the student is the child of a retired military member or an active duty member currently serving with at least eight years of service, they should also contact the academy directly to apply for a presidential nomination. Furthermore, a child would also qualify for the presidential process if their parent is currently in the Reserves serving as a member of a Reserve component and credited with at least eight full years of service (a minimum of 2,880 points). Both of our sons competed to receive these nominations. They are limited in number and highly competitive, but well worth the effort.

To apply for a nomination through a congressional office, you will be required to completely fill out an application packet (see your representative's website). To be eligible for appointment, you must be an American citizen, and at least seventeen years old and not yet twenty-three years old on July 1 of the year you enter an academy. Also, you must have no legal obligation to support children or other dependents.

All applications are usually due in October. Then the offices will conduct interviews during the months of November and December. The nominations will be announced in January.

The Liaison Officer

Each military academy will assign an officer to assist you in the process of applying. Each academy has a different title for their respective liaisons:

USNA: Blue and Gold Officer
USAFA: Admissions Liaison Officer (ALO)
USMA: Military Academy Liaison Officers (MALO)
Merchant Marine Academy: Admissions Field Representatives
Coast Guard Academy: Military Affairs Liaison Officer—(Please note this academy does not require a congressional nomination.)

In addition to having to meet certain physical requirements, you will also have to be interviewed by this intermediary. I would encourage you to attend service academy nights that are hosted in your community, where you can speak with these officers. Our son's Blue and Gold representative, LTC Jerry Geil, USMC (Ret), was an outstanding inspiration as he interviewed Philip for his candidate requirement. Make good use of your liaison. One will be assigned to you and should contact you once you have applied.

Summer Leadership Seminar—For High School Juniors

In the summer between a student's junior and senior year, each institution hosts an excellent program that provides an up-close-and-personal view of the academy. These seminars are where your hero at home can compete to attend that will give them an idea of what life is like at that institution, and it will also look great on a résumé. These applications are usually available in January at the academy's website and should be turned in as early as possible. The applications are so involved that some have said they are an excellent precursor to the final academy application. Also, you will be in the system, and a lot of this information will transfer over into that directory. Two of our sons attended two different academy summer seminars, and it actually changed the mind of one of our sons as to where he would attend. So feel free to look at more than one option. You will have to pay transportation to/from the academy as well as a camp fee ($300 to $400).

The Résumé

Once in high school, the résumé fodder begins. Keep in mind that these schools are looking for the "whole person" approach, and the résumé will need to show accomplishments in academics, athletics, community involvement, and leadership. One winning résumé garnered one million dollars in college scholarships from USNA ($450,000), USAFA ($450,000), and UCLA ROTC ($180,000).

The Essay

It is never too early to begin to think about what you would like to write in your admissions application essay. These are very important and should be well thought out before submitting. Be sure to have your liaison officer review it before you submit it, or ask an academy graduate to help. It also wouldn't hurt to have a faculty member from your school review it as well. More eyes on the project can mean a broader perspective, but it still needs to be your own voice, so you will have the final word on the essay. Go to the beginning of this chapter to see the essay that garnered Philip's nomination to both USNA and USMA.

ROTC

ROTC can be a legitimate option even if you are still in high school, already in college, or serving as an enlisted service member. If you want to become a military officer, researching an ROTC scholarship is a good option. As I said earlier, a lot of the academic and "whole person" elements that are involved in getting into a military academy are the same qualities that are valued in an ROTC scholarship. They want to see motivated young people who are athletic, academically inclined, with leadership skills and involvement in their community. These are also offered based on a student's merit and grades, not financial need.

Most ROTC scholarships consist of two-, three-, or four-year scholarship options based on the time remaining to complete your degree. There are full tuition scholarships available or an option for room and board in place of tuition, if you should qualify. Plus, there are additional allowances for books and fees as well. Another great benefit of most ROTC scholarships is that they also provide monthly living allowances for each school year. You can earn certain amounts depending on your level in the ROTC curriculum. For example, at press time, a first-year cadet would get $300 per month and a fourth-year cadet could get $500 per month.

There are opportunities for active duty or the Reserve component when you become a military officer through ROTC.

Enlisted Signing Bonuses and Education Money

Every child is different, and it may be that your child doesn't want to go to college right away but does desire to experience the real world right away. If they enlist in military service, there are various kinds of education benefits and signing bonuses that might be available to them, including the GI bill, found at www.gibill.va.gov. But all are not created equal. You may get $50,000 for education in the Navy and $30,000 in the Air Force. It would be wise for the enlistee to go to a recruiter with a former military member who understands the process so there aren't any surprises after he signs on the dotted line. Or, he can review the various kinds of education programs each branch of the service offers at www.military.com or www.militaryonesource.com.

Besides money to attend college, all branches also offer education to enlistees so that they can work on their associate's (or bachelor's) degree while they are serving out their enlistment. They can be on a ship or in port and still have a lot of educational options. Plus, a lot of the mandatory courses they take as part of their specialized service may count as college credits once they are ready to transfer them to a college or university. This makes enlisting in the military a very good way to get an education while serving your country at the same time.

☆ *Hidden Hero Profile* ☆

Keri Powers Pye*

* Keri is a part of what is fondly called the 2 Percent Club. When a cadet or midshipman enters their respective military academy and has a girlfriend or boyfriend, only 2 percent will have that same significant other upon graduation. Keri not only survived the club, she led it by organizing different events and support groups for girlfriends of midshipmen.

Name: Keri Powers Pye

Spouse's Name: 2nd LT Luke Pye

Branch of Service: United States Marine Corps

Kids: None for quite a while!

Number of Moves: One, so far

Years in Service: Four years at the United States Naval Academy and two-plus months in USMC

Work/Employer: Luke is currently working for the Marine Corps Recruiting Command at Headquarters Marine Corps. I am finishing the last year of my master's program in clinical counseling and interning full time at two free counseling clinics. I also teach Zumba classes.

Hobbies: Luke loves working out, hiking, kayaking, and watching the Atlanta Braves. I love working out, teaching Zumba, baking, making homemade ice cream, and traveling.

Do you have any military family stories you can share?

The weekend after Plebe Parent Weekend at USNA, Luke wanted to be a proper midshipman and take me out on a sailboat. Though we had been dating for over a year at the time, Luke still looked for any chance he could find to impress me. He was manning the sailboat by himself, and I could tell he was in a little over his head, but I remained very impressed. It took quite a while to actually get out on the water, and just as we reached the open seas, Luke realized he had to be back on deck in ten minutes for a "chow call." He frantically brought the sailboat back to the dock but didn't have time to properly store it, so he asked me to sit in the sailboat for "about fifteen minutes" while he ran back on deck for his chow call. He promised he would be back soon. So there I sat on a sailboat that was not quite close enough to the dock, and sunset was drawing near . . . and so were the rain clouds. The wind picked up at about the same speed as my seasickness, and I began looking around the boat for a makeshift umbrella. After half an hour, several strange looks from passersby, and some light drizzle, Luke came running back to the boat in his summer whites. He looked slightly mortified when he saw the pale shade of green my face had turned. Because the boat was too far from the dock for my short legs to reach, Luke had to carry me off of the boat before he properly stored the craft. He spent the rest of the night apologizing, but I ultimately decided to marry him anyway!

Least Favorite Aspect of Military Life:

Because I am a planner, the lack of uncertainty and frequent changes in military life are not exactly my favorite aspect. We have changed the dates of at least three vacations or visits with family and almost had to change our wedding date after last-minute changes in orders. But I can't complain too much; the last-minute changes in Luke's most recent orders led to an extra week of leave!

Favorite Aspect of Military Life:

I have loved developing a new family within the military. Because of Luke's time at the United States Naval Academy, we have friends all over the country and compassionate brothers and sisters who understand our life. While I dread leaving behind the friends we've made at Luke's current duty station, I look forward to expanding our family with every move ahead.

Favorite quote:

"Freedom prospers when religion is vibrant and the rule of law under God is acknowledged." Former President Ronald Reagan

☆ 18 ☆

HIDDEN HERO PORTRAIT—
WENDY WENDLER

A Scuba-Diving Sheriff Conquers Spain

Once a cop, always a cop.

Granted, she wasn't your typical cop. I mean, when a crook looks down a gun barrel, he doesn't expect to see violet eyes with thick black lashes at the other end. When you add lovely raven hair to the mix, the bad guy would probably expect Elizabeth Taylor with a glass of champagne—not James Bond with a .45 magnum.

Deputy Sheriff Wendy Wendler sounds like the lead in a Peter Pan remake, but that's her real name, and don't let the doll-like eyes fool you—she's no pushover. Not everyone who meets her believes that, but she can be convincing. Very convincing. Some guys find that out the hard way.

Wendy married Tom, who left his job as a city policeman to become an Air Force Airman, and they moved to Torrejon Air Base in Spain, where he had a unique assignment in downtown Madrid. It was expensive to live downtown, but Wendy said, "I learned to invent tasty meals on a small budget and I became a great baker." This proved to be a skill that served her well later in life when she made cakes as a part-time job.

☆ *Profile* ☆

Name: Wendy Wendler

Spouse's Name: MSGT Tom Wendler

Branch of Service: USAF

Kids: Austin and Taylor (two natural children). I am also "Mimi" to ten "adopted" grandsons and two granddaughters.

Number of Moves: sixteen

Years in Service: twenty-four

Work: Entrepreneur, Wonderworks Media, at www.wendywendler.com, Civil Service.

Awards: After working only two months at the 58th Maintenance Operations Squadron, I was selected Civilian of the Year for the squadron, group, and 58th Special Operations Wing. Volunteer Excellence Award—lifetime achievement for volunteer hours exceeding 2,000. Best airman's attic in the Air Force as recognized by Assistant AF Chief of Staff's spouse. Diamond Superior Award—Kirtland First Sergeant's Council.

Hobbies: scrapbooking, stamping, baking, cooking, scuba diving, quilting, and the performing arts

Least Favorite Aspect of Military Life:
not having a home to call my own for more than a few years and moving away from friends

Favorite Aspect of Military Life:
the ability to meet new people and touch their lives for the better, and seeing all the world God has created by moving to and visiting different places

Describe your military experience before 9/11 and after:
Our service in the military has always been full of pride and integrity. We do not view the military as a paycheck but a commitment to our country to protect and defend. After 9/11, those feelings became all the more real in our lives. We do as duty calls, and one thing we know as a family: "Mission first, family always." We have pulled together to support our troops fighting on the front lines, and to not forget the ones left behind. As a veteran spouse of twenty years, I feel it is my duty to support the young spouses coming into this way of life. Military life is not for the faint of heart. I am so proud of my husband and all of his accomplishments. He truly is my HERO.

But there were a few more surprises to be had in Spain. Their car was stolen within the first month. "Welcome to Europe," she thought. It was recovered two days later—sans the radio and tires.

Her main concern was "How are we going to see all of Europe on an airman's salary? I wanted to see every nook and cranny of France, Spain, Italy, England, and Germany that we could cram into our two-year tour." Her ability to stretch a peseta came into play in the form of two backpacks, a Eurail pass, and the adventuresome spirit of a cop. They took fifteen days to see Frankfurt and Munich, Germany; Innsbruck, Austria; Florence, Italy; Switzerland; Paris; the Riviera; and Costa Brava. It's been said, "If you leave an overseas tour without being in the hole on leave—you're doing something wrong." Tom and Wendy were determined "not to do anything wrong" on that tour.

They rode the rails to castles, cathedrals, and craftsmen. They ate Parisian pastries, Italian escargot, and German chocolate. They saw gypsies and royal gems, museums and monks, and hostels and horses. It was a tour that almost went off without a proverbial hitch.

At one point during the tour, Tom's dad and stepmom joined them in Italy and were anxious to see some of the country. The two couples were in the train station in Rome, when a pair of professional crooks approached them. One man asked directions of the men, and he slowly drew them away from Wendy, who was propped up against a brick wall. Behind her back was the video camera that she was holding in place with her body. Distracted by the action in front of her, she moved slightly, but her professional training made her aware that a hand was v-e-r-y slowly reaching in for the camera behind her back.

There was a quick motion as the thief tried to snatch the prize and quickly run away with his booty. But he wasn't prepared for something that happened more swiftly than his ability to escape. Wendy's instincts took over as she reached out, grabbed the thief by the arm, pinned him up against the wall, and began to twist his arm with her strong hand. His eyes bulged in terror under her startlingly strong grip, as he couldn't believe a woman had caught him in this way. He dropped the camera in the pain of her power hold. She bent down to retrieve it, lest the other thief snatch it away. As she did, she loosened her grip long enough for the criminal to break free and run. And he ran and he ran and he ran . . .

Wendy looked up to see other train passengers with their jaws dropped open as they witnessed "Jane Bond" in action. She smiled, looked at the Spaniards in the crowd, and said in fluent Spanish, "Si eres policia una vez, siempre seras un policia." Which means, "Once a cop, always a cop."

* * * * * * *

Wendy is an amazing individual. She's profiled in this section on balanced budgets because she's learned to be the master of a balanced budget on an enlisted salary in an expensive world. She's as tough on where her money goes as she was on that video camera thief. She's also learned to be resourceful by bringing money into her home using her varied talents.

But she also has a lot of courage, which is evidenced in her hobbies: She was a semi-pro softball player for four years, and she is an avid scuba diver. She conquered her claustrophobia by going into a cavern on one memorable dive. She said she felt water in her mouth, and the next time she breathed, it was all water! She was thirty-two feet down, and all she could think about was that she wouldn't see her little girls again. She remembers, "It scared me, and I wondered how Tom would raise my children without me. Then I heard the voice of my instructor in my head. I fell back on my training by throwing my mouthpiece to the bottom of the cavern and replacing it with my back-up regulator. I purged the valve and began to breathe.

"When I swam out of the cave and surfaced, I was truly shaken with my brush with death—particularly when my girls came running up to me. Boy, was I glad to be back! But I dived again, and I continue to enjoy the beauty and adventure of the exciting sport."

That about sums up Wendy's philosophy of life—when experiencing some of the challenges she's been through, she just dives into life again and keeps trying until it works out beautifully. She sent her husband into harm's way in Somalia for six months when her first child was five months old. While he was gone to Cuba, she was home with a toddler and a baby, and she experienced an emergency situation when a degenerative disc disease rendered her bedridden for two weeks.

Wendy is not only cautious, tough, and savvy, she's also very much in touch with her feminine side. Her entrepreneurial spirit helps her family financially as she dives into areas that interest her—but they also have a dual function in that they usually help others as well. She has a business called Wonderworks Media at www.wendywendler.com, in which she shares her expertise in interior design, and it houses her herb business, as well. Her tips have been published in national books as she creatively shows families how to do more with less.

Wendy's most recent endeavor is that of a doula. The word *doula* comes from the Greek word for the most important female slave or servant in an ancient Greek household: the woman who probably helped the lady of the house through her childbearing. The word has come to refer to "a woman experienced in childbirth, who provides continuous physical, emotional, and informational support to the mother before, during, and just after childbirth" (Klaus, Kennell, and Klaus, *Mothering the Mother*). The acceptance of doulas in maternity care is growing rapidly with the recognition of their important contribution to the well-being of mothers and infants.

Wendy has not been hindered by the military lifestyle, as is evident in her choices in life. She faces life as a marathon race, not a 100-yard dash. In doing so, she takes the circumstances she's been dealt, cuts the dead weight, and presses forward with her goals. Along the way, she touches the lives of everyone she meets. Of course, if you're a camera thief, you probably wouldn't want to meet up with Wendy. She's definitely the kind of homeland hero you would want on *your* side in a fight.

★ ★ ★ ★ ★ ★ ★

Wendy is a lot like many of you reading this profile, in that she would never call herself a hero for rising to the financial and geographical challenges of the military lifestyle. But that is the point exactly: You are a hero because of the sacrifices you so willingly make without a thought for your own desires or comfort. Which of us would *choose* to move, as Wendy has? You'll notice a recurring theme in these profiles, in that the most difficult part of military life is leaving friends when you move. But Wendy and many of the people reading this page do it on a regular basis. It's not easy, but you keep going anyway.

There's the phrase that is repeated when a family member is presented with a flag upon the death of a loved one: "On behalf of a grateful nation, we thank you." About 25 percent of our nation remembers this. During war, or events like 9/11, that same nation rises boldly in its support of our military and their families. But it is by and large the military families—not only the spouses, but the kids, moms, dads, sisters, and brothers, who must keep this gratitude alive and consistent for the military member. You lead the way in this fight by living out a life of sacrifice and support for your family and spouse, and in doing so, you serve a grateful nation.

★ ★ ★ ★ ★ ★ ★

*Take your corner of the world and enjoy each day you are given;
you never know what your next adventure might be.*

—Wendy Wendler

Celebrating
Memories

☆ 19 ☆

OPERATION HEARTS APART

Creative Coping During Military Separations

W*hen the Heroes at Home Tour went to Europe, we made it a habit to meet with the Commanding General or the Wing Commander at the beginning of the tour on that particular base or post. We asked this officer in charge one question: What would you say is the greatest challenge your military members and their families face while in Europe? Without fail, they would answer two things: their financial challenge while living abroad, and the operations tempo that keeps families apart. One of these spouses, Joann Patrick, wrote her feelings about these separations:*

"Big Girls Don't Cry" by Joann Patrick

"Big girls don't cry" are the exact words my husband used the day he deployed. *But they do,* I thought, as I choked back the tears. It was our first deployment. As amazing as it sounds, in thirteen years of marriage, we had never had to face the big "D." There were lots of separations, of course: too-many-to-count TDYs and the dreaded yearlong remote to Korea. So I wasn't entirely unprepared for this four-month separation. In fact, I felt it would make me stronger.

With my hubby gone, I had no choice but to be strong and self-reliant. Throw anything my way and I would handle it with my big-girl britches on. Big hairy spiders . . . no problem! That's what combat boots are for. Stopped-up toilet . . . no big deal! That's what that red plungy thingy is for. I was, after all, Superwoman!

Yet a week before my hubby left, I felt them—those unmistakable feelings of panic and dread. They overwhelmed me, but I couldn't tell him that. I wouldn't. He already had too much on his mind. So with a heavy heart, I sent the man I loved more than anything in this world off to war. He left knowing that everything at home would be OK.

And I didn't cry, at least not in front of him. I waited until I drove away, until I could no longer see his tan-clad frame waving at me in my rearview mirror. Then this big girl cried herself a river.

* * * * * * *

Whether you are separated from your spouse due to travel, work situations, or military duties, it's important to stay connected while you're apart. Separation is such a regular part of the military family's lifestyle, it is easy to get buried under the busyness and forget to take purposeful steps toward staying connected. There's a tendency to get so caught up in the woes of single parenting and endless "messes" that we forget the responsibility we have to ourself, our spouse, and our kids to stay in touch.

Another problem that arises when families are geographically split is that household budgets may get sidetracked, and the family gets into serious financial trouble in the process. Whether the separation is twelve days or twelve months, here are some practical and inexpensive ways to keep the home fires burning—even if it's from five thousand miles away.

Before They Go

There are some meaningful things you can do before your spouse leaves that will help you stay connected throughout the departure. Here are a few ideas to get your creative juices flowing:

Notes-to-Go

Depending upon how long they're gone, send a bundle of notes with them. If they're gone for three months, make them weekly notes with a special memory, a word of encouragement, or a funny cartoon. If allowed, you'll also be making Skype calls, sending them emails, texts, and snail-mail letters, but this bundle will give your spouse a sense of taking a bit of you (and the kids) with him.

Watch Out for Fireworks

Part of the classic pre-TDY syndrome is that each person begins to emotionally separate him/herself for what lies ahead. Expect the tensions to be high and be on guard for potential fireworks over the littlest things. Simply being aware of these emotions and potential disagreements can go a long way toward diffusing the situation.

Letters/Gifts/Flowers With Friends

One thing the service member can do before his/her departure is to leave letters and gifts with friends, to be distributed each week to his or her spouse. Or they can arrange to have flowers delivered on special dates. This bit of forethought means the world to the one(s) left behind. Make sure to see the Wish List at the end of this chapter for some great ideas.

Family Photos

This is a good idea no matter how long or short the TDY or deployment. Get a good family photo and put it in a sturdy frame with a stand of its own. I even take one of these photos with me when I travel for business and speaking engagements. Have your spouse place the photo in the hotel room or barracks as a reminder of two things: (1) his actions today will affect his family tomorrow, and (2) there's someone counting on him at home.

Recording Memories

Jody Dale, Army chaplain wife, says, "About a week before Garry went to Somalia, we gathered as a family in the kids' bedrooms, and Garry read stories to them while I ran the video camera. I captured their faces, the pre-bedtime prayers, and even some of the songs they sang with their daddy. We watched the video while he was gone and still do, occasionally, even to this day. Each time we watch, it makes us thankful he came home."

Recording Stories

If you have young children, consider making an audio or digital recording of the deployed parent reading their favorite stories. Army Chaplain Egert recorded stories and family devotions before he left so his children could hear him read nightly. Even young babies will benefit from hearing that parent's voice, and upon their return will adapt more easily because they are familiar with that voice. But be prepared to explain that Mommy or Daddy cannot hear them if they talk to the player!

Cards Home

There seems to be a gazillion and one things the service member has to do before he or she deploys, and buying cards to send back home can easily get overlooked. Buy some stationery, some cards for kids, or even postcards, and self-address them, including postage (if they'll be near a U.S. military base with a post office). Emails and texts are great, but kids love regular mail. Be sure to have an ample supply of cards for each individual child, because the kids will love receiving this mail.

Investment

Consider investing in a Webcam for your computer as well as one for your spouse so that you can see each other online via Skype or even on your smartphone. You might even consider an investment in a digital camera that will allow you to send both stills and moving footage to your spouse (or vice versa if you want to let them take the camera over and if it's allowed by the regulation in their deployed area). I have a FLIP phone that is simple to use for video and easily downloaded into my computer. You might even want to consider investing in a phone plan that allows for email or instant messaging so your spouse will not be dependent on getting to a computer and a line in order to "talk" to you. Once again, you will have to verify that the deployed installation commander allows such devices.

Phone Cards

Buy a renewable, prepaid calling card for your spouse; they have special ones for overseas, and this could greatly reduce long-distance calling expenses.

Follow the List

There is a pre-deployment briefing that your spouse is required to attend. They will bring home documents, such as power-of-attorney and notification paper work. Be sure you take the time to go over these with your spouse and make plans accordingly. You will find a more detailed list in the next chapter.

While They Are Gone

Email, Texts, Cards, Facebook, Tweets, and Letters

Even remote military assignments very often have access to email. This is an excellent way to tell your loved one about your day and to ask questions and advice. Be sure you reread your emails or texts before you send them, especially if you're venting or feeling sad when you write. Be very careful about what you post on your Facebook wall as well or what you may tweet. You may want to wait until the next day to send your email, because this kind of correspondence tends to be one-dimensional and will often communicate a tone or message that you will regret once you are in a better frame of mind. Remember to be honest and yet keep your notes as positive as possible. Proverbs 25:25 says, "Like cold water to a weary soul, so is good news from a distant land." Do jabber on about the day, the routine, what you did—these things seem meaningless to you but are part of the fiber of life that your mate is likely missing and looking forward to upon his return.

Routines

It's important to stick with your normal routine as much as possible, especially if you have children. When your spouse is away, there's a tendency to order pizza every night, let the house go, and allow the children to break bedtime curfews. But consistency will keep you on track and give your children the stability that can only come with a regular schedule.

Top Twelve Don'ts for Deployment

I asked a database of military families for their input in much of this book, which provides a diversity of interests and ideas. Quite a few of them came up with important "don'ts."

1. *Don't have a negative attitude;* it will hurt you, your kids, and everyone who is unfortunate enough to be around you!

2. *Don't spend time alone with people of the opposite sex;* establish boundaries during this particularly vulnerable time.

3. *Don't listen to your favorite love songs* or romantic movies if it makes you nostalgic for your mate. Instead, watch a comedy with a friend.

4. *Don't buy big-ticket items* without your spouse's approval—no matter how depressed you are!

5. *Don't give in to impulse buying* on the smaller-ticket items either; they will surely add up to big debts!

6. *Don't clean out your spouse's "stuff,"* even if he never does listen to those old CDs!

7. *Don't stay home alone*—especially if you have little ones. Join a MOPS (Mothers of Preschoolers) group in your area. For more information on attending or starting a MOPS group in your area, go to www.mops.org or call 1–888–910-MOPS.

8. *Don't turn down offers for help.* Take people up on their offers to take you to lunch, come over for dinner, baby-sit your kids (if you trust them), and even bring you a casserole. Now is the time to accept help!

9. *Don't overdose on news shows,* especially when your spouse is involved in a "hot news" conflict. Don't let your kids hear much (if any) of the news involving your spouse's deployment. Madeline Brazell says, "Andrew, who was only two when Duane went to war, started to exhibit disturbing behavior during the first days of the war when we kept the news on almost all day."

10. *Don't overdo it on TV in general*—too much of it makes your brain turn to mush and your morals turn maudlin.

11. *Don't use TV, DVDs, computers, or game systems as a baby-sitter.* Limit their use to one show or one hour a day, and your child will have a better outlook on life.

12. *Don't list your physical address in the phone book or on any registration information.* When a Stealth went down in Kosovo, and they didn't know who the pilot was, CNN was standing curbside at every pilot's house listed in the phone book!

The list continues for the "do's" while they're gone.

Build Something!

Leigh Ann Trevillion is a mother of two-year-old twins, and her husband travels frequently. She's an unusual gal who likes to ride live bulls, go skydiving, and hang from the top of the 100-foot skeleton of a construction site. Therefore, her method of coping while her husband is gone may or may not fit your personality. She says, "My way of getting through is to take on building projects to surprise him with on his return. . . . I've built a room addition, painted a room a new color, and built a storage shed."

Enjoy the Downtime

Army spouse Jill Mingear says, "My husband, Darren, was gone at least one week per month when we were stationed at Fort Campbell, Kentucky. I worked, and we had one child at the time. I actually enjoyed the downtime of less laundry, cooking, and a lightened schedule."

Independence Day

The truth is if you are highly dependent upon your spouse for your emotional well-being, your ability to explore new things, or your happiness in general, you're going to have a harder time of it. Military spouses learn to be flexible, and this characteristic is never more needed than when the unit is deployed or they are TDY. Jill Mingear puts it well: "When the boys were preschoolers, I'd plan a trip home to see my family. I would take all kinds of road trips. If I had waited for Darren to take me everywhere, I never would have gone *anywhere*!"

New Adventures

While routines are important to families, it doesn't mean you have to exclude new adventures. Try taking the kids downhill skiing, castle hopping (if you're stationed in Europe), and exploring your geographical part of the world. The kids can tell the deployed parent about their adventures, and when they are exploring fun new areas, they are less likely to feel they are missing life.

Installation Resources

Every military base, regardless of the branch of service, has programs and resources for the families of deployed military members. Make sure you take advantage of these! Depending upon the base and the program, perks can include everything from free oil changes to regular audiovisual telephone calls, where your entire family can talk with your spouse at a prearranged time.

Extended Family

While it's important to visit extended family, especially during deployments of three months or more, it's also important to keep a balance on these visits. It's very easy to shift the *interdependence* that exists between a husband and wife to a *dependence* upon extended family. Your real home is where the military sends you, or where your *nuclear* family—your spouse and kids—is. If you're visiting your parents' home during each deployment and calling that "home," the potential to depend on *extended family* more than your *nuclear family* could possibly undermine that primary family relationship. Jill Mingear says, "I feel it is important to get away from the post when the spouse is deployed, but if you make a habit of running to your parents every time your spouse deploys, that can be unhealthy. You have to be independent for yourself and your spouse's sake. They don't need to worry about things falling apart on the home front."

Gifts

Sometimes your friends or parents may want to help *you* by buying special gifts or treats. They will sometimes ask you what you want or need. Give them a copy of this book and direct them to this section. Suggested gift items are: phone cards, movie tickets, restaurant gift cards, free baby-sitting, magazine subscriptions, and humorous or inspirational books.

Teachers

Let your children's teachers know the deployment/TDY schedule so they will be aware of potential mood swings or "acting out" in a child who may be missing his/her parent. This helps the teacher to be more understanding without damaging the child's spirit.

Class Projects

Consider approaching your kids' teachers and asking if their class-mates can use some of the English or writing course time to write letters to the deployed spouse. Your children will be proud of Mommy or Daddy's important job, and the fact that others are concerned for their safety as well.

Sticky-Note Fun

Madeline Brazell, Air Force spouse, says, "When Duane would leave on a TDY, I would make a calendar and mark off the days until he returned with small sticky notes over the dates. Andrew and Chris were preschoolers, and they enjoyed removing a sticky note each day. I was relieved from being asked constantly how much longer Daddy would be gone!"

If you are particularly crafty, you could take Madeline's idea and make an "advent calendar," marking each day in a special way.

Special Treats

I've noticed that when the guys deploy on a mission, some of the wives "treat" themselves in destructive ways. It's the feeling that "I have to do this alone, so I deserve this (fill-in-the-blank)." If some of those indulgences include overspending on credit cards, over-indulging in comfort foods, or going to nightclubs, then you will not feel better in the long run. Instead of unhealthy outlets, treat yourself to an occasional massage at the massage therapy school or a manicure or pedicure at a cosmetology college. Go out to lunch with an encouraging girl friend (go to my website at www.elliekay.com for links to restaurant coupons). Take the kids to the dollar theater (or matinee), zoo, museum, or on a nature walk.

Exercise

I've always made exercise a priority—even with five kids! The result is that I have more energy, a lifted mood, and better ability to cope with the pressures of being a single mom while Bob is gone. Even a brisk three-mile walk three times a week is enough to keep your body healthy and keep those extra pounds at bay. Try listening to uplifting music while you exercise.

The New You!

Madeline Brazell also offered this idea: "Make plans to do those things you never get around to doing while your spouse is at home. Start a new exercise program and surprise him when he returns. Change the color of your bedroom; buy a new pet for your kids (we got small ones like fish or birds). Organize closets, photo albums, recipes. Get in touch with old friends and relatives; start a neighborhood women's Bible study; or have a garage sale." Or buy a new SUV. (Just kidding!)

Kindred Spirits

A kindred spirit is someone you can confide in about virtually anything—fears, temptations, dreams, or desires. I've found that while these true friends are precious and rare, they are also crucial to my emotional health while Bob is flying afar. There's nothing like a friend who has a knack for saying the right thing at the right time.

Gripe-Free Zone

Jody Dale, Army chaplain wife, says, "NEVER gripe to your spouse when talking to him/her while he/she is deployed. They can't do anything about it and feel helpless. Take your problems to God and to a good friend. Report the good things, fun events, wishes and hopes for tomorrow. Always let them know they are missed, but not to the point where you are devastated and cannot cope. The truth is—you can!"

Laughter Is Good Medicine

Loved ones need to laugh while they are gone, so send pictures, jokes, cartoons, or goofy packages from home while encouraging the deployed member to do the same.

Volunteer

This is a fantastic way to take your mind off your loneliness: helping others. Most military-sponsored programs offer child-care reimbursement, so it serves the dual function of providing a break from the kiddies. If your children are school age, consider watching the preschoolers up the street for another mom whose spouse is deployed. Even if you only offered this service once or twice a month, it's a great feeling to give someone else a break.

Get a Whine Cellar for Your Kids

Dr. Kevin Leman, a friend who endorses my books and is the best-selling author of a gazillion books and DVDs, including *Making Your Children Mind Without Losing Yours,* says that it's important to our kids to keep set boundaries when routines may be disrupted by change. So that means if your spouse is deployed and little junior starts to act out by throwing tantrums or getting whiney, it's important to respond to that behavior immediately. In fact, he recommends putting them in a "whine cellar," a place in your home that is dedicated to giving them a time-out when they whine or otherwise act out. I found, as a mom of many kids, that consistency was the key and insanity was the key to consistency!

Anonymous Gifts

Brighten the life of the spouse who is having a particularly tough time by leaving or mailing anonymous gifts. For ideas, see the Wish List at the end of this chapter.

Homecoming and Reunions

One Family Support director that I spoke with, Lenn Furrow, said, "The best advice I could give the military member who is deployed for a long period of time is: Do not come home early and unannounced. Your spouse has imagined the reunion countless times in her mind, and if you suddenly surprise her a day or a week early, the house will not be as clean as she wanted it to be, your favorite meal won't be prepared, and she might look a sight. Don't rob her of the joy of the homecoming by arriving early and unannounced!"

Pace Yourself

Deployment and TDY orders change all the time. Don't zero in on a specific date. Instead, be prepared (as much as you can) to have your spouse call and announce a change in the arrival date (either earlier or later).

Expect the Unexpected

During long separations, we women tend to glamorize the reunion, and it's rarely quite as wonderful as it was in our minds. Plan all you want and make it special, but realize that it may not go off exactly the way you wanted it to, and decide ahead of time that it will be all right.

Rough Landings

The post-deployment adjustment can be a severe bummer. You've been independent and in charge at home, while your spouse has only been responsible for him/herself while deployed. Have your spouse read this section so that you will both be prepared for the adjustments that happen upon reunion. The deployed spouse needs to give the homebound spouse room to move from independence back into interdependence. It is best to turn over areas of responsibility slowly. *Very slowly.* The deployed spouse may feel as if they're just sitting on the sidelines for the first few days, and that is all right. Sometimes it's the best place for them to be as "normalcy" returns to your reunited household.

Red Flags: Signs of Post-Traumatic Stress Disorder

Occasionally after military members come back from war where they have experienced trauma, they may show signs of PTSD. Not everyone reacts the same way to stress, and some may not be looking forward to their homecoming at all. Some military members may show signs of depression as they transition into life back home. If you observe one or many of the following signs, ask your chaplain or your Life Skills Support Center (LSSC) for help:

- hopelessness/despair
- lack of interest in activities
- lack of energy
- change in weight
- change in duty performance, such as being late or not getting the job done
- sleep disturbance
- intrusive thoughts
- anxiety or panic attacks, such as persistent fear, flashbacks, avoiding people, nightmares, or jumpiness

Remember that it is always better to talk to someone sooner than later, and your military spouse may need your help to get the help he or she needs.

Special Times

The events you've been anticipating for weeks or months are now about to happen. It's important to realize that you don't have to do everything in the first few days your spouse is home. Consider it a mini-vacation that lasts a couple of weeks. Throughout that time you can farm out the kids for a night, create a candlelight dinner with favorite foods another night, buy a new outfit for another night (I like *Victoria's Secret,* and so does Bob!), or rent a favorite new movie for yet another night.

Extended Family

Try to discourage extended family from visiting the first week or two your spouse is home. Once again, you could give them their own copy of this book and ask them to read this section. You deserve some time alone, and you will need the space to adjust to being a family again. Madeline Brazell says, "After Duane was gone four months, some well-meaning relatives wanted to drive down to the base and meet him on the runway. I gently asked them to please wait a week. I was so thankful they understood."

Bonus Section—The Service Member's Wish Book

When I was a kid, Sears published a HUGE Christmas Wish Book catalog. I remember sitting on the couch, playing a game in which I wished that Santa would give me a gift on each page; all I had to do was choose. You can make it Christmas for your service member any time of the year by creating a Wish Book. You could send several wishes at once or create a new page each week.

This might be a good project for your Family Support Group/Family Readiness Group or your spouses coffee group. The emphasis can be on either romance or family bonding (or both). Some of these will be items they can use right away, while others hold a promise for the future. You can send a note with a special gift attached or enclose it in the envelope or package. Here are some ideas to get you started:

- I Wish for You . . . Laughter With Friends
  (Write an account of something cute the kids did that week.)
- I Wish for You . . . Beauty for Ashes
  (Something lovely made out of something unusual. The kids once made "angels" out of spray-painted Coke cans that were folded in the center, using the top of the can as the angel's head and the opening as its mouth.)
- I Wish for You . . . Peace and Tranquility
  (A mood music CD with a note that you will be listening to the same music)
- I Wish for You . . . A Special Evening
  (A gift certificate to their favorite restaurant to be redeemed upon their return)
- I Wish for You . . . Health
  (Vitamins or a power nutrition bar)
- I Wish for You . . . Thin Thighs
  (Firming gel or support hose as a gag gift)
- I Wish for You . . . Good Hair Days
  (Any hair-care product, preferably one they use!)
- I Wish for You . . . A Rainbow After the Storm
  (Anything with a rainbow on it, or have the kids draw and color a rainbow)
- I Wish for You . . . Special Moments and Good Memories
  (A photo album—to keep photos they take while they're away as well as the ones you send)

- I Wish for You . . . Good Conversation
  (A phone card)
- I Wish for You . . . Warm Connections
  (Stationery)
- I Wish for You . . . A Breath of Freshness
  (A supply of Altoids or other breath mints)
- I Wish for You . . . Wisdom
  (A book to challenge their mind)
- I Wish for You . . . Love
  (A big chocolate kiss)
- I Wish for You . . . Kodak Moments
  (A disposable camera)
- I Wish for You . . . A Stamp of Approval
  (Stamps)
- I Wish for You . . . Happy Surprises
  (Anything . . . try to make it something they enjoy, and be creative!)
- I Wish for You . . . Light at the End of the Tunnel
  (A candle)
- I Wish for You . . . The Promise of Spring
  (Any bulb plant)
- I Wish for You . . . A Quiet Afternoon
  (Hot-cocoa packets or tea)
- I Wish for You . . . Quiet Moments With God
  (A good devotional book, such as *My Utmost for His Highest* by Oswald Chambers)
- I Wish for You . . . Romantic Moments in a "Tub for Two"
  (Bubble bath to be brought back home in anticipation of your reunion)
- I Wish for You . . . No Postponed Returns or Extended Moments Apart
  (A travel alarm clock, showing that the time will pass)
- I Wish for You . . . Healthy Competition
  (A game; maybe one they can play with other soldiers on deployment)
- I Wish for You . . . Good Scents
  (Their favorite cologne or the scent you usually wear for them to spray on their pillow and remember you by)

- I Wish for You . . . Self-Sufficiency
  (A mini tool kit or Swiss Army knife if you're allowed to send them)
- I Wish for You . . . A Platform for Praise
  (A platform shoe purchased at the local thrift shop as a gag gift)
- I Wish for You . . . Someone to Help You Bear Your Burdens
  (A stuffed Teddy bear)
- I Wish for You . . . Good Therapy
  (Aromatherapy candle or lotion)
- I Wish for You . . . Roses Without Thorns
  (A rose potpourri ball or silk rose, or one drawn by the kids)
- I Wish for You . . . A Clean House
  (Homemade gift certificate guaranteeing a clean house—if they don't arrive early and unannounced!)
- I Wish for You . . . No More "Ring Around the Collar"
  (A bottle of Shout or Spray 'n' Wash spot cleaner)
- I Wish for You . . . No More Headaches
  (Tylenol PM or Excedrin)
- I Wish for You . . . Ageless Beauty
  (A night cream or aftershave lotion)

★　★　★　★　★　★　★

Chuck Swindoll, bestselling author of many books, once said, "Words can never adequately convey the incredible impact of our attitude toward life. The longer I live, the more convinced I am that life is 10 percent what happens to us and 90 percent how we respond to it" (*Strengthening Your Grip,* Word, 1983). This is true for all military families, and it is never truer than when your spouse is gone. There are lots of tips in this section, and even if you learned just a few things, it could make all the difference in the next deployment—because the next one will come, and . . .

It will never be convenient timing.

It will never be short enough.

It will never be over until your spouse separates or retires from the military, and even then there will be unique problems and challenges.

But . . . I don't want to end this important chapter on a negative note. So let's put some perspective on the topic . . .

Even though the timing isn't perfect, you can make the most of the time.

Even though it's longer than you'd like, it isn't forever.

Even though it's part of military life, you will likely miss some aspects about the lifestyle when you're through.

The most important thing to remember, as much as we joke about "serving your country in Hawaii," is that there is genuine and abiding *purpose* in the service member's going. It's a much bigger perspective than we can imagine, because . . .

If it weren't for their mission, we wouldn't have freedom.

If it weren't for the tears of farewell, we'd never shed tears of joy for a safe homecoming.

If it weren't for your sacrifice at home, we wouldn't have America as we now know it.

Perspective makes all the difference.

☆ 20 ☆

COURAGE UNDER FIRE

Facing Fear With Faith

Life in the trenches demands courage, but sometimes life at home requires just as much bravery as the battlefront. This was the case when we were called in to Fort Wainwright, near Fairbanks, Alaska, to help the spouses of the 172nd Stryker Brigade Combat Team. This Army unit was deployed in Iraq for twelve months, and at the last minute their deployment was extended four months. In addition, they were moved from a green zone to a red zone in Iraq. Many of the families were very young and had gone to the expense of flying down to the "lower forty-eight" to pass the long year with the support of extended family members. These spouses had returned to Alaska, awaiting the joyful reunion of those they loved and missed so much. But life changed literally overnight for them.

A significant number of soldiers had already come home and were immediately sent back to the desert for the extension while the other half were not allowed to return home at all, but were informed that they would stay another 120 days.

Most of the spouses were wives with young children, and dozens of them had babies who had not yet met their fathers. They were outraged at how the situation was handled. In fact, it was so unprecedented that the president sent the Secretary of Defense to Alaska to talk to these family members and offer an explanation. But no explanation would take away the devastation of the moment. The community in Fairbanks wanted to do something to help, and they brought in our team to give a special Heroes at Home presentation and provide free books to the participants. Michelle Cuthrell, one of the Stryker Brigade spouses, looked beyond her own pain to help put on the Heroes at Home event and bring comfort to her fellow wives in the unit.

As it turned out, I spoke in the morning in the city of Fairbanks, and the Secretary of Defense spoke in the afternoon at Fort Wainright. It was a tough audience, as they were angry, frustrated, scared, and confused. When I shared "The Top Ten Qualities of a Hidden Hero," I lingered on the characteristic of courage, as I felt the need to drive home an important aspect of being courageous.

"I know it's hard on you right now and you are angry," I told these young women. "I know you want to vent to your husband in an email or the next time you talk on the phone."

It was then that my mama finger came out and started wagging.

"But don't do that! That's not what he needs. You vent to your mama, your chaplain, or a girl friend, but don't you dare vent on your husband! He is already worried about you and your babies. He doesn't need to add your frustration to his already over-tasked emotions."

My eyes filled with unbidden tears as the message welled up in me and flowed over to the audience.

"The next time you talk to your husband, you tell him three things: 'I love you, I'm proud of you, and we'll be all right.'"

I wiped my eyes and continued, "When these military men and women are concerned about overwhelming issues at home, they have trouble concentrating on their jobs over there. When they cannot concentrate as well, it translates into potential accidents. When there are accidents, there is death. So if you want to do your part to save lives in Iraq, then you tell your husband that you love him, you're proud of him, and you're going to be all right. Then when he gets home safely, you can vent all you want, and even make him change a few diapers too."

The audience was so engaged, they were sitting on the edge of their seats as if the words they heard were their own personal lifeline for the months to come. Some women were overheard saying after the event, "Now I know what I need to do. I didn't know what to do before I came to this conference, but now I know what my part is and I know what to do."

After we got back from Alaska, we watched CNN, along with all of America, and in horror we saw our military soldiers being killed by sharpshooters in downtown Baghdad. We received a call that one of the first men killed was the husband of a woman who had been in our audience when we spoke to the Stryker Brigade. When this wife and mother received notification that her husband would not be coming home, she said, "I'm so glad that I went to the Heroes at Home conference. When I talked to my husband, I was going to vent. After all, he's my best friend and I tell him everything. Instead, I decided to speak affirming words to him. Now I can live with the fact that the last words I ever spoke to him were: 'I love you, I'm proud of you, and I'm going to be all right.'"

I know what it's like to live on the edge of life and death. In Bob's military career, and even now, we face the fact that what he does is dangerous, and people can die while doing the kind of work he does. We lost too many friends when their jets went down.

★ ★ ★ ★ ★ ★ ★

Bob and I had a code we used for accidents. Before the squadron would go on "shut down," if he had any chance at all, he would call and say, "Hi, I had a good flight, and I love you. Good-bye." Then he would abruptly hang up.

He made that call too many times, but the fact that he was the one calling meant that he *wasn't* the one in the "jet gone down."

I think it's a blessing the way memories from those harrowing days fade as we veterans on the home front keep moving forward in this life we call "the service." But it only takes another phone call for the past to thrust its ugly face into our conscious mind and come rushing forward again.

★ ★ ★ ★ ★ ★ ★

Sending a spouse on a deployment, out on a ship, or to the field, is hard enough, but sending them into harm's way is doubly difficult. Military spouses cope with these life-and-death situations as a matter of course, but that doesn't mean it is easy. There are some practical "housekeeping" issues you can take care of to make sure your affairs are in order, and I've listed those below. However, even more important are the emotional, psychological, and spiritual preparations that can make the difference between your personal success or failure as you handle these critical issues.

Some of the greatest personal growth I've seen in myself and in my friends has occurred during a time of extended separation. Listen to how other military spouses have coped.

You're Not Falling Apart!

There may be times when the pressure of the firefight gets to you and you think you're falling apart! But you're not. No, you're really not. We all feel that way at times, and that's when we need a strong faith and a good friend. If you don't have a strong faith, then now would be a good time to explore that aspect of your spirituality through the resources listed in this book—starting as near as your installation's chapel. An Army spouse said, "Sad days will come, but that does not mean you are falling apart. Recognize them for what they are. Use those days to appreciate all that you have, for the sadness comes due to the fact that you are missing someone special. You can be thankful you have someone to miss. Memories of our loved ones affect us, and that is a good thing."

Wendy, an Air Force spouse whose husband was sent to Somalia when she had a new baby, said, "Be confident in who you are when your spouse leaves. Some women feel that they are not capable of many things that their husbands normally handle. Look deep inside yourself. You can handle anything they can, and if not, you can find someone to help out. Look to your unit, friends, or church for the help you need. You may not know this, but the military trains you in a strange way for many obstacles that most civilians do not understand and could not handle."

Of Death and Dying

We saw in the earlier story of this chapter that pilots learn to compartmentalize death in order to do their jobs. This is true of soldiers and sailors as well. If your spouse goes into a dangerous situation and experiences war and death, they will be forever changed. But not all change is bad. One of the things that comforted me when I was a new bride was the peace that comes from knowing where Bob would go if he were to die. At PWOC, I went to a study on the names of God and it changed the way I viewed God. One wife who sent her husband into such a situation said, "Be aware that your spouse will never be the same person after being faced with war and death. You must allow him to slowly reenter the world you live in. Things will be different for them, and they may not talk about it. Don't push them by always asking 'why?' In their own time they will open up."

If you have a spouse who has been involved in life-and-death situations, there are counseling programs at your local chapel or Family Support Center equivalent to help the service member as well as the family. Brig. Gen. Dick Abel (Ret.) said, "Different situations can be a springboard to spiritual growth." Take advantage of these early in the situation. If your spouse is overseas and involved in war and death, visit the counseling center before they get home so that a trained professional can tell you what to expect and how you can make reentry easier on your spouse.

One important aspect of reentry after such a dramatic experience is for the spouse not to turn over responsibilities too quickly to the return-ing service member. It needs to be a slow transition, and sometimes certain activities trigger painful memories for them. No matter how innocuous the activity seems, it may be something they simply cannot handle for a while, or ever. It could be something as simple as reading a child's favorite storybook that reminds them of how their friend who died read to his kids. Or a trip to the zoo could trigger a memory of where a fellow fallen soldier used to work as a second job. Be sensitive to your spouse, whether the issues make sense to you or not. That is why counseling programs, such as the Military Family Life Counselor (MFLC), are very important for both parties after a combat situation.

Chapel Programs

Pray, Pray, Pray

There is a diversity of faiths among military families, but most people find comfort in prayer regardless of their religious affiliation. Prayer can actually lower blood pressure, release tension, and contribute to an individual's mental, emotional, and physical health. Give your fam-ily this incredible gift by setting up a regular time in the morning (to start your day) or evening (to prepare for the long nights) for prayer. Let your spouse know that you are all praying for him or her; you might even consider praying for the same things on the same nights to create a feeling of unity.

Jody Dale, wife of an Army chaplain, said this about her husband's tour in Somalia: "My strength was my prayer group and knowing to Whom I was praying. Friends who truly cared and prayed made me get involved and get out to the gym. I had a friend, Judy, who insisted that I get moving when I least felt like it. At times I was so mean to her and unthankful, but as I look back, she helped me keep my mind and body active, and our friendship was strengthened."

Defending the Military Marriage

Defending the Military Marriage is an outstanding study currently available to military members through the HomeBuilders Couples Series (www.homebuilders.com). The topics include: "Basic Training," "Communicating in the Trenches," "More-Month-Than-Money Blues," and "SEAL Training: Sexual Accountability and Love." It is a short course that you go through with other couples to help strengthen your marriage before those trial-by-fire situations occur. (Another good resource is *Loving Your Military Man* by Bea Fishback.)

For more information on this time-friendly study, go to www .milmin.com. The inexpensive study book was written by Lt. Col. Jim Fishback, USA (Ret.) and his wife, Bea. I had a chance to meet them while I was with our Heroes at Home Tour in Europe. They are great people who practice what they preach.

Catholic and Protestant Women of the Chapel—Other Programs

These are only a couple of the military-sponsored programs that offer assistance to those who are seeking a deeper faith. Bible studies, religious education programs for kids, youth groups, summer vacation Bible school, chapel services for all denominations, and spiritual counseling are all as close as your nearest installation chapel.

Referrals

Military Ministry
P.O. Box 120124
Newport News, VA 23612-0124
(800) 444–6006
www.milmin.com
    This ministry is an outreach to all military families.

Navigators
P.O. Box 6000
Colorado Springs, CO 80934

(719) 598-1212
Fax: (719) 260–0479
www.navigators.org

This ministry is composed of over 250 staff and more than 1,200 active-duty workers serving Army, Navy, Air Force, Marine Corps, and Coast Guard personnel on more than 117 U.S. and overseas military bases and posts.

Officer's Christian Fellowship of the USA
3784 South Inca
Englewood, CO 80110
(303) 761-1984
(800) 424-1984
Fax: (303) 761-6226
www.ocfusa.org

The objectives of this fellowship are to build the spiritual maturity of member military officers and to provide support, especially for transient officers. A quarterly magazine, *Command*, is offered.

Military Community Youth Ministries
P.O. Box 2486
Colorado Springs, CO 80901-2484
(719) 381-1831
(800) 832-9098
Fax: (719) 381-1754
www.mcym.org

By combining the vision and skills of Youth for Christ, Young Life, and Catholic Network Ministry, this group focuses on ministering to teens of military parents. Activities include Bible studies, camps, and retreats.

Cadence International
P.O. Box 1268
Englewood, CO 80150
(800) 396-6680
Fax: (303) 788-0661
www.cadence.org

With forty-two centers worldwide, this nonprofit organization reaches out to U.S. military singles, families, and youth. They do this through hospitality houses, retreat and Bible study ministries, and youth groups. The future looks bright for Cadence and for new ministry outreaches. Plans include concentrated ministries to people of color, dependent children, women in uniform, deployed persons and their families, as well as militaries of other nations.

Christian Military Fellowship (CMF)
P.O. Box 1207
Englewood, CO 80150-1207
(303) 761-1959
(800) 798-7875
Fax: (303) 761-4577 or (800) 682-4206
www.cmfhq.org

This association is committed to reaching out to military members. CMF involves all elements of that society, including all ranks, family members, and civilian employees.

Digging the Well

We were told that Bob had orders to Saudi Arabia, and he was 95 percent sure he was going for a yearlong remote by himself. After waiting twelve weeks on the confirmation of the assignment, we discovered it had been canceled. This happened repeatedly throughout our military lives. That is the nature of the life of a military family. It is frustrating at times, but it is vital that we continue to support our spouses in their commitment to our country.

I would like to leave you with the quote of a woman I greatly admire, Lenn Furrow. She has seen both sides of the military family fence—as an Army spouse and as the director of a family support center. Her words express briefly and powerfully why *you* are so important to the welfare of our nation and why *you* are a hero—the hero at home.

She says, "As soon as a family stops supporting the service member and is no longer willing to sacrifice, we will lose the best we have."

Digging the Well Before You Need It

The Family Checklist (Recommended by the ACS/Family Program Coordinator)

Medical

- Get up-to-date immunizations for each family member.
- Know the location of health and dental records for each member.

- Know who is to be contacted in the case of a medical emergency.
- Know who has the medical power of attorney.

Finance

- Make sure there will be money immediately available on a continuing basis while the sponsor is gone.
- Set up an allotment to be sent to the family's bank and sign up for Sure-Pay/Direct Deposit.
- Will the direct deposit provide for all the necessities to maintain a household?
- If moving away from the installation during the deployment, is there money for this move?
- What types of accounts does the family have, and with what banks?
- Know where the bank books and account numbers are.
- Know if there is a safety deposit box and where the key is.
- Have credit card names and numbers written in a safe place along with the companies' numbers and addresses in the event of loss.
- Make sure the spouse knows how to manage and balance a checkbook.
- Establish a budget with information on the following payments and their schedules:
    1. Mortgage
    2. Telephone
    3. Water and sewage
    4. Electricity
    5. Trash
    6. Insurance
    7. Taxes
    8. Gas
    9. Credit cards
    10. Auto payments
    11. Other debts
- Know who is to be contacted regarding direct pay problems.

Automobile

- Know the responsibilities associated with the car.
- Know the name/address of lienholder.

- Locate the vehicle's title and make sure a copy of the registration is in the vehicle.
- Make sure the spouse is insured to drive the vehicle.
- Know renewal dates for license plates and safety inspection.
- Have a valid driver's license and know when it expires.
- Set aside a duplicate set of keys in a safe place.
- Become acquainted with how to make emergency repairs on a car (flat tire, overheating, dead battery, etc.).
- If spouse cannot drive, make arrangements for transportation.
- Know phone number of emergency transportation contact.

Housing

- Know where the following are located and how to use them:
    1. Electrical control box (fuse box), including how to replace fuses
    2. The water control valve for shutting off the water in case of an emergency (broken or leaking pipes)
    3. The gas control valve
    4. How to turn the water off on an overflowing toilet
    5. The names and phone numbers of repairmen
    6. Duplicate set of house keys

Legal/Administrative

- Have up-to-date identification cards.
- Know where and how the cards are replaced if lost or stolen.
- Have power of attorney of deploying member and know how to use it to take necessary action regarding an important family matter or a special legal situation.
- Know where the power of attorney is kept.
- Have a copy of everyone's birth certificate.
- Have a copy of marriage license.
- Have copies of adoption papers, divorce decrees, court orders, and know where they are kept.
- Make sure everyone over the age of two has a social security number, and know where they are kept.
- Know where the copies of state and federal income tax records are kept.
- Have copies of insurance policies.

- Know where any stocks, bonds, or securities are kept.
- Know where deeds to land are kept.
- Safeguard important papers (fire-safe box or safe-deposit box at bank).
- Make sure wills are up-to-date for both spouses, and know where they are kept.
- Send copies of wills to the person who will have guardianship of the children and to the person who will execute the will for your children and your spouse.
- Make sure base housing knows where the family member and deployed member can be located in the event of an emergency.
- Know where passports are kept.
- Have a current photo of all family members (full face, clearly visible) together with information about height and weight.

★ ★ ★ ★ ★ ★ ★

On 9/11, while the president talked of war, all military bases went to "Delta Alert," the most severe alert possible. All leaves were canceled as we, along with the rest of the nation, held our breath and awaited orders from the Commander in Chief. As a fighter pilot and wife, Bob and I had long had our affairs in order. Yet this time I didn't expect my husband's reaction. Later that week Bob came home from flying, closed the doors to my home office, and sat on the couch. We were alone, and I waited for him to speak.

He looked as if he were carrying a heavy weight, his shoulders sagging under the pressure of the burden. He abruptly asked the question that was obviously bothering him—one that he had never asked before in our military lives together: "Beloved, what if I don't come back?"

I was surprised, because he'd always taken his job in stride. But there is something different about this war on terrorism. Suddenly I felt courage well up within me, the courage of many women who stood in my shoes decades before me as they sent their men into harm's way. The courage was one that had been molded in deep faith and perfected in the fire of fifteen years' experience.

I confidently answered him, "I believe you WILL come back, Beloved. I believe that if you go, you'll have a job to do over there—you'll fly and fight and accomplish your mission. But I believe God still has a job for you back here too. I believe you'll come back."

My conviction and faith acted as a balm for Bob. He let out a heavy sigh, relaxed his shoulders, and said, "All right." He had confidence in his wife's faith, and that's all he needed. He got up and left the room. His concerns quelled, he could now move on to the next task of the day: the perpetual search for his other black sock.

As soon as Bob left the room, I sensed another profound thought coming from deep within. It was a still, small voice, filled with comfort and grace. The words strangely held both reality and reassurance. But I knew they were thoughts I could *not* speak to Bob. Not then. Not there.

The simple words were: "And even if he doesn't come back, it will *still* be all right."

★　★　★　★　★　★　★

Learn as if you're going to live forever. Live as if you're going to die tomorrow.

—John Wooden

(Eddie Pells, AP sportswriter, "Wooden still living life's lessons," May 14, 2002)

✩ 21 ✩

RUFFLES AND FLOURISHES

A Salute to the Hero at Home

There is usually a baptism by fire that happens in the life of most military families. This is the moment when the military member deploys and the remaining spouse realizes that he or she really can live without their loved one for a while. This can happen after you've been in the military for ten years, or it could happen after ten days. But on the other side of this baptism there is a new birth, when the spouse feels empowered by his or her ability to cope in the midst of the fire of challenge. For Michelle Cuthrell, author of Behind the Blue Star Banner, this new awakening was to happen in her first week of marriage. As you read her story, why don't you think of how you would write your own? Everyone reading this book has a story, one that is uniquely yours and deserving of as much attention as anyone else's experience. But first, let's hear from Michelle:

I wasn't commissioned, and I didn't enlist, but on May 22, a couple of years ago, I joined the Army. My uniform was my white wedding dress, my oath of office, my wedding vows. And though I'd heard an awful lot about becoming an Army wife before I walked down that aisle, when I said, "I do," I really had no idea just how much I would be "doing."

Three days before we were married, I got my first clue.

That's when my soon-to-be husband received his very first set of orders as a commissioned officer in the United States Army. He had graduated two weeks earlier from the University of Dayton, and we had been eagerly awaiting the announcement of our very first duty station.

In the civilian world, most couples figure out where they're going to live and work, and then get married. Some even start making moving arrangements before the big wedding day. But with the Army it's never quite that simple. Not only do you have to wait on the Army to figure out when you can move and where you're going to live, but you have to work around the entire system just to plan your own wedding.

After many long nights and lots of frustrated tears, we'd finally ironed out the wedding details, but three days before that Cinderella event, we still had no idea about all our other life details—like where we were going to live for the next three or four years of our lives.

As we walked hand in hand into the University of Dayton ROTC office, I started to shake. The Army wouldn't really send us somewhere crazy, would they? We were just hometown Ohio kids starting our lives together. They wouldn't move us any farther than driving distance from the family we'd been surrounded by our entire lives—or would they? As Matt picked up his first set of orders, I closed my eyes and clenched my fists and prayed a quick prayer that we'd be living somewhere calm, somewhere normal, somewhere that I could at least bathe in the sun on long, lonely days away from family.

My husband took the orders and pointed to the abbreviation AK—for Alaska.

Good-bye sunshine, hello Last Frontier. Not exactly the close-to-home, familiar culture, sunshine paradise I'd hoped for.

So one week after we said "I do," I had a whole lot of other "doing" to do. For being the most famous bureaucracy on the face of the planet, the Army sure didn't take long to put the paper work through on that motion. I went from "Michelle" to "military dependent" in less than a week.

Michelle isn't alone. You may not have gone from your hometown to living halfway across the world in a week, but you've faced your own trial by fire. You experience your own kind of challenges every week. You rise to the task even though you don't wear the rank. You haven't taken the oath. And you often stand alone (or with a few babies on your hips). I wish I could give every last one of you a medal!

In the military, there is a tradition that offers "Ruffles and Flourishes" to Very Important People. This is a musical honor reserved for general officers and equivalent ranking officials. At the 10th Mountain Division, they had a ceremony that was similar in that it paid special honor to high-ranking division officers. They called it a "tattoo." Bob and I witnessed the majesty of this event several times, and it was singularly impressive. Every military member is in his/her formal dress uniform, there's a red carpet for guests of honor, and their spouses are in formal attire, standing with them on the carpet. A full band plays music that makes our hearts beat with pride and brings tears to our eyes.

A Salute

If you will indulge me for a minute, I'd like to salute you, the military spouse, with your own special event. But I'll need your cooperation.

I would like you to imagine with me a special dream scene: *You* are the one standing on that carpet. This tribute is to the homeland hero.

Your spouse is dressed formally in respect for *you* tonight, his eyes filled with pride as he looks at you lovingly. If his buttons were not sewn on tightly, they would surely burst.

Your spouse starts the series of toasts: "I propose a toast!" He smiles at you proudly and holds out his champagne glass. "To her bravery and courage in the face of uncertainty and doubt."

"Hear, Hear!" the audience replies. "To bravery and courage!"

The congressman in the audience is next: "I propose a toast!" He looks into your eyes and speaks with polish and confidence. "To her strength and valor above and beyond the call of duty!"

The crowd shouts a hearty "Hear, Hear!" as the sound of crystal tapping crystal is heard. "To strength and valor!"

Suddenly you hear the band strike up "Hail to the Chief" as the audience ripples with gasps of astonishment!

The Commander in Chief suddenly parts the crowd and strides purposefully toward you, with the Secret Service following at a safe distance. There is a motion for silence: "I'd like to propose a toast!" The audience is spellbound, awaiting the words of the most powerful person in the world.

"I'm here to pay honor to the hidden hero in this room."

The president looks into your astonished face and smiles a warm grin that makes you feel as if you're the only one in the room.

The Commander in Chief holds a champagne glass high and shouts boldly to the crowd, "I propose a toast!" Everyone raises his or her glass. "To the hero at home! We love you, we're proud of you, and together we'll be all right. *America salutes you!*"

Afterword

At Thermopylae, a rocky mountain pass in northern Greece, the feared and admired Spartan soldiers stood three hundred strong. Theirs was a suicide mission, to hold the pass against the invading millions of the mighty Persian Army. Day after bloody day they withstood the terrible onslaught, buying time for the Greeks to rally their forces. Born into a cult of spiritual courage, physical endurance, and unmatched battle skill, the Spartans would be remembered for the greatest military stand in history. . . .

[The King speaks to Dienekes, a woman who has lost both husband and son in the siege.]

"The city speculates, my lady," King Leonidas resumes, "as to why I elected those I did to the three hundred. . . . But I now tell you.

"I chose them not for their own valor, but for that of their women. . . . When the battle is over, when the three hundred have gone down to death, then will all Greece look to the Spartans, to see how they bear it.

"But who, lady, who will the Spartans look to? To you. To you, the other wives, daughters, sisters, and mothers of the fallen.

"If they behold your hearts riven and broken with grief, they, too, will break. And Greece will break with them. But if you bear up, dry-eyed, not alone enduring your loss but seizing it with contempt for its agony and embracing it as the honor that it is in truth, then Sparta will stand. And all Hellas will stand behind her. . . . You and your sisters of the Three Hundred are the mothers now of all Greece and of freedom itself."

—From *Gates of Fire* by Steven Pressfield
(Bantam Books, 1999)

BIBLIOGRAPHY

Air Force Reserve Command Fact Sheet. www.afre.af.mil, 2007.

Anstett, Patricia. "Do You Need More Sleep?" from *The Oregonian,* 1999.

Army Family Team Building Levels I, II, III. Department of the Army, 2007.

ESGR Factsheet. www.esgr.mil, Employer Support of Guard and Reserve, 2007.

Farrell, Pam. *Men Are Like Waffles—Women Are Like Spaghetti.* Harvest House, 2007.

Fishback, Jim. *Defending the Military Marriage.* Family Life Publications, 2002.

Gray, Alice, et al. *Lists to Live By.* Multnomah, 2004.

Kay, Ellie. *Shop, Save, and Share.* Bethany House Publishers, 1998.

———. *How to Save Money Every Day.* Bethany House Publishers, 2001.

———. *Money Doesn't Grow on Trees.* Bethany House Publishers, 2002.

MetLife. *All-Season Exercise.* MetLife Consumer Education Center, 2000.

Miller, Susan. *After the Boxes Are Unpacked.* Tyndale, 1998.

NavyReserve.com, 2007. "About the Reserve."

Pressfield, Steven. *Gates of Fire.* Bantam Books, 1999.

Stack, Debi. *Martha to the Max*. Moody Press, 2000.

Swindoll, Chuck. *Tale of the Tardy Oxcart*. Word Publishing, 1998.

———. *Strengthening Your Grip*. Word Publishing, 1983.

United States Chaplain Service. "Reunion and Reintegration." Quick Series Press, 2006.

Ellie Kay, author of fourteen books, popular speaker, and mother of a large family, has walked her own talk. Married to Bob Kay—a former Stealth fighter pilot—and proud mom of sons in the military, Ellie understands the circumstances of military families. She has appeared on or in over 600 media outlets, including a regular slot on ABC *News Now* as well as *Nightline,* CNBC, Fox News, MSNBC, and the *Today Show.* Her Heroes at Home message has been heard by military families around the world. She and her family live in Southern California.

For more information, visit www.elliekay.com

Twitter: @elliekay

Facebook: Ellie Kay, facebook@elliekay.com

Twitter: @elliekay

www.elliekay.com

Facebook: Ellie Kay, facebook@elliekay.com